The Bible
INTERPRETED IN
Dream Symbols

Collected Interpretations by

Barbara Condron
Daniel R. Condron
Gayle B. Matthes
Jerry L. Rothermel

SOM Publishing
Windyville, Missouri 65783

© May 2000
by the School of Metaphysics No. 100164

ISBN: 0-944386-23-7
Library of Congress Catalogue Number pending

PRINTED IN THE UNITED STATES OF AMERICA

If you desire to learn more about the teachings
in this book, write to School of Metaphysics,
World Headquarters, Windyville, Missouri
65783. Or call 417-345-8411.
Or visit us on the internet at www.som.org

The Illustrated *Bible*

Front cover...
The Ascension of Christ by John Crainshaw
The Woman and the Dragon by Dianne Brady

Back cover...
Creation by Barbara Condron
Song of Solomon by Sharka Glet

Foreword

From the time I was born, I learned about the truths recorded in the best-selling book of all time – The Holy Bible. I was a babe of only a few weeks when my mother and father took me before a tent full of literally thousands of people so my grandfather, a faith-healing evangelist, could dedicate my life to the Lord. So began my acquaintance with the supernatural, the meta-physical.

My initial recognition of a connection between dreams and the Bible came not in partnering the two but rather in wanting to know the meaning of my dreams. I came across the story of Joseph and his brothers in the *Old Testament*, how he saved himself from slavery by interpreting the dreams of the Pharaoh. Having many dreams myself, some which troubled me, upon hearing this I believed I might have found my savior in a beloved minister. Surely if Joseph interpreted dreams, Rev. Rhode could as well. It was not to be.

This disappointment came only a few months before the darkest period of my life. I was entering the creativity of adolescence with little insightful guidance for my spirit. Don't get me wrong, I did very well by all outwardly determinable means, in most cases a model daughter, but I was spiritually adrift. In a most undisciplined fashion I rebelled against that which I did not understand.

What I didn't understand the most was the inconsistencies in a religion which produced, from where I had placed myself, a great deal of hypocrisy in its adherents. For years in my deceitfully-independent mind, Truth became dogma, guidance became coercion, love became manipulation. Off to college I went looking for the answers to life among strangers. The <u>Bible</u> was a book I never opened, but I took it with me all the same.

Months went by. My understanding of life did not improve, in fact a profound depression was setting in because the purpose of my life eluded my grasp. Shortly after graduating from the university, I took a class in metaphysics as a favor to a friend. We had been studying several weeks when the president of the school visited us and agreed to teach our class. We were quite honored by his visit and quite excited by the prospect of learning directly from him.

As fate would have it – or luck, or change, or God's will, they all refer to the workings of Universal Law – the lesson of the evening was the nature of consciousness and the structure of the mind. For the latter he drew a diagram of the mind on a blackboard explaining there are three divisions of the mind: the Conscious Mind, the Subconscious Mind and the Superconscious Mind, each having a purpose, function, and duty to perform in order for the whole mind to thrive. For the nature of consciousness, he pulled out a <u>Bible</u> and began to read a story I had not heard for years.

I immediately felt a hardening, the residue of years of practicing shutting out rhetoric which piqued my conscience. The practiced resistance pushed away even at the mention of the <u>Bible</u>. Thankfully I was not trapped by prejudice to the extent that my mind would close down. My mind went to the facts. I knew this was not a Sunday School class and I was no longer twelve years old. I did some quick admitting that night. I knew from experience that the <u>Bible</u> contained Truth. I just didn't understand its contradictions, and no one else I knew did either. That was why I had put the book aside, seeking truth elsewhere. Now, ten years later, I had an opportunity to revisit what I had been told was "original sin", the woman eating the fruit from the tree in the Garden of Eden.

What I learned that night is presented in these pages in much the same way Dr. Jerry L. Rothermel gave it to our class that night over a quarter century ago. Here are fresh ways to understand the Universal Truths in the Bible. Here were ways to answer some of those questions I'd been carrying around for years, "Why did God put the tree in the garden and then tell them not to touch it?" "Why was I being punished for something I had nothing to do with?" "If Jesus came to save us from our sins, what happened to all those people who lived before him?" "If Christ is coming again, what in Heaven is he waiting for?"

That night I understood what the gospels meant when their authors would say, let him who has eyes see and ears hear.

The beauty to me of that evening of illumination was the teacher did not give me answers to believe, he offered a way of learning that would lead to knowing. Many times in the years following that class I would hear him say, "the <u>Bible</u> is written in a language, a language of the mind, the language of our dreams. Learn the language and you can decode your dreams and the <u>Bible</u>."

This is how the <u>Bible</u> is presented here, and through the eyes of not just one but four very different individuals. These modern-day disciples bring the entire <u>Bible</u> to life and in so doing give a picture of the growth of consciousness possible for humanity. Here is evolution and creation unified through spiritual disciplines taught in the School of Metaphysics during its first thirty years of existence as a school openly teaching the inner secrets of creation.

Four distinct movements of consciousness beginning with the origin, *Genesis*, and culminating in John's dream of the *Revelation*, places you and your growing awareness at the center of the Biblical Truths. Here is the journey of every individual, the hope of every person, the evolution of humanity. Here is the meaning, revealed in the universal language of mind, of man's past and his future. It is the story of the making of a Christ, the manifestation of a Christ, and the reappearance of the Christ. The eternal quest for enlightenment. It is your story and it is mine.

It is simply the <u>Bible</u> interpreted in dream symbols.

–Barbara Condron
College of Metaphysics
Spring 2000

Contents

The Bible
INTERPRETED IN
Dream Symbols

The Bible in a Nutshell

by Daniel R. Condron

from a sermon originally given in 1986 in Detroit, Michigan

There is an old adage that says, "As Above, so Below." The meaning of this is that physical existence follows the mental existence and that thought is cause. You cause your life with your thoughts. Your environment does not cause your life. You chose to be born into a specific family. You chose your job and the place where you go to work. You chose to be married or single. You chose the food you eat, whether a carrot or a slice of bread.

You make changes with the inner Self, then you bring those changes and growth outward ,applying them in your life. You apply them outwardly in your physical life. Then you have knowledge and experience you can receive inward and add to your storehouse of permanent understandings stored in Subconscious mind.

The Universe operates in repeating cycles and can become an upward spiral when the life is dedicated to soul growth and spiritual transformation. As energy goes out in any form it is important to receive it back in return. To receive it means to use what is available and to use it to the fullest. Use every opportunity to keep the energy in your life moving, alive, and in motion. Money is a good tool for understanding the movement of energy because it represents an exchange of energy. So do not just hoard money, even if it is just depositing it in the bank. Do something with the energy of money. Keep it in motion. The piece of paper that money, such as a dollar bill, is printed on really does not have much intrinsic value, or value of its own.

Money is a little bit of ink and a little bit of paper. Money represents an exchange of energy. Gold and silver are real money because they have intrinsic value. An exchange of energy is presented all throughout the Bible. In fact, the Bible presents an image of the building up of forms and structure, and an exchange of energy. That exchange of energy is understood or utilized to a full degree by spiritually enlightened beings. Then there is a need for a higher or greater structure built upon the previous one so that we may have a larger field of experiencing and learning. Soul growth and spiritual development are worth more than money because they are permanent.

When you went to first grade or kindergarten you had one type of learning and you mastered certain abilities. Going through grades, you created a field of learning in which you needed a greater structure and a more expanded freedom for learning. This was prepared for by the responsibility of learning the previous steps. You entered high school. You went from room to room for classes. After high school you went to college or trade school or a job where you learned other skills. Each one was a step towards gaining greater freedom. You earned this greater freedom from having used and understood the structure of the previous step and incorporating them into yourself. Each involved a higher level of responsibility.

Around us in different stages of evolution are the gases, then the minerals, then the plants and animals, then human man.

Evolution shows us the building up of a structure of form that has come before and been utilized. Then there is a need for a greater form and structure to use in order for the soul to evolve. The Bible uses a symbology to present these ideas.

The first symbology of the Bible is presented in the *Book of Genesis.* It says *In the beginning God created the heavens and the earth and the earth was without form.* Then there started to be forms created. First there was the light and the dark, then the sun and the stars, then the plants, and then the animals. Finally something was created *"in the image and likeness of the Creator,"* meaning with like attributes and ability to create using will power and imagination. There are three factors to reasoning. The first factor is attention. Attention so that the present can be used effectively. Memory so that the past can be can be drawn upon, drawn out, and used, and imagination so that those two can be used together in order to create the next step for the individual. Our Creator, while endowing us in his likeness and image, gave us the ability to create the next step for ourselves. That implies free will and the ability to make decisions. When you got up this morning you made decisions about whether you were going to write your dream down, whether you were going to remember your dream, whether you were going to eat break-fast, what you were going to eat for breakfast, whether you were going to brush your teeth, or if you were going to turn the light off or leave it on, and what you were going to wear. You made decisions. In order to become compatible to our Creator we were given free will. Free will is the ability to initiate motion in the direction we have imaged.

Sin in the Bible symbolizes mistake, and a mistake is that which does not produce for the permanent learning of the Self. *Righteous* symbolizes right or correct use of experience which adds to the permanent learning of the Self. The permanent learning of the Self comes from the inner soul urge which draws, pulls, and pushes each individual closer to compatibility with their maker as referred to in *Genesis*. The various steps of creation are outlined in great detail starting with Adam and his descendants. Adam begat Seth. This lineage continues through Enoch to Methusael to Noah, then on to Abraham and Isaac and Jacob.

There are correspondences between this lineage and the physical evolution of the human body from homo erectus to homo habilus to Neanderthal. There have been a lot of side tracks. Human physical body evolution veered off from the great apes. We veered off from the different dead lines or dead ends that had come about in producing the homo sapiens physical body.

Finally we added the most important component which was imagination to the brain so the thinker could inhabit the body. We became entrapped. Entrapment in a physical body shows up in a couple of places in the Bible. One of them is *Abraham* who represents the Conscious mind and an honest ego. Abraham begat Isaac. *Isaac* represents the Subconscious mind and he begat Jacob who became Israel. Israel was the father of the lineage called Israelites. The *Israelites* represent the teacher aspects. They represent the parts of you that are using the opportunities for permanent learning and teaching this to others. Thus you prepare to receive the learning inside yourself and create the next form and structure.

Israel had 12 sons. Joseph was his favorite. Joseph and his brothers went down to Egypt because it was the time of a famine. They lived there for many years. They did very well but they became entrapped or became *slaves* which symbolizes our entrapment in the physical body. At our point of evolution, the physical body is a vehicle for our souls to use for a lifetime.

Each night we practice dying and each morning we practice being reborn. The soul that is you moves out of your body each night and enters Subconscious mind, the land of dreams. The dream state gives us information about the previous day's experience. We assimilate and we write the dream down in a notebook the next morning and we are prepared for the next one day's lifetime. At the end of many one day lifetimes we go into the Subconscious mind again, but we don't come back out to that physical body. This we refer to as death. We assimilate the previous day's lifetime experience. We do this for a while then it is time to once again come out with a purpose drawing upon and adding to our soul growth, with a message from those previous lifetimes.

From the learning of that previous lifetime the soul creates its new lifetime and its new physical body. And how is that dream expressed? It's expressed in your choice, male or female body, of your sun sign, of your time of birth, and place of birth. It's expressed in race, in the country, in the physical malfunctions of your body or being in a body that is healthy in many ways. It is expressed in the numbers in your name. It becomes expressed in the lines on your hands, and in various ways as you form your body. It shows in the choices you have made.

The movement out of entrapment as symbolized in the Bible was led by a man named Moses. He was a prophet and has at times been called the greatest of prophets. A *prophet* represents a goal setter. That goal is to reach the *promised land* and, in fact the Israelites do reach the promised land. Later, Moses died and the Israelites had a new leader named Joshua to lead them into the promised land. *They conquer it*, which symbolizes your own efforts.

There is a need to understand your attention, to control it, and to choose the messages that you receive through the five senses which are your vehicles for receiving information. The will together with the attention and the imagination are your tools for expressing your inner Self in your environment through forms we call creations or manifestations. This is exactly what the Israelites did. They created a nation that ruled the land. It rose up and it had a mighty mind, and we call that mind *Solomon's temple*. There was a lot of wisdom produced in this stage of evolution. *Solomon* symbolizes wisdom.

The <u>Bible</u> presents more knowledge about the entrapment of the soul in the physical body. Then the <u>Bible</u> presents the *New Testament*. The *New Testament* presents and discusses the time of Jesus. The book of *Matthew* of the *New Testament* presents the lineage that led to Jesus. This lineage begins with Abraham and includes Isaac, Jacob, David, and Solomon. *David* represents the quality of reasoning in adolescence.

The plan of creation is outlined very well in the <u>Bible</u>. But we deviated from that plan. We were supposed to learn from observation as souls in the Subconscious mind or the inner mind, as we observed the physical existence. We created a good body to experience in. Imagine if you had been working for a long time to create the perfect car for yourself. Cadillac, Lincoln, Corvette, a Mercedes. Whatever you would image as the perfect vehicle to get you from one point to another. You liked it so well that you got in it and drove around. You liked it so much, that you got in it one too many times and you found that you couldn't get back out of it any more. So you stayed in the vehicle, and the only way you could get out of it was to die. But if you died after a while you would only get stuck in another car, and you got to drive it for a while and you stayed in it until you died again, and so on and so on. This is an analogy of what we did.

The *New Testament* presents the story of the reasoner from the point of entrapment, instead of from the point of observation. We did however create a pretty good vehicle. There is a certain leveling factor that I really liked once I saw this, and that leveling or evening factor is death. Death evens things out to where you always get the opportunity that you need and nobody gets too much or an unfair advantage. That great evener or that great leveler/balancer is called death. No matter how many accumulations of factories, cars or money, how big and powerful you are, at death you leave all those physical things behind.

The next lifetime you come in naked and start from scratch again. Everybody has to start from scratch. You have no physical possessions when you come in. You come in the way you are. That's the way we leave also, with no possessions. So, in our short time on this earth each lifetime it is important for us to learn the lessons that the physical existence provides. To do our duty to the fullest by building permanent understandings and teaching others to do the same.

In the Bhagavad Gita, one of the Holy Books of India, Krishna says to Arjuna, "Do your duty." *Arjuna* represents the leader of the five senses and understanding the Conscious mind, *Krishna* is your own I AM. When you listen to your inner self, your I AM, when you look to see where the greatest learning is, and give it your whole heart you are doing your duty.

In the Bible, *Jesus* represents the knowing quality. *John the Baptist* represents the believing quality while *Jesus* represents the knowing quality, which is the action of knowing. Believing always comes before knowing. John the Baptist, who was the harbinger, prepared the way for Jesus. Jesus went down to the river Jordan where John the Baptist was baptizing people. John the Baptist baptized people by immersing them in the water. John's baptism was submersion in water. Jesus walked up and John did not want to dunk Jesus in the water because Jesus was greater than he. John said, "Are you the one?" Jesus replied, "Yes, I'm the one. I'm the one you've been talking about and preparing the way for." So John says, "Will you baptize me? Why don't you baptize me because you are greater than me." Jesus says "You baptize me." John said, "Well, I'm not even good enough to tie your shoe. I'm not even that good. I can't do it."

Believing is just as good a quality as knowing because without believing you never get to knowing. If you go around acting like you know it all, you never get to knowing. You don't even stay in believing because if you think you know it all you really secretly doubt that you know anything and that's called a superiority complex sometimes manifested as an inferiority complex and it's a refusal to learn. When Jesus said "baptize me," he indicated his willingness to complete and come to terms with this step called believing because he was ready for the next step. So John baptized Jesus in the Jordan River. Jesus came up out of the water, a dove descended from Heaven and a voice from God boomed, *This is my beloved son in whom I am well pleased.*"

John said, *"I baptize you with water, but the one that comes after me will baptize with the fire and the spirit."* The Bible uses the word *"spirit"* a lot but in looking at the meaning of *spirit* we recognize another word that can be used with spirit interchangeably is Mind.

Baptizing the Mind and the *spirit* gives you a clear picture of commitment to use the whole *Spirit* and the whole Mind. *Water* represents, in the language of mind, the symbolic language, our conscious waking, physical experience. A *baptism* is a commitment to cause something to happen. The commitment of a baptism in water is the commitment to cause physical creations to occur. The way you set the learning process in motion is activity towards the goal.

Jesus baptized with the whole Mind, the holy spirit and the fire. *Fire* represents expansion, and it is a greater baptism. *Baptism by fire* means to create not only with the physical, but the whole Mind. You create the physical experience and from that experience you receive into the Self, the understanding of the whole Self. You add permanent learning to yourself so that you prosper in your soul development, in your spiritual awareness, in your motion toward enlightenment. The baptism of fire is in effect a quickening, an enabling for that individual, causing more attention and more awareness and more emphasis on learning and soul growth from each experience. Also more emphasis on using the will and more emphasis on developing the perceptive abilities, that include reasoning and perception.

Jesus, before he began his ministry and after he had this baptism, is pictured as confronting the Devil in the wilderness. The *Devil or Satan* symbolizes the conscious ego. Ego is identity. When you identify who you are, where you are, where you have come from, then you know where you want to go. You are motivated to cause forward motion, to become like your mental parent.

Then Jesus began his ministry. Jesus is a teacher. He goes before crowds, but he's not called a preacher. He is called a teacher. Because he who teaches learns. This is the way learning occurs. You gain some information, you pass it on through words, you hear what you say, you find out what you know and what you are learning and what you need to learn. This information builds to knowledge. This you do again, and again, and again so the information leads to knowledge which leads to wisdom which leads to permanent understandings being added to the whole Self.

This same process is true concerning anything you are
building. You learn from it, receive it, and then send it back out
again. This is exactly what occurrs when Jesus does his
healings. One of the first things Jesus asked was if the person
believed he could be healed, or sometimes he would say, *"Go
your way and sin no more."* Meaning don't make that same
mistake again, don't have that same attitude that caused the
illness. There is a corresponding attitude with each illness.
When you know the illness you can connect with the attitude that
is causing the illness. When the attitude is changed, the physical
illness, which is the effect, goes away.

When your primary goal is to know cause and forward
motion you begin correcting the unproductive attitudes, healing
yourself, and changing the cause of the disorder. There is a
maturity that goes on and on, forward and forward. Until it
finally climaxes in the Bible as the crucifixion. The crucifixion
shows power over the physical body and the ability to remove
any barriers, remove any limitations and accomplish soul growth
and spiritual development. You have the ability to clear out of
the unconscious part of your brain, all the fears, all the doubts,
anything that is not understood.

The large *rock* over Jesus' grave symbolizes the will that
you use to change any unclear picture, any repetitive unproductive motion to learning and soul growth. You need to build the
ability to cause your mind and your whole attention to be any-
where that you direct it.

After the crucifixion Jesus appeared, on the road to
Jerusalem, and finally to the whole eleven apostles. By this time
Judas had killed himself and was replaced by Mathias. Jesus
said to the 12 apostles, *Full power has been given to you. Go
therefore and preach the good news to all the nations in the
name of the Father, the Son and the Holy Ghost,* The *Holy*

Ghost is the Whole Mind.

The Father, Son, and the Holy Ghost or Spirit are sometimes referred to as the three aspects of God or the triune Godhead. You identify something by naming it, so *name* represents identity. The Father, Son, and Holy Spirit are ways of identifying different aspects of Mind and Creation. *God the Father* indicates Superconscious Mind or an aspect of Superconscious Mind. *Father* symbolizes authority. *Father in heaven* symbolizes the Superconscious Aspect in Superconscious Mind. *The Son* represents the aggressive quality. *Male* symbolizes the quality of initiating action. *Female* indicates the receptive and nurturing quality. *The Holy Spirit* is the whole Mind. *Holy*, means whole. *Spirit* means Mind. *Go therefore, unto all the nations in the name of the Father, Son, and the Holy Spirit* is a symbolic command to teach all aspects of yourSelf to be enlightened in fulfillment of the plan held in Superconscious Mind. This grand plan is designed to give each individual the opportunity to cause rapid soul growth and spiritual development. It is a blueprint that each of us can follow in order to become enlightened and compatible to our Creator at a greatly accelerated rate.

There is another part in the Bible, another symbol or group of symbols that is very important to understand. This symbol is the *serpent* or *snake*. In the book of *Genesis* the snake or serpent is presented as tempting Eve, the mother of all living, to eat of the tree of good and evil. In the gospels the serpent, the tempter, appears again. This time in the guise of the devil or Satan. In the last book of the Bible this serpent symbol appears again in a much more powerful form as the dragon which is the ancient serpent from *Genesis*. In *Revelation* the dragon attempts to take control by trying to destroy the woman who is about to give birth to a son that is to shepherd the nations.

In all three cases, the *serpent*, the *devil*, and the *dragon,* the symbolic meaning that is being portrayed is the use or misuse, growth or expansion of the ego. The ego was originally known as I AM, above and beyond Mind, above and beyond time and space. I AM originally moved outward from the Creator into Superconscious Mind and from there to Subconscious Mind to observe and learn from activity in the physical existence. Through meddling and interfering with the natural growth of events, animals, and animal man in the physical environment we, as I AM's or egos became entrapped in the physical existence. Thereby, we placed ourselves under the cycle of reincarnation and the law of Karma.

As we have grown as ego so has the power of our ego grown. Now we can either be very destructive as a child throwing a temper tantrum or an adolescent who has no emotional control or we can use motivation wisely creating learning and growth for ourselves and others while continuing to use our emotions productively. The dragon ego is the one who has learned to be a responsible Creator and is causing learning and growth in their life every day. Such a one is aiding and is causing learning, growth and spiritual development. Such a one is a teacher.

Your small limited conscious ego must align with I AM and the plan held in Superconscious Mind for you to be like a Creator, for you to be enlightened. Otherwise, you remain engrossed and entrapped in physical existence awaiting another lifetime to possibly progress in spiritual evolution.

The book of *Revelation* presents the *book of life.* Not everyone's name is written in the book of life or the book of the living. This is because not everyone is causing directed forward motion that produces accelerated soul growth. Likewise, not all aspects of yourself are producing rapid soul growth and spiritual development. Since the <u>Bible</u> is about you and all parts or aspects of yourself, you must learn to use this guidebook for soul growth and rapid spiritual transformation in order to gain the highest fulfillment this lifetime and for eternity.

The Book of Awareness

GENESIS

The Book of Awareness

GENESIS

by Jerry L. Rothermel

first published in Thresholds Magazine in fall 1975

Our first work with the Bible will be the *Book of Genesis*. The title *Genesis* was given to the Septuagint, which means Greek translation of the Book, because of its concern with the origin of the world and of the physical human race, and particularly with the Hebrew people. It is evident that the translator was either ignorant that *Genesis* is speaking of the whole man and not just the physical man, or that they were following along the lines of keeping the written word so that only "those who had eyes" would understand what was being presented.

We understand the word *man* to be a derivative from the word *manu*, which means thinker. The thinking processes take place on all levels of consciousness whether it be through the brain of the physical, conscious man or through the soul of the subconscious man. All being one and the same. Thinking is not uniquely exclusive to the physical man, but takes place in each level of consciousness. For generations, we have had others think for us. Even at this present time, we are continually bombarded with the media presenting the idea that it isn't necessary for man to think. With this we totally disagree. For man to fulfill his purpose and destiny, it is very necessary that man think, and come to conclusions and understandings for himself, for his own soul progression.

We find in existence throughout the Universe that there is nothing existing without a purpose. So in discovering the purpose of man's existence it would be necessary to understand the total make-up of man.

Genesis, in a very beautiful way, has presented the total make-up of man, and how man became physical, conscious man.

We find in *Revelation* the way the physical conscious man can become aware of the total selves. All of the books in between *Genesis* and *Revelation* are merely ways in which the thinker can become aware of the total self with full experience.

I understand man's purpose for existence to be that of becoming compatible with the parent, or the Creator of all existence. You will find your children, once they have reached the age of maturity and have produced children, becoming more compatible with you. This is because you have had experiences that were basically alike and you are able to relate to each other in companionship. This is my understanding of the purpose of man's existence.

Chapter One
Primeval History

With each purpose a set of plans is generally drawn up. So if we would consider the first chapter of *Genesis* as being that set of plans for man, or as we understand it Light, to begin the existence in time and space. I consider the first chapter of *Genesis* as being primeval history, *primeval* meaning the drawing up of the blueprints, or the rules and regulations, in which man can exist and become knowledgeable, and with experience become compatible with the Creator.

First Story of Creation verses 1-31. In the beginning God created the heavens and earth, and the earth was a formless wasteland. We understand the *formless wasteland* as meaning there was no earth. There was nothing of form or shape.

The darkness covered the abyss while a mighty wind swept over the waters.
I can readily see the *darkness* as being the desire or thoughts of our Creator moving across the *water*, which would be mind substance, beginning to form the very first creation.

Let there be light, and there was light. God saw how good the light was.
I understand *light* to be the first and only begotten son of our Creator. *And God saw how good the Light was,* meaning that the creation of light through thought had been complete.

God then separated the light from the darkness. God called the light "day," and the darkness he called "night." Thus evening came and, morning followed—the first day.
Throughout the <u>Bible</u> we find references to "light" and "day." We understand the light to be the original emanation and therefore called *day. Night* is the first separation or first layer of consciousness, and would therefore create a darkness or an unawareness of the origin or light of man.

I understand the separation of the light from the darkness to indicate the first death as presented in the <u>Bible</u>. Every individual who has ever been born into the physical has gone through that very first *death,* or lack of awareness of the origin of existence. Light is of Universal origin and anything that physical man can see within the skies in the Universe is a part of that emanation of the original Light of Creation.

We as individuals were particles of the original emanation of Light, and through the desire to be individual, took on — through the original free choice — the identity of individuality. We began moving out from the original emanation of Light for the purpose of gaining experience and knowledge. We find the first indication of individuality in the verse, *God separated the Light from the darkness.*

In verse five, *God called the light "day," and the darkness he called "night." Thus evening came and morning followed—the first day.* Remember that we referred to the *waters* as mind substance.

Let there be a dome in the middle of the waters, to separate one body of water from the other. And so it happened.

In the separating of the *waters above the dome* (some Bibles present it as *firmament*, and they all present it as *sky*) from the *waters below the dome* we see the separating of different levels of mind. We understand the *waters above the dome* or the *firmament* to be the Superconscious mind. The *waters below the dome* represent the beginning of the Subconscious mind. God made the dome, and it separated the water above the dome from the water below it.

God called the dome "the sky." Evening came, and morning followed—the first day.

Remember that when the apostles were looking after Jesus' ascension, they were looking into the sky. And the man who talked to them asked them why they were looking after the Master into the sky. Does this begin to make sense, now? Jesus' ascension was toward the high self and total awareness. We see the *dome,* or the *firmament,* as being the separation point where the outward thinker [from the Subconscious into the Conscious mind] is separated from the total inner thinker.

Then God said, "Let the water under the sky be gathered into a single basin, so that the dry land may appear." And so it happened: the water under the sky was gathered into its basin, and the dry land appeared.

If you will understand this to be the beginning of the Subconscious mind, and the *water gathered into a single basin* to be the beginning of Subconscious individuality, the *water* still represents mind. When you see this, you have begun to understand the significance of the clay, or the ground, from which God created man.

God called the dry land "the earth," and the basin of water he called "the sea." God saw how good it was.

Can you see how *water* means mind substance and *basin* would be individual subconscious mind? Remember that we have said the *dry land* was the beginning of the forming of the Subconscious mind, and the *seas* are still *water,* or mind substance. So the Subconscious man began to form in its appearance but still with mind substance with which to think.

Then God said, "Let the earth bring forth vegetation: every kind of plant that bears seed and every kind of fruit tree on earth that bears fruit with its seed in it." And so it happened.

Consider that the way our Creator created was through desire. If man, or Light, is an offspring of our Creator, then the Light must also create, or learn through desire. We understand the *vegetation* and the *trees* to be experiences within the Subconscious mind. The *trees that have seed* within them would be seed-thoughts, or ideas, that would be planted within that Subconscious mind and produce *fruit,* or an experience, as an understood experience for the Subconscious mind.

The earth brought forth every kind of plant that bears seed and every kind of fruit tree on earth that bears fruit with its seed in it. God saw how good it was. Evening came, and morning followed—the third day.

Understand that the *seeds in the plants* and the *trees* were all a part of man, or the inner man's Subconscious thinking and experiences.

Then God said: "Let there be lights in the dome of the sky, to separate day from night."

Remember I told you to remember the earlier reference to light and day, darkness and night. Now we're producing an illuminary that will separate the awareness of the inner self from the awareness of the outer self. We understand these to be divisions of mind. The *greater light* is the awareness of the Superconscious mind, and the *lesser light* is the awareness of the Subconscious mind.

"Let them mark the fixed times, the days and the years, and serve as luminaries in the dome of the sky, to shed light upon the earth." And so it happened.

As you reach each level of consciousness, and become aware of the experiences and how they relate through these levels of consciousness, you come in contact with the different luminaries, or different shades of light, while experiencing. The different luminaries serve as marked times, or understandings, and help you to understand where you are in understanding within the earth cycle. And experiencing upon the earth cycle is necessary in order for there to be understanding of the Light, or the origin of existence.

God made the two great lights, the greater one to govern the day,

and the lesser one to govern the night; and he made the stars.
We have already talked about the greater light and the lesser light
and now we'll discuss the *stars,* which refer to the Conscious mind.
In *Revelation* there is a place where the serpent sweeps one-third of
the stars out of the skies and onto the earth. This is the one-third of
man that is trapped within physical existence. When the astrologers
came looking for Jesus, they said that they had *seen the birth of his
star,* or become aware of the new mind in the physical.

*God set them in the dome of the sky, to shed light upon the earth, to
govern the day and the night, and to separate the light from the
darkness. God saw how good it was. Evening came, and morning
followed—the fourth day. Then God said, "Let the water teem with
an abundance of living creatures, and on the earth let birds fly
beneath the dome of the sky." And so it happened.*
The *living creatures* are the different experiences that light is going
through. A *bird* always refers to the soul. Going back to the
Egyptian time period, you will find that even they, in their reference
to the soul, presented it as a bird. So this *bird that is flying beneath
the dome* is soul.

*God created the great sea monsters and all kinds of swimming
creatures with which the water teems, and all kinds of winged birds.
God saw how good it was, and God blessed them, saying, "Be
fertile, multiply, and fill the water of the seas; and let the birds
multiply on the earth." Evening came, and morning followed—the
fifth day.*
These *teeming monsters* would be the different experiences, errors
and ideas that man, or Light, is going through within the Subconscious mind.

Then God said, "Let the earth bring forth all kinds of living

*creatures: cattle, creeping things, and wild animals of all kinds."
And so it happened. God made all kinds of wild animals, all kinds
of cattle, and all kinds of creeping things of the earth. God saw how
good it was.*

These are the different experiences that Light has gone through.
They are experiences within animal forms. If you will remember,
God's creation was done through desire. Light, or man's creation,
also is done through desire. When there is need for a vehicle to
experience in, Light, or man, begins to imagine or image, into
existence different vehicles. So I think this refers to the Light
imaging, or imagining, the different animals as vehicles for experiencing.

Then God said, "Let us make man in our image, after our likeness."
Here we see another creation created. I think that God is talking to
the high self, or the Superconscious mind here. If you will notice,
this is the sixth day of creation. *Let us make man in our image,* in
our image-maker, or in our imagination, *after our likeness,* with the
same capabilities that God has.

*Let them have dominion over the fish of the sea, the birds of the air,
and the cattle, and over all the wild animals and all the creatures
that crawl on the ground.*

To have dominion over something, you must be able to understand
its complete expression of energy. This is why I think that man, or
light, in its soul progression has experienced through all of the
animal forms and has created them. If he has dominion over them,
he does understand their expression of energy and the way it
presents itself.

*God created man in his image; in the divine image he created him;
male and female he created them.*

This is where I really come to an understanding of the creating through desire by God creating man in his image. I think the first extension of man was both male and female, having both the positive and negative attributes of energy's expression. This would be the Superconscious mind.

God blessed them, saying; "Be fertile and multiply; fill the earth and subdue it. Have dominion over the fish of the sea, the birds of the air, and all the living things that live on the earth."
I believe this reference to the *earth* is within the Subconscious mind.

God also said: "See, I give you every seed-bearing plant all over the earth and every tree that has seed-bearing fruit on it to be your food."
I understand this to be man's right to use all of the organs and glands of the brain of the animal, in other words, the old brain, to learn from, the *food* being knowledge, or experiences.

"And to all the animals of the land, all the birds of the air, and all the living creatures that crawl on the ground, I give all the green plants for food." And so it happened.
The *green plants* are the Subconscious experiencing. The animal's progression can only be to the Subconscious level in understanding.

God looked at everything he had made, and he found it very good. Evening came, and morning followed—the sixth day.
That is the end of the first chapter of *Genesis*, which is called the first creation, or the first story of creation. I want to present the beginning of the second chapter of *Genesis* because I think it finishes the first chapter.

Verses 1-4. Thus the heavens and the earth and all their array were completed. Since on the seventh day God was finished with the work he had been doing, he rested on the seventh day from all the work he had undertaken. So God blessed the seventh day and made it holy, because on it he rested from all the work he had done in creation. Such is the story of the heavens and the earth at their creation.

I understand each *day* to be a different time period, or a generation of the progress of man the thinker, or Light, into understanding and maturity. If we take them as they are presented in daily form, we find a complete cycle that Light, or man, has gone through to become human man.

We find that man is presently in the fifth day of creation and learning through the animal body that Conscious man experiences in.

The sixth day of creation will see the evolvement of man into the intuitive, or spiritual, man. This will be a more refined body. Man is now in the process of desiring that more refined body and through this desire is bringing about the coming of the spiritual man, or intuitive man. We have about reached the age of change. We're about to go through the end of time that Jesus spoke of. This will not be the end of the world, but the end of a time period, which is the fifth day of creation of man. I think that the sixth day of creation will emerge over some fifteen hundred years.

God rested on the seventh day and made it holy and this will be true of man also. We learn for six days, or six time periods of maturity, and on the seventh day we are finished with our schooling, or our preparation for companionship with the Creator. Since the seventh day is holy, we should look forward to experiencing with compatibility with our Creator.

Although the seventh day has not happened yet, we can begin practicing for the seventh day in the physical by going to churches, or assembling in any place where we find people of like minds. The *seventh day*, or the *Sabbath*, I believe to be the final progression of Light, or man.

Chapter Two

The first chapter of *Genesis* was our God's intention of the way Light should progress outward into human man, through experiencing.

All of the rules and regulations for Light's experiences to be fulfilled had been brought into being so that Light could be compatible with the parent, or with God. We concluded by working with the first four verses of the second chapter of *Genesis*.

The first chapter of *Genesis* is titled the first story of creation and the second chapter is called the second story of creation. We understand this to mean that the first chapter was the intention of our Creator, or the blueprint, so that the construction of the Earth and the Universe could manifest through thought into physical reality and thus become a place of learning for Light, or those particles of Light that we call Human Man.

Verses one through four. Thus the heavens and the earth and all their array were completed. Since on the seventh day God was finished with the work he had been doing, he rested on the seventh day from all the work he had undertaken. So God blessed the seventh day and made it holy, because on it he rested from all the work he had done in creation.

Such is the story of the heavens and the earth and their creation. A set of blueprints are drawn before any building can be built. Then the building is constructed from the blueprints. We consider the first chapter of *Genesis* as that set of blueprints with all of the regulations and the recognition of the stress and strain that would be applied to man, so that he could mature and become compatible with his God, or the Creator.

We recognize the *seventh day*, or *Sabbath*, as a time period, or as the end of a learning time period for Light and experiencing in matter such as Earth or even other planets, for we do believe that there is Light upon each of the planets. Their existence emanates a type of energy that influences everyone upon the Earth and the Earth also emanates an energy that influences other planets.

Second Story of Creation verses 4-25. At the time when the Lord God made the earth and the heavens while as yet there was not field shrub on earth and no grass of the field had sprouted, for the Lord God had sent no rain upon the earth and there was no man to till the soil,

Notice that the first chapter of *Genesis* had indicated God, or a Creator. We find indication of Lord God in the second chapter. We think that in the interpretation from the original Aramaic language, the word, *God* and *Lord God* were translated as being so close that they began using them interchangeably. But our understanding of this differentiating factor is that *Lord God* refers to Light, and Light's working into matter of the very highest essence of Light.

but a stream was welling up out of the earth and was watering all the surface of the ground.

We understand this *stream* to be the energy, or attention, emanating from our Creator to each particle of Light. *Watering all parts of the earth* refers to the energy that Light uses to exist and experience while maturing and learning to become compatible with God.

The Lord God formed man out of the clay of the ground and blew into his nostrils the breath of life, and so man became a living being. This *breath of life* is the attention given by our Creator to those individual particles of Light. From that moment on the particles of life become individuals, or living entities.

Then the Lord God planted a garden in Eden, in the east, and he placed there the man whom he had formed.
We understand the *garden of Eden* to represent the old part of the brain of the physical man. The old part of the brain is the different glands within the head that keep the rest of the physical body in motion. *East* in the Bible always refers to the controlling area, or head area, of the physical man. The passage about the *garden and man being made from the ground,* is referring to the very substance from which intelligence comes. We understand the *ground* that man was made from to be the mind substance of Light.

Out of the ground the Lord God made various trees grow that were delightful to look at and good for food, with the tree of life in the middle of the garden and the tree of knowledge of good and bad.
We indicated earlier that *food* refers to knowledge, or a place where experience can be derived from. We understand the *tree of life* to be the medulla oblongata. The medulla oblongata is the one point in the brain that cannot be operated upon. It is here that all the nerve cells work outward to the physical body, or inward to the brain.

The medulla oblongata is in the middle of the garden area, or in the middle of the head. The *tree of knowledge of good and bad* would be the pituitary gland. The pituitary gland's purpose is to interpret energy. To interpret means to determine whether a thing would be pleasant or unpleasant. Consider this then to be the reasoning that Light used in experiencing.

A river rises in Eden to water the garden; beyond there it divides and becomes four branches.
We come again to that stream welling up out of the Earth that was

presented in verse six. Again we recognize this as the attention from our Creator to the individual that will give energy to the physical existence, or to the substance or essence of the total man.

Beyond there it divides into four branches. Look at the anatomy of the physical structure and you will find four major energy streams that flow throughout the physical body.

The name of the first is the Pishon;
We recognize this river as being the essence of man's existence in the physical. For example consider the chromosomes. There are two shapes in the form of a horseshoe that begin to form the chromosome. The shapes do not touch to form the chromosome. The shapes do not touch to form the perfect circle but they close together forming two half U's. Within those outer rings you find two more rings, turned ninety degrees, again not touching each other, but forming a space between the two heels of the U's. As the chromosomes split, they form a stacking-like process, one on top of the other until a group of cells have formed together. At the place where the U's do not come together there is a river like bed, or a place where energy can flow through.

it is the one that winds through the whole land of Havilah,
We understand *Havilah* to represent the physical body. If you will, remember the acupuncture meridians that we have learned about. The Chinese have long used this science to control pain, emotions, and the receptivity of the physical body to pain and pleasure. *Pishon* then, refers to the acupuncture meridians. *Havilah* is the whole physical body of the human man.

where there is gold. The gold of that land is excellent;
Gold indicates value. In other words, without this energy of the first river, there could be no life, or existence of the human man.

bdellium and lapis lazuli are also there.

The *bdellium* indicates yang and the *lapis lazuli* indicates yin. This is the balance of the positive and negative factors that flow throughout the entire system of the human man.

The name of the second river is the Gihon;

We believe that the *Gihon* refers to the parasympathetic nervous system. This is the nervous system that begins in the brain and flows down the spinal column separating at the points of the vertebrae joints. The energy then flows outward from the spinal column to each organ and gland within the physical body. This is the outward flow of energy and a part of the yin and yang system.

it is the one that winds all through the land of Cush.

We understand the *land of Cush* to be the area of the spinal column.

The name of the third river is the Tigris; it is the one that flows east of Asshur.

The *Tigris River* indicates the sympathetic nervous system. It is the sympathetic nervous system that returns energy from each organ and gland to the brain. This energy basically forms in the solar plexus and carries the signals from the various organs back to the brain via the spinal column to indicate where the physical body is in need of attention. *"East of Asshur"* indicates out into the physical, or from the neck level down.

The fourth river is the Euphrates.

The *Euphrates* is what many refer to as the Kundalini energy. Farther on in *Genesis* we read of Moses raising the serpent in the wilderness. It was the Kundalini energy that Moses raised. This energy begins at the base of the tail bone and is always available to be used in the physical.

The Lord God then took the man and settled him in the garden of Eden, to cultivate and care for it.

In other words, the physical body of animal man was used for experiencing in the physical so that Light could gain knowledge and thus become compatible with the Creator.

The Lord God gave man this order: "You are free to eat from any of the trees of the garden

You can experience through the glands and organs of the head.

except the tree of knowledge of good and bad.

Remember we said that the *tree of knowledge of good and bad* was the reasoning ability, or conscious reasoning ability within the physical.

From that tree you shall not eat;

This was a commandment. You do not have enough strength yet to use conscious reasoning, so don't partake of the reasoning qualities of human man yet.

the moment you eat from it you are surely doomed to die."

We understand this to be the indication of the second death, or the entrapment into the physical. We believe that Light at that point was not entrapped within the physical but was merely using the physical existence as a means of experiencing. Light itself, or that particle of Light that we call man, had the ability to enter and leave the animal man body at will and experience those things that were necessary to enable him to fulfill his learning at whatever level he was on at that particular time.

The Lord God said: "It is not good for the man to be alone. I will make a suitable partner for him."

At this point, Light was existing in the Superconscious mind and in the Subconscious mind. But there was a need for further experiencing, or for conscious reasoning in the physical. In the beginning, before the physical conscious reasoning had become a part of Light, there was a recognition that the Lord God or what we call the Superconscious, was beginning to recognize that total experience could not be fulfilled only through the Subconscious mind. It would be necessary for Light, or man, to have a further extension of Self for greater learning.

So the Lord God formed out of the ground various wild animals and various birds of the air,
We understand these animals to be Light's various experiences.

and he brought them to the man to see what he would call them;
Unless Light, or man, had experienced within those animals and birds, why would the Lord God bring the animals to the man to name them? In order to name something you would have had to experience that particular thing, or have gone through an experience with that particular thing, in order that you might be able to give a definition, or an explanation, of how it functions.

whatever the man called each of them would be its name. The man gave names to all the cattle, all the birds of the air, and all the wild animals;
He had experienced within each of those existences up to that point; so he was able to explain the energy as it expressed itself in each of those forms of energy. The physical body is only energy in the process of expressing itself in the physical.

but none proved to be the suitable partner for the man.
The animal did not have a great enough reasoning capacity, or a

great enough area for storing knowledge. Notice that in the physical, the brain of the animal does not have as great a gray area as does the animal man, or even human man. We think that the prehistoric man, or the Aborigine or animal man, was the first suitable partner for man.

So the Lord God cast a deep sleep on the man,
We believe this deep sleep is that transitional time that the individual goes through as he is being born into the physical.

and while he was asleep, he took out one of his ribs and closed up its place with flesh.
We understand the *rib* to be the connecting link between the Subconscious and Conscious minds. Emotion is the one thing that is experienced within the Subconscious and Conscious minds during the time of all experiencing in the physical. The *rib* is the emotional level of consciousness that is a part of the total man. Since it is the first inner level of consciousness, we can readily recognize the value in the expression and experiencing of emotion in the physical or conscious mind and in the sub-physical or Subconscious mind.

The Lord God then built up into a woman the rib that he had taken from the man.
The word *man* is a derivative from the word *manu,* which means thinker. So if we have a thinker from which a *rib was taken,* and a *woman,* or a further thinker that had been formed, then we find that it gives value to both Conscious and Subconscious mind. We do not think that the <u>Bible</u> is talking about an individual man, Adam, but is talking about the thinker, Ad-Am, or first thinker.

When he brought her to the man the man said: "This one, at last, is bone of my bones and flesh of my flesh;

This indicates that they are both made of the same substance, and that substance is mind. This gives value to the Conscious mind as well as the Subconscious mind. However, it also gives responsibility for maintaining that substance, or the utilization of the mental qualities of expressing energy.

this one shall be called 'woman,'
Woman means outer thinker, or conscious thinking.

for out of 'her man' this one had been taken."
This indicates that the Conscious mind is merely an extension of the Subconscious mind. I do not think that this is talking about physical man or woman, but about the qualities of expression of each man, or the division of the total mind. *Man* suggests the aggressive act of thinking and *woman* suggests the receptive act of thinking. Unless there is a receiver, how can there be a giver? Unless there is a giver, how can there be a receiver? Look at a light bulb. There is both a positive and negative quality of expression of light energy in the light bulb. The light could not be produced without these positive and negative qualities.

That is why a man leaves his father and mother and clings to his wife, and the two of them become one body.
The Conscious mind is an important part of experience within the physical realm because there is free conscious choice in the physical thinking of man.

The two should function in unison because they are one body. It is also the Subconscious mind that stores understood past experiences. This should give rise to the thought of the origin of genius. What brings about a Da Vinci, a Marconi, or a Bell? These individuals displayed characteristics of ancient wisdom and of lasting experiences that would be unable to be obtained in a single lifetime.

We see that the Subconscious mind stores understood experiences in a permanent Light memory. This should be an everlasting part of man because *man*, or the Subconscious thinker, is a product of our Creator. This is what most theologians call the soul, or the body of the thinker in the Subconscious levels. We find that *woman*, or Conscious mind, is an extension of the Subconscious thinker, but is not everlasting and will deteriorate at the end of each physical lifetime or existence.

The man and his wife were both naked,
Nakedness refers to being pure, but without experience. Therefore the Subconscious and Conscious minds were both without experiences. The minds at that time had not yet had the experiences of reasoning. They had not experienced in the physical where errors could be committed that could entrap them into the physical.

We understand that *sin* is error and not something that is unforgivable. It is merely a mistake that Light has experienced; and therefore there is a need to re-experience it to bring about a complete understanding and produce a maturity within mind.

yet they felt no shame.
We think that chapter two of *Genesis* is a most beautiful explanation of the total man. It gives value and dignity to the thinker. The thinker, or man, has been conditioned to think that he has no value and no worth. Yet we're conditioned to think that we're made in the likeness of our Creator, which would give little or no value to that Creator.

The Conscious and Subconscious minds, being a product of creative intelligence of our God, deserve dignity and recognition of their value and worth.

We are giving our interpretation of *Genesis* so that humanity will begin to recognize the value and the worth of themselves. We find that within the blueprint of the creative experiencing for Light, or man, there is no indication that man has no value, or that man's thoughts are unworthy of being shared with the rest of creation, or with our Creator.

We hope that you are beginning to see your value and worth and that you will continue to expand your mind and learn more about yourself. If you can learn about your own self, you can learn that the rest of humanity also has equal value. You have as much value as any other individual regardless of your relative positions within the physical life.

Chapter Three

As we come to Chapter Three, we have determined that the first chapter of *Genesis* is our Creator's intention of the way that life should progress outward into human man through experiencing. These are the rules and regulations for the son of God, or Light, to use in experiencing.

In the second chapter, we determined that Light was in the process of experiencing and therefore was in the process of Creating also, and that each day of the six days were time periods of Light's progression through experiencing.

In the seventeenth verse of the second chapter of *Genesis,* we read,

"Except of the tree of the knowledge of Good and Evil you may eat of all the other fruits. From that tree you shall not eat. The moment you eat from it you are surely doomed to die."

The Creator did not lie when he told Adam that he would die if he partook of the fruit of the *Tree of Knowledge of Good and Evil.* He was telling him of another way of Life that he would be responsible for if he began to use the reasoning capability before he had some other basic experiences.

The Fall of Man verses 1-21. Now the serpent was the most cunning of all the animals that the Lord God had made. The serpent asked the woman, "Did God really tell you not to eat from any of the trees in the garden?"
Notice the serpent is beginning to tempt or intimidate the woman. Remember that *woman* represents the Conscious mind.

"Did God really tell you not to eat from any of the trees in the garden?"
Notice that "any" is the key word in the sentence.

The woman answered the serpent: "We may eat of the fruit of the trees in the garden; it is only about the fruit of the tree in the middle of the garden that God said, 'You shall not eat it or even touch it, lest you die.'"
Here the Conscious mind begins to use reasoning, but again the serpent tempts the Conscious mind.

But the serpent said to the woman: "You certainly will not die! No, God knows well that the moment you eat of it your eyes will be opened and you will be like gods who know what is good and what is bad."
Again, refer to reasoning.

The woman saw that the tree was good for food,
Good for understanding,

pleasing to the eyes, and desirable for gaining wisdom.

Reasoning and understanding are necessary for wisdom.

So she took some of the fruit and ate it; and she also gave some to her husband, who was with her, and he ate it.
In the second chapter, the man and the woman became one flesh.

The duty of the Subconscious mind is to fulfill all conscious desires, and the duty of the Conscious mind is to add understood experiences to the Subconscious mind. So when it says,

So she took some of the fruit and ate it;
She gained experience from it,

and also gave some to her husband, who was with her, and he ate it.
Which means that through the placing of the understood experience from the Conscious mind into the Subconscious mind there was soul growth.

Then the eyes of both of them were opened, and they realized that they were naked;
Before you can realize anything, you must experience it and make it a part of yourself.

so they sewed fig leaves together and made loincloths for themselves.
In other words, this was a false outer presentation; it was not a natural garment for the souls.

When they heard the sound of the Lord God moving about in the garden at the breezy time of the day,
The *breezy time of day* would be the early part of that particular time period, or the beginning of reasoning man.

the man and his wife hid themselves from the Lord God among the trees of the garden.
They became a part of the brain area in their experiencing because the trees in the garden represent the pituitary, the gland of perception.

The Lord God then called to the man and asked him,
Recognize that the Lord God is mostly working through the Subconscious mind.

"Where are you?"   He answered, "I heard you in the garden; but I was afraid, because I was naked, so I hid myself." Then he asked, "Who told you that you were naked?"
Notice here that the man is beginning to use reasoning.

"I heard you......so I hid myself."
It seems so plain that the Subconscious reasoning was beginning to become a part of the outer presentation of man or the Subconscious mind was beginning to make itself known through its experiences.

"You have eaten, then, from the tree of which I had forbidden you to eat?" The man replied, "The woman whom you put here with me she gave me fruit from the tree, and so I ate it."
Here the Subconscious mind explains that the Conscious mind, in the fulfillment of its duty, had made conscious experiencing a permanent part of the Subconscious memory.

The Lord God then asked the woman,
Now we see the Lord God coming out toward the Conscious mind.

The woman answered, "The serpent tricked me into it, so I ate it."
As far as I can see, this is the very beginning of passing the buck.

Then the Lord God said to the serpent:
It is necessary for us to determine where the serpent could possibly fit into life's experiences. The twelfth chapter of *Revelation* mentions the ancient serpent, the old dragon, the one called Satan, or the devil. This *dragon* is a consumer of offspring, or of children. I recognize *children* to be new ways of life, or new ideas, so you might consider the *serpent* to represent conscious ego. The most beautiful angel, Lucifer, or Satan, was thrown out of heaven. We find that an individual who has a low opinion of himself will develop a false ego in order to hide a negative evaluation of self. The false ego can make you think you are something that you are not, or at least pretend to others that you are something you are not.

"Because you have done this, you shall be banned
In other words, the ego now splits, and it not only is part of the total self but also it is a separate part of the conscious self.

"Because you have done this, you shall be banned from all the animals
From all of the experiences and habits

and from all the wild creatures; on your belly shall you crawl,
Basically, this is exactly what the ego does until it comes into a full awareness of its value and its beauty.

and dirt shall you eat all the days of your life. I will put enmity between you and the woman, and between your offspring and hers; he will strike your head, while you strike at his heel."
By placing hatred between new ways of life in the conscious ego, you are putting inharmony between control or lack of control of the Conscious and Subconscious minds. New ideas do strike at the very head of the ego, while the ego strikes at the very spiritual foundation

of man. (The *heels* or the *feet* should be considered as being spiritual foundation; otherwise, why would Jesus have wanted to wash the feet of the apostles at the last supper?)

To the woman he said: "I will intensify the pangs of your childbearing;
It is very painful and difficult to make changes in your life.

Yet your urge shall be for your husband, and he shall be your master."
The Subconscious mind is the master over the Conscious mind. It is the Subconscious mind that determines the time to incarn physically and the time to withdraw from the physical, or the time to remove the attention from the Conscious mind.

Yet your urge shall be for your husband,
The Conscious mind shall continually strive for the harmony between Conscious and Subconscious minds.

To the man he said: "Because you listened to your wife and ate from the tree of which I had forbidden you to eat,
Because you have used reasoning out into the Conscious mind and it wasn't time yet, here is what is going to happen.

"Cursed be the ground because of you!
Cursed be the mind substance because of you; in other words, you are going to have to form it yourself.

In toil shall you eat its yield all the days of your life.
The Subconscious mind must gain understood experiences through the conscious mind; therefore, it must wait patiently for the Conscious mind to finally harmonize with it.

Thorns and thistles shall it bring forth to you, as you eat of the plants of the field.
Plants of the fields refer to the gland of the old brain with which man reasons.

By the sweat of your face shall you get bread to eat,
Bread represents knowledge.

until you return to the ground, from which you were taken; for you are dirt and to dirt you shall return."
The *dirt* is Subconscious mind substance and therefore *man*, or *Adam*, is from the Subconscious; *woman* or *Eve* is from the Conscious mind.

The man called his wife Eve, because she became the mother of all living.
Now the attention is focused in the Conscious mind, or the five senses. This is where you live.

Remember in Chapter Two, the Lord God told the man that if he even touched the fruit of the tree of knowledge of good and bad that he would die. Yet in verse twenty of the third chapter, we find that neither man nor woman is dying, but are being told how they will experience and the way in which they can work back toward compatibility with the Lord God. The *man* is calling his *wife*; that is, the Subconscious is calling the Conscious mind Eve because she became the mother of all the living and this makes me think that this was another layer of consciousness that was attached to the total light principle or the I Am principle. So the outward mind, or the Conscious mind, at that time became the part where man must experience for compatibility. They do not die physically but change their consciousness in a further pushing outward for experiences.

Then the Lord God said: "See! The man has become like one of us, knowing what is good and what is bad!
The Subconscious mind has become aware of the reasoning ability and has become like a god.

Therefore, he must not be allowed to put out his hand to take fruit from the tree of life also, and thus eat of it forever."
In our discussion of the second chapter of *Genesis*, we determined that the phrase *"from the river"* (verse 10) referred to life. Man can greatly extend his physical life by effectively utilizing the medulla oblongata and can consciously determine the time of withdrawal from the physical existence.

The Lord God therefore banished him from the garden of Eden,
Remember that we considered the *garden of Eden* to be experiencing with the Subconscious mind through the glands of the animal man, that is, through the glands of the old brain of animal man.

to till the ground from which he had been taken. When he expelled the man, he settled him east of the garden of Eden;
East is the head area, so *East of,* would be being responsible for the physical body or the lower half of man. This makes sense because the thyroid gland is located at the throat, and this is the energy transformer which functions in the physical; and your utilization of the will determines the rate of your soul growth.

When he expelled the man, he settled him east of the garden; and he stationed the cherubim
Which I believe to be the throat chakra.

and the fiery revolving sword, to guard the way to the tree of life.
I consider the *revolving sword* to be the law of karma. The third

chapter, in talking about man dying and yet continuing to live gives credibility to what Jesus said when he talked to his apostle, *"Once I was dead and now I live forever."* I think he was saying that once He too was trapped in the physical, the same as you and I are right now, but that He had overcome the physical magnets or impulses through experiencing in the physical and had become aware of His sonship to the Creator, or oneness with the Father. Now his attention was continual and no longer withdrew into the Subconscious mind at death but continued in an awareness of eternal life. It is my belief that eternal life did not begin with the physical birth in that incarnation but began many eons of years ago when Light first came into existence. I think that Light is the only begotten Son of our Creator, and that we, as individuals, are particles of that Light. Once we become aware of our Sonship and our place in the scheme of all creation we can truly claim to be children of God.

These interpretations of the *Book of Genesis* are reprinted from *Thresholds Magazine* with permission from the Board of Governors of the School of Metaphysics.

Is Keeping the Commandments Enough?

by Barbara Condron

from a sermon given on June 7, 1987 in Des Moines, Iowa

When I was young I was taught that there were ten commandments. I do not even remember the first time I was introduced to
them. It was probably during Sunday school, that regular
weekend time when Christians of like ages gather to learn about
Godly matters. The child part of my memory recalls the commandments as a list of things you were supposed to not do. As I
grew older this troubled me, because I wanted to know why.

My adult eyes would see them years later in much the
same light. When read for physical meaning, the Biblical
commandments given to Moses do not tell you what to do, they
describe what you are not to do. Even so, they are at the very
least a good system of rules to live by, a sound code of ethics that
encourages civilization to progress. As I got older I began to
realize this. The commandments are an intelligent list of ideas
that encourages us to refrain from hurting someone else. "Thou

shalt not... take the Lord's name in vain, kill, commit adultery, steal, bear false witness (lie)." Each takes from someone else. At one point I began to believe the ten commandments were really good laws to live by. The first one addressed Man's relationship with his Maker, with his God, so these are holy laws. This elevated them above and beyond human laws – our speed limits and our places to park or not park, those kind of manmade laws. These commandments were a covenant beginning with God and reaching through our dealings with all others, giving them an element of importance to all of us no matter who we were, how old, where we were.

As I kept seeking answers to my questions about life and existence, I learned about the other Holy Works of the world. I was raised on the Bible by people who believe it is God's word, that God inspired the men who wrote the Bible. It would be a long, sometimes arduous, always rewarding journey to come to terms with the truth in that. As a result when I went off to college I thought that the Bible was all there was, take it or leave it, and I had left it several years before. When I learned there are all these other religions, each with their own Holy books, I began to wonder what made the Bible so special. I wondered if it was the only book that was special in that way. I found the answer when I began studying metaphysics.

The Rosetta Stone was learning the language that all minds speak, the language used in our dreams. This is a Universal Language, a communication from mind to mind, transcending our physicalness. I started reading the Holy Scriptures from throughout the world, interpreting them like a dream, in the universal symbols I was learning. My life changed. I saw that, indeed, there was no particular book, there was no particular person, there was no particular place on the earth, past or present, that had exclusive rights to the Truth. Beyond the dogma of religion where sometimes such rights are claimed was a greater, Universal Truth. I learned that each of the Holy Scriptures of the world talk about the "ten commandments" and my desire to understand their inner meaning at last began to be fulfilled.

If we are going to know if keeping the commandments is enough or if there is not a little bit more that we are to do, we first need to study those ten commandments. If you have got a <u>Bible</u> you may want to turn to *Exodus 20* because as we go through these, some of these you are going to recognize and have right before you in your <u>Bible</u>; some of them are going to shock you, because it will not be necessarily the words in front of you. *Exodus* is the second book in the <u>Bible</u>. Chapter 20 begins like this: *Then God delivered all these commandments. "I, the Lord, am your God, who brought you out of the land of Egypt, that place of slavery."* This we understand to be the first commandment.

The second commandment reads like this: *"And now, oh prince of Pandu, Arjuna my well beloved student listen unto my further supremely and mysterious teachings, which now I shall reveal unto thee, for thy good and because of my love for thee. Give unto thy heart and mind and soul and understanding and thought and interest and attention, oh Arjuna my beloved, place them all upon me, who hath declared my true being unto thee. Serve me alone, worship only me, bow down to me alone and pledge thee that thou shall surely come to me, thou who are my loved one."* (from the <u>Bhagavad Gita</u>)

Third commandment from *Exodus* you find at verse 7: *"You shall not take the name of the Lord, your God, in vain; for the Lord will not leave unpunished him who takes his name in vain."*

The fourth commandment comes from the <u>Koran</u>: *"Children of Israel remember my blessing, wherewith I blessed you and fulfill my covenant, and have all of me, and believe in that I have sent down, confirming that this is with you and be not the first to disbelieve in it, and sell not my signs for a little price, and fear you me, and do not confound the truth with vanity and do not conceal the truth willingly, and perform the prayer and pay the alms, and bow with those that bow. Will you bid others to piety and forget yourselves while you recite the book? Do you not understand? Seek you help in patience and prayer, for grievous it is save to the humble who reckon that they shall meet their Lord, and unto him they are returning."*

The fifth commandment from *Exodus* in verse 12: *"Honor your father and your mother, that you may have a long life in the land which the Lord, your God, has given you."*

From the Buddha scriptures, commandment six: *"Those who are suffering or who fear suffering think of nirvana as an escape and a recompense. They imagine that nirvana consists in the future annihilation of the senses and the sense minds. They are not aware that universal mind and nirvana are one and that this life and death world and nirvana are not to be separated. These ignorant ones, instead of meditating on the imagelessness of nirvana talk of different ways of emancipation; being ignorant of and not understanding of the teaching they cling to the notion of nirvana that is outside of what is seen of the mind and thus go on rolling themselves along with the wheel of life and death."*

The seventh commandment is: *"You shall not commit adultery." (Exodus 20:14)*

The eighth is: *"You shall not steal." (Exodus 20:15)*

The ninth, from the Pali Sources: *"What now is right speech? There someone avoids lying and abstains from it; he speaks the truth and is devoted to the truth, reliable, worthy of confidence, is not a deceiver of men. Being at a meeting or amongst people or in the midst of his relatives or in society or in*

*the king's court and called upon and asked as witness to tell
what he knows he answers, 'I know nothing' and if he knows, he
answers, 'I know for I have experienced.' If he has seen nothing,
he answers, 'I have seen nothing' and if he has seen, he answers,
'I have seen.' Thus he never knowingly speaks a lie, neither for
the sake of his own advantage nor for the sake of another
person's advantage, nor for the sake of any advantage what so
ever."*

    The tenth commandment: *"You shall not covet your
neighbor's house, you shall not covet your neighbor's wife, nor
his male or female slave, nor his ox or ass, nor anything else that
belongs to him." (Exodus 20:17)*

    When we get into the *New Testament* of the <u>Bible</u> we
find that Jesus adds another commandment. He says that there
are two great commandments and the second one that he quotes
does not appear in *Exodus.* That commandment that he gives us
is *"love ye one another"* and I think that is best described in the
<u>Tao Te Ching</u>: *"In the world many call me great, yet I seem to
have no intelligence. The master, indeed, is great, yet he also
seems to have no intelligence. As regards our intelligence its
smallness is of long continuum. The master and I have three
treasures, we hold them and prize them. The first is called deep
love. The second is called protectiveness and the third is called
not planning to be first. Having deep love you then have courage. Having protectiveness you then can give freely. Not
planning to be first you will be a perfect instrument that will
endure. Now, men neglect deep love and seek courage, they put
aside protectiveness and seek extravagance, they leave the
second place and seek the first, then death comes. The master
fights by means of love, then he conquers, he keeps guard by
means of it then he is impregnable; heaven will save him and by
love will defend him."*

When you expand your awareness of the commandments and you see them as more than just physical rules of what not to do, you reach in yourself to know how the truth is touching you. Only from this inner, self-revelatory state can you can begin to see that all the Holy scriptures in the world convey the idea of the commandments. Different people, different languages, different ways of speaking but the same ideas. In some areas certain rules are stressed while others are fallow, but the spiritual codes have always existed in progressive societies. This is why humanity has evolved throughout thousands of years. The development, the spiritual evolution of understanding the essence of these commands is intrinsic to the health and well-being of every person on the planet. The reality of interfaith is expanding the mind to embrace all so the unifying Truth can illumine individual awareness. This happens when the commandments are held in high regard as the governor of our thoughts and actions.

When we endeavor to live up to these commandments there is still something else that we need to do. Jesus talked about this in the *New Testament, Luke, Chapter 18.*

Jesus of Nazareth was a man who walked on the Earth, as you and I, over 2000 years ago. He became known as the Christ, coming from the Greek *Christos* which means "anointed." Christ is a title. If we wrote the Bible today we might call someone "Dr." or "Mother." The title denotes a certain position attained in life. The same is true with the title of Christ. This title signifies not the attainment of physical knowledge, nor even physical skill, rather Christ signifies an illumined awareness, a state of being. I believe this is the ideal for everyone on this planet. This enlightened state of being displayed by Jesus, and Gautama, and Zarathustra, and Mohammed, and others before us.

Jesus learned throughout his life, beginning his teaching and ministry around the age of thirty. The New Testament includes four records, written by different males, primarily about the last years of his life. As is true of many great masters of consciousness, Jesus taught in parables. Many times the disciples would ask why he spoke in parables, wondering "why do you not just come out with the truth?" He had a response for that and it is in the gospels if you want to find it. This is understanding the Bible on one level.

Jesus also in this book represents you and I. You and I reaching toward the state of knowing. Not just believing who we are or where we came from or why we are here or what we are supposed to be doing and having really good beliefs about it, but taking that belief and putting action to it so that we *know* who we are and we *know* where we came from and we *know* what we are here to do. Such knowing brings Christ awareness to the seeker. This is what Jesus addresses when he meets the man who wants eternal life.

Starting with verse 18: *Of the ruling class one of the ruling class asked him then, "Good teacher, what must I do to share an everlasting life?" Luke 18:18-30. Everlasting life* in the language of mind symbolizes the awareness that there is indeed more than just the physical existence. We tend to look at our physical existence as the end all, be all, so we direct much of our love, our energy, our attention into physical pursuits. We tend to stop there which makes physical death a demon lurking at our door waiting to catch up with us any moment. We live much of our life trying to escape the fact of physical death. An ignorance of everlasting life is perpetuated by our fears. The more engrossed we are in materiality the more easily we forget our existence prior to this lifetime. The more our senses are engrossed in physical pleasures, the easier it is to stop imagining

existence following this plane's experience. This man wants to
know what he has to do to have everlasting life.

*Jesus responded to him, "Why call me good, none is
good but God alone. You know the commandments, you shall
not commit adultery, you shall not steal, you shall not kill, you
shall not bear false witness or be dishonest, you shall honor thy
father and thy mother." He replied, "I have kept these since I
was a boy."*

I was really impressed when I first read this; that there
would be someone who would come up to this man Jesus, that
could say to him knowing that he had a lot of awareness, knowing that he could read people's minds because he knows people's
thoughts, and say "I have kept all of these commandments."
This is something that I aspire to. So whatever you can imagine
someone like that being – *that* is what this man is and he is also a
ruler.

*When Jesus heard this he said to him, "There is one
thing further that you must do."* How often have you heard that?
Maybe you are at work and you have done all the work that
you're supposed to do and then somebody comes in and says,
"Can you do one more thing?" One more thing that you must
do; how else are you ever going to learn what your limitations
are, and learn that you can conquer them? How are you ever
going to know what your true essence is, what you are capable of
unless you do everything that you can do and you think you need
to do, and you do it well, and then there is an opportunity to do
even more. That is the condition this man is in. He has kept all
the commandments, but there is "one thing further you must do."

*"Sell all you have and give to the poor. You will have
treasure in heaven, then come and follow me."* Now I know that
there are a lot of ministers in churches who have used this quote
as well as others in the <u>Bible</u> to fill church coffers. I do not think

that is what Jesus is talking about. What is most important is what are you going to sell? If you sell everything that you have, what are you going to be left with? I think most of you would probably think nothing, but not so. In the Universal Language of Mind *"selling all that you have"* is using everything that you have got. Everything that you already possess. What you possess as a thinker are all the understood experiences from many lifetimes, from many experiences. If you do not *"sell"* them – if you do not use them and give of and from them – then you hoard. You are like the miser, separated and alone. So you have to sell all that you have and give it to the poor.

Who are the *poor?* What are you going to do with these understandings? Do you realize right now there are things that you would like to do but you are really not sure that you can? But you would really like to do them? That there are things you want in life, there are ways that you want to be, ways you want to express? Things that you want to accomplish, but you have not done it yet? This is *being poor.* When you sell what you have, what you already possess, what you have already built, and you give to the *poor,* you are growing in understanding, you are growing in awareness. The Subconscious Mind is a half of a whole. It has space for more and more understanding of how to become compatible with the Creator who brought us into existence. Right now we have many of those understandings completed and there are only just a few left to discover and make a part of ourselves. We are very close to the second coming of Christ. We must keep the commandments, see value in them, live by them, grow in our awareness and understanding of what *to do* instead of what not to do. Then we must respond, using those understandings so that the *poor,* the weak, the inexperienced parts of you can become filled. Doesn't sound so bad now does it? Doesn't sound like you are going to have to say goodbye to something and never see it again.

Unfortunately, like most in his day and time, this man doesn't know the language of mind so *on hearing this he grew melancholy.* He probably thought Jesus wanted all of his money for he was a very rich man. *When Jesus observed this he said, "How hard it will be for the rich to go into the Kingdom of God. Indeed, it is easier for a camel to go through the needle's eye than a rich man to enter the Kingdom of Heaven."*

How many times has someone complimented you on the way you look, on the way you talk, on a gift that you gave, on a job well done? What was your response? "Oh, it was nothing. Oh, anybody can do that. Oh, they probably are not sincere, or they probably want something from me. They are just saying that to get on my good side, because they want something in return." When you are *rich*, when you can do things well, you have got to admit it in order to cause spiritual evolution, *to enter the Kingdom of Heaven.*

His listeners asked him, "Who then can be saved?" to which he replied, *"Things that are impossible for men, are possible for God."* Mankind's physical history is filled with stories of genius crucified. There have always been people who ridicule, mock, and condemn evolution accelerating ideas. Be it the idea that the earth is round or man can fly or that dreams meaning something important or that we can think of something and have it materialize, those who have not, cannot, and will not conceive such concepts try to make themselves look bigger by destroying the progressive among us. Why is that? There are many people who have been excommunicated through the Catholic Church throughout history because they were innovative thinkers, because they went outside what was normally accepted. The truth is it is the imaginative thinkers, the ones filled with genius, who we remember throughout time. Many, like Jesus and Gandhi, were willing to give their physical lives in exchange for the work they were here to do. Everything we now enjoy, and too often take for granted, was created by an innovative thinker whose vision was beyond that of the mass of people.

To be aware is to realize you are one of these people. There are ideas that you have every day that could lift you beyond what the mass of people think. What do you do with those thoughts? How do you make them alive in your life? Answer this and you will go beyond keeping the ten commandments, you will begin using the wealth only you possess, wealth beyond physical metals and possessions. Things that are impossible for *men*, those who only think physically, are possible for God, a creator.

Peter said, "We have left all we own to become your followers." His answer was, "I assure you that there is no one who has left home, or wife, or brothers or parents or children for the sake of the Kingdom of God who will not receive a plentiful return in this age and life everlasting in the age to come." The present age describes our point of spiritual evolution. It is a time to move from believing into knowing, to apply reasoning to produce intuition. Peter is the connecting link. *Peter* signifying will recognizes the need to continue motion in the life to which Jesus teaches that all that has become known, all that has been made a permanent part of Self through understanding will produce in two ways. First, the pentiful return is the alignment with Universal Laws which assures everyone in harmony with them abundance. Kindness begets kindness, giving respect opens the door for receiving respect. Like attracts like. Secondly, those understandings you make a part of self today will endure for they are the ones needed to become compatible to your Creator. *This age* is the time of developing Spiritual Man. *The age to come* is Godman, compatibility with our Maker. To *follow Jesus* is to commit to the consciousness of a knower, one who understands Universal Truth from experience. Such consciousness is that of a sage.

The Bible teaches how to be that wise, that rich. This is one of my favorite passages. The richest man in the Bible, the one who had any woman he ever wanted, any number of offspring, hundreds of men at his command, advisors, counselors, priests, military people, every possession available. The one who was able to build the temple for the Lord was also the wisest man in the Bible. *Solomon* represents a stage in the cycle of awareness, a stage that enables the man Jesus to teach as he did and frees you and I to believe and know that we, too, can become enlightened, a Christ.

"That night God appeared to Solomon and said to him, "Make a request of me and I will grant it to you." Solomon answered God, "You have shown great favor to my father, David, and you have allowed me to succeed him as King. Now, Lord God, may your promise to my father David be fulfilled. For you have made me King over people as numerous as the dust of the earth. Give me, therefore, wisdom and knowledge to lead these people, for otherwise who can rule these great people of yours?" God then replied to Solomon, "Since this has been your wish and you have not asked for riches, treasures and glory, nor for the life of those who hate you, nor even for a long life for yourself, but have asked for wisdom and knowledge to rule my people over whom I have made you King, wisdom and knowledge are given you. But I will also give you riches, treasures and glory such as Kings before you never had, nor will those who come after you have." (II Chronicles 1:7-12)

These are the steps we must take for illumination. The development of reasoning symbolized through the life of the Biblical David produces the direct grasp of truth – intuition –

symbolized by David's son, Solomon. It is this direct grasp of truth that displays itself outwardly as wisdom. It is the wisdom, the Solomon within you and I, that we must be willing to give completely, freely. Then we will uphold the ten commandments and they will become a guideline for our personal evolution, a light upon our path in our journey to reach the Christ Consciousness.

The Book of Commitment

The SONG of SOLOMON

The Book of Commitment

The SONG of SOLOMON

by Daniel R. Condron

originally published in 1982 as a single volume entitled
The Most Beautiful Book in the World

This book is a treatise on love, beauty, and wisdom. I have studied many of the great books of religion and many of the great spiritual works throughout the ages as well as the more contemporary writers and authors of poetry and prose, historical and spiritual. Never have I found a book so striking in its beauty, its simplicity and the pictures it paints of love. I thought to myself, many times, how sad for many people to never be aware of the value, knowledge, wisdom, and beauty contained within *The Song of Solomon*. Thus, a real need for a book that utilizes the Universal Language of Mind to interpret the deeper meanings.

The *Song of Solomon,* sometimes called the *Song of Songs* (meaning greatest of songs), is so beautiful because, as with most of the books of the <u>Bible</u>, it can be interpreted physically and literally or mentally and spiritually. Anyone, no matter what their degree of evolution and mental or spiritual attainment, can gain value from this book and see the extreme beauty of the love expressed.

If the *Song of Solomon* is interpreted in a physical way, one can recognize the manner with which love expresses in our lives or in the exchange between two people. I will be presenting this book in a manner, that concerns you, the reader, on a very deep level. I will show how each person can learn to attain and gain spiritual harmony within the different parts of oneself and within the different parts of Mind. This begins to reveal the beauty that lies within the foundation necessary to develop the understandings of a creator, and like Solomon, to attain the great wisdom. Wisdom comes from applying, practicing, and teaching that which we have understood to be true to a point of knowing. Otherwise we remain in the believing state of intellectualism, always quoting other people, so called authorities. We never become a true authority on the most important thing, Self.

The *Song of Solomon* is a book that teaches how to cause an inner harmony and an inner growth, which naturally will be expressed outwardly in your daily life, as it becomes a part of each of us. The picture of an alignment of the minds of the individual and the clear, precise, and concise way it is portrayed is the reason for this book's longevity and beauty.

Although all the great spiritual works present Mind and how it functions, for those who have eyes to see, the <u>Bible</u>, in many ways is the most practical. It gives the most detailed, step by step process by which man progresses from a mental child, being created whole and perfect but without experience, to the mental adult, the thinker. This process covers many millions of years and carries us through many cycles of evolution, which is beyond the purpose of this particular book. This presentation will cover one book of many of the <u>Bible</u>. This one I find to be the most beautiful, perhaps you will also.

Introduction

Dreams and the Bible have much in common. Dreams are presented to us in the form of pictures, which are then interpreted into words by the Conscious mind for use in our waking lives. Dreams are the movies of the Mind. To describe a dream entails using words that form a complete picture, so the person hearing the dream will get a good idea (picture) of what the dreamer is describing. For successful communication, a picture must first be formed in the Mind of the speaker. Next, words are used to convey the picture. The listener hears the words and formulates a picture of what is being said in his own brain. The degree to which the pictures of the speaker and listener match is the degree to which the communication is successful.

The same holds true with Bible interpretation except the steps are reversed. When interpreting a dream, the picture is changed to the spoken or written word. When interpreting the Bible in the language of Mind, (which is pictures), the words are seen as a whole picture. This is similar to being on the receiving end of communication and attempting to put the words into a cohesive picture. The reason the Bible may be interpreted in this manner is due to the fact that the people who wrote the Bible understood Mind and how it works. They, therefore, wrote the Bible in words, to describe how Mind functions. Some of the Bible is also historically accurate. Therefore, each would receive from a reading of the Bible exactly what his spiritual and mental development permitted. For those with eyes to see, the deepest secrets of creation are contained within the Bible. For those who identify only with the physical body and the world of effect, the laws of Moses still contain value.

There are three great divisions of Mind. The division we identify with the most, and use during our waking life, we call the physical or Conscious mind. This is the division of Mind where the electro-magnetic light waves have become slowed down to such a rate as to be called physical matter. The things we experience with the five physical senses are energy slowed down to such a rate as to be perceived by the crude physical senses. Even the things we observe around us, such as cars, houses, and a person's physical body are made up of a bundle of energy which we perceive. It is interesting to note here that even a seemingly dense physical body will not stop x-rays or gamma rays from passing through it because the atoms are so far apart.

The next great division of Mind will be referred to as the Subconscious mind. Here "sub" means that which is behind rather than that which is below. For the Subconscious mind is what the Conscious mind was formed out of. This is the part of Mind we use while asleep and dreaming. It is the part that holds all our past understood experiences from both this lifetime and others. Therefore, the Subconscious mind knows only truth. The Subconscious mind is also the intuitive part of each of us. The Conscious and Subconscious divisions of Mind are the parts which will be most heavily discussed in this book.

The third division of Mind is called the Superconscious mind and contains the seed idea to become a creator. It is your mental blueprint for building a complete Self, a Creator, a Christ within you. *The Mystery of Christ in you, your hope of glory (Col. 1:27).* Your duty is to fulfill your blueprint, the perfect plan for you as an individual held in Superconscious mind. This blueprint must be fulfilled through productive, learning-filled activity within the physical environment. In the same way a blueprint for a bridge is fulfilled through the construction of the bridge through the efforts of the laborers. The bridge being analogous to the Subconscious mind and the efforts of the laborers being the efforts of each individual in the physical, conscious life.

The Old Testament of the Bible symbolically presents the so-called descent of man, the movement outward through the levels of

Mind, slowing the vibration down until we became finally entrapped or engrossed within a physical body. To appreciate this fact you might begin to consider the body, your body, as a vehicle, as you would a car. You might consider that your thoughts do not originate from your body, but from a deeper place called Mind. Everything around us was created from a thought.

Chapter one of *Song of Solomon* explains that Solomon was the son of David. Let us consider that *David* indicates reasoning, the beginning or infancy that is moving to adolescence of the use of reasoning, as we, humanity, began using more constructively the physical level of Mind. *Solomon*, being the son of David, indicates the further use of reasoning to gain understandings and applying those understandings to move from just intellectual and physical reasoning toward the foremost goal, to develop wisdom. *Solomon* symbolizes the full flowering of adulthood in reasoning and the movement into wisdom.

The mother of Solomon, was Bathsheba. *Bathsheba*, a Hebrew word, means seventh daughter or measure of fullness. *"Bath"* means daughter. *"Sheba"* is a form of Hebrew which means swear by the seven. This is a declaration that the things promised would be fulfilled. So *Bathsheba* is the fulfillment of what has been promised. Those who use the physical environment and apply themselves within the physical experience to receive and build understandings shall develop wisdom. They shall learn how to control happenings within the environment, shall gain control of the Conscious or outer mind and shall become "like gods" or creators. Solomon used his wisdom to create a country as each person shall create a great Mind – their own Mind. This is a part of the fulfillment of the covenant that was made in the book of *Genesis 9:8*.

And God said to Noah and to his sons with him. "See I am now establishing my covenant that was with your descendents after you and with every living creature that was with you, all the birds and various tame and wild animals that were with you and came out of the ark. I will establish my covenant with you that never again will all bodily creatures be destroyed by the waters of a flood; there shall not be another flood to devastate the earth. God added, this is the sign that I am giving for all the years to come of the covenant between me and you and every living creature with you. I set my bow in the clouds to serve as a sign of the covenant between me and the earth. When I bring clouds over the earth, and the bow appears in the clouds, I will recall the covenant I have made between me and you and all living beings, so that the waters shall never again become a flood to destroy all mortal beings."

This is saying the seventh level or the physical will be the place of experience for humanity. The *covenant* is that each of us have ability for control over what the living creatures and the birds, and various tame and wild animals that came out of the ark represent. *Animals* symbolize habits. In other words, the thinker has the right to use the physical experience and to apply this to develop reasoning to a very high degree. Reasoning may be applied and used by the thinker when returning and working into Mind aggressively with control and awareness. *Solomon* symbolizes the use of understanding and reasoning to such a high degree that wisdom is developed.

This is a good point within this book to explain the Subconscious mind. Subconscious mind is a storehouse for each individual's permanent understandings. The Conscious mind is the part of Mind most people identify with during the waking hours. The Subconscious mind you may comprehend as being that part which is used in the dreaming time. Your level of degree of control and awareness within the dream state is a good indicator of your degree of mental evolution. Since your Subconscious mind is where understandings

are stored, you may readily see that this part of Mind is what enables
you to be intuitive or to experience things that are not explainable
through physical law such as dreams. Being successful and a creator
involves using not just your conscious mind but your subconscious
mind as well.

Solomon was perhaps the greatest king that Israel ever had.
Israel represents the teacher aspects of the Self. Solomon expanded
the boundaries of Israel and caused it to take in the largest territory
in its history. This is a picture of the expanded use of Mind, which
must follow naturally from the use of reasoning and the application
of understandings.

*In Gideon the Lord appeared to Solomon in a dream by night, God
said, "Ask what I shall give thee." And Solomon said, "Thou hast
showed unto thy servant David my father great mercy, according as
he walked before in truth, and in righteousness, and in uprightness
of heart with thee; and thou hast kept for him this great kindness, that
thou hast given him a son to sit on his throne as it is this day. And
now, O Lord my God, thou hast made thy servant king instead of
David my father; and I am but a little child: I know not how to go
out or come in. And thy servant is in the midst of thy people which
thou hast chosen, a great people that cannot be numbered nor
counted. Give therefore thy servant an understanding heart to
judge thy people, that I may discern between good and bad: for who
is able to judge this thy so great a people?" And his speech pleased
the Lord, that Solomon had asked this thing. And God said unto him,
"Because thou hast asked this thing, and hast not asked of thyself
long life, neither hast asked riches for thyself, nor hast the life of
thine enemies; but hast asked for thyself understanding to discern
judgement; Behold, I have done according to thy word: lo, I have
given thee a wise and an understanding heart so that there was none
like thee before thee, neither after thee shall any arise like unto thee.*

*I have also given thee that which thou hast not asked, both riches,
and honor: so that there shall not be any among the kings like unto
thee all thy days." (I Kings 3:5)*

The productive use of the Heart chakra is indicated here. The quality
of the Heart chakra is love and understanding. The wisdom of
Solomon is therefore intimately tied in with the ability to draw
permanently stored understandings out of Subconscious mind for
use in our physical life. Solomon was a master of the Heart chakra.

Wisdom is the result of using reasoning to gain understandings
through the use of first, gathering information; second, use of
reasoning to draw conclusions; third, gathering and receiving
understandings and fourth, gaining wisdom from the repeated
success from using the understandings, especially in teaching others
what you have learned.

Solomon was a great judge. Solomon chose wisdom above
riches of the earthly type. When a person sets as their singular ideal
and purpose, or the single heart as it is referred to in the Bible, or the
single eye, then that one can use every opportunity in life to learn
from and to gain understandings. *Matthew 5:8* says, *Blessed are the
single hearted for they shall see God.* Also in *Matthew 6:22* I have
found, *The eye is the body's lamp. If your eyes are good, your body
will be filled with light.*

If you live the life for the sole purpose of accumulating
possessions while not fully using them you will have a very lonely
and empty life indeed. However, by using the experiences to draw
conclusions and then to use the conclusions constructively you can
begin to feel a satisfaction that surpasses any peace or contentment
that might be gained from owning great physical riches. Now I want
to explain that there is nothing wrong with being rich, being
physically wealthy, owning property, etc. The rub comes when we
allow possessions to use us. For example, you may decide that self

development may require physically relocating but feel tied down by possessions. This is where things own and misuse you rather than you using them. By using the physical life with the purpose of learning we begin to feel satisfied and to grow inwardly and outwardly. Your money cannot be taken with you from lifetime to lifetime but you can take permanent understandings that have been developed through your commitment to the whole Self.

In *I Chronicles 22:7*, David is speaking to his son Solomon saying:

"My son it was my purpose to build a house myself for the honor of the Lord but this word of the Lord came to me. You have shed much blood and you have waged great wars. You may not build a house in my honor because you have shed too much blood upon the earth in my sight. However, a son is to be born to you. He will be a peaceful man and I will give him rest from all his enemies on every side. For Solomon shall be his name and in his time I will bestow peace and tranquility on Israel. It is he who shall build a house in my honor. He shall be a son to me and I will be a father to him and I will establish the throne of his kingship over Israel forever. Now my son, the Lord be with you and may you succeed in building the house of the Lord your God as he has said you shall. May the Lord give you prudence and discernment when he brings you to rule over Israel, so that you keep the law of the Lord your God. Only then shall you succeed, if you are careful to observe the precepts and decrees which the Lord gave Moses for Israel. Be brave and steadfast: Do not fear or lose heart."

This passage is indicating that reasoning (symbolized by *David*) is not enough by itself. Reasoning has to be applied to produce wisdom. To use reasoning correctly means to trace cause back to yourself. To place the blame for failure or success on someone or something outside or in your environment is a disrespect for yourself, for you have denied your very sonship, the creator within yourself. This is tantamount to admitting you have no value and everything and everyone controls you rather than you controlling the situations and circumstances and causing things to happen. Place then the blame for failure or success, squarely where it belongs, on your own shoulders. As adult, reasoning individuals, we are responsible for ourselves and the environment we choose and create. The person who *builds the house of the Lord* is the one who traces to himself the cause as creator of the situations and circumstances within his life and, therefore knows how to change and improve them. Do not remain in the adolescence of reasoning nor in the compulsive stage, rather, create anew and for the better, and move to adulthood in reasoning!

A house is where we live and since we are not a physical body but a mental being, Mind is where we live. *House* refers to Mind. Building the *house of the Lord* must be done by and for yourself. No one else can build your *house*-Mind for you but yourself, the thinker. Each one can only achieve understandings for the real Self not for someone else. We may aid others, yet the learning can only be accomplished by the Self. This is the way each of us can begin to fill up the Subconscious mind of Self. The Conscious mind is here, to glean understandings for the Subconscious mind. Through this process you and I become *Solomon*! Through this manner we build the *temple to the Lord. The* Lord, when used in the <u>Bible</u> refers to the "I AM," the individuality within each of us.

Chapter One

*Love's Desires
verses one through four.
Let him kiss me with
kisses of his mouth!
More delightful is your
love than wine! Your
name spoken is a
spreading perfume-that
is why the maidens love
you. Draw me! We will
follow you eagerly!
Bring me, O King, to*

*your chambers. With you we rejoice and exult, we extol your love;
it is beyond wine, how rightly you are loved!*

In the second verse the words are spoken as if they are coming from
a woman speaking to Solomon. When we find a *woman* being referred
to in the Bible, there is reference being made to the Conscious mind
and aspects of the Conscious mind. When the word *man* is used in
the Bible, there is a reference being made to the aspects of the
Subconscious mind. To clarify the why of the statement I have
made, it is necessary to read from the Bible book of *Genesis 2: 21
25. So the Lord God cast a deep sleep on the man, and while he was
asleep, he took out one of his ribs and closed up its place with flesh.
The Lord God then built up into a woman the rib that he had taken
from the man. When he brought her to the man, the man said: "This
one, at last, is bone of my bones and flesh of my flesh: This one shall
be called Woman for out of her man this one has been taken." That
is why a man leaves his father and mother and clings to his wife and*

the two of them become one body. The man and his wife were both
naked, yet they felt no shame.

Lord indicates the "I AM" and the *man* indicates the Subconscious mind's aspect. For *man* which comes from the Sanskrit word *manu* means thinker and the true thinker uses both the Subconscious and Conscious minds. To be able to accurately perceive cause, you need to be aware of how thoughts and desires are formed in the Conscious mind and then transferred to the Subconscious mind where they begin to move outward into our daily lives. The I Am is striving to fulfill the purpose of becoming a whole functioning Self. The I Am principle when first created was whole and perfect yet without experience, much like a baby. This presentation is one indicating the effort put forth by the I Am, the individuality, to follow through by maturing to be as the mental parent, a creator.

The *rib* is the emotional level of Mind, much like the ribs that contain the organs within the physical body. So it can be seen, that the Conscious mind and its aspects were created from the Subconscious mind and its aspects with the emotional level of the Subconscious mind serving as the binder, the *rib*, holding the two together. This is why emotions can be felt even though they are not, strictly speaking, a physical phenomenon. The woman had to be created out of the Subconscious mind for the Subconscious mind was created prior to the creation of the Conscious mind–*Woman*, i.e.: coming from or out of man, the thinker. The *man* or Subconscious mind and its aspects leave the Superconscious mind–*father and mother* and clings to his *wife*-Conscious mind. The individual must use the Conscious mind to glean knowledge to add to the Subconscious mind. So the individual may return triumphantly to the Superconscious mind with wisdom and as an adult. The two of them become one body. The Subconscious and Conscious become one body or work together for the growth of the person until enough understandings are completed to enable the individual to return home to the Superconscious mind. By returning home to the Superconscious mind we fulfill the seed idea of becoming a creator, an enlightened one.

If the Superconscious mind is your blueprint for becoming a creator, then the Subconscious, becomes the bridge and the Conscious mind the tools, materials, and labor where the bridge is constructed. For the Conscious mind is where we practice being a creator. It is in the Conscious mind that we build our bridge of awareness to the Superconscious mind.

The *woman* was created from the *rib* of *man* signifying that the Conscious mind was created from the emotional level of the Subconscious mind. The emotional level serves as a motor to cause thoughts to manifest or push out into the physical. Thus the emotions can be felt, even though they are not a physical thing.

It is sometimes difficult to grasp the true difference between understanding and information. For example, a friend may mention to you the fact that milk comes from cows. To which you reply, I know. Yet, unless you have actually milked a cow or at least seen a cow being milked, you do not <u>know</u> milk comes from cows, you only <u>believe</u>, what someone has told you verbally or with the written word.

When I was in college I would stay up late at night reading books, preparing for tests. I would memorize information from these books night and day, even on weekends. Then I would take tests where I would write some of the information I had memorized on a paper designed to find out how much information the students had memorized. In all my years in college I never received an understanding from reading a book. All that I gained was memorized information placed in the brain to be forgotten at a later date. In fact, most of the information I memorized for the test, I had forgotten within a week of the test!

I built understandings outside of the classroom. Only after I began the serious study of Mind was I able to see the difference and thus I began to consciously speed up the rate of learning of respect, authority, confidence, pride, love, receptivity, aggressiveness, determination, purpose, reasoning and power within myself. You need to use information to draw conclusions and then apply them in your day to day life. You can read all the best books about how to drive a car but there will still need to be the practice of getting in and actually driving that car before you can say, I know how to drive a car.

The Conscious and the Subconscious minds are to work together as a team so they may mature and become as their mental parents. Using reasoning and the understandings together creates wisdom. At this point, *the man and his wife were both naked, yet they felt no shame* indicating both the Conscious and Subconscious minds were without experience. Yet we see the descendents of Adam and Eve getting more and more experience and understandings. Following the lineage, this learning is seen to lead to *David* (reasoning) and then to *Solomon* (wisdom, further extension and fulfillment of reasoning). Verse 2 indicates the desire of the Conscious mind for harmony with the Subconscious mind.

More delightful is your love than wine, is indicating that nothing is more satisfying than harmonizing the Conscious and Subconscious minds. More delightful than wisdom itself is the act of gaining harmony between the Conscious and Subconscious minds, for your subconscious mind is your soul. All the *maidens* (conscious aspects) love to be in harmony and at peace with themselves. The Subconscious mind draws the attention of the Conscious mind to it. If you will watch your dreams you will find the Subconscious mind is striving to work in harmony with the Conscious mind and this is one way in which it draws the attention of the Conscious mind to it. Listen to your inner desire and yearning for truth and learning. There is always a searching, a desire for something more until the point where there is the realization that what you sought is within. This is the beginning of consciously developing the inner self. The Conscious mind does follow the Subconscious mind. The Subconscious mind determines the point of incarnation and it determines and sets up the situations and circumstances for the upcoming lifetime at the point of birth.

King indicates control within the Conscious and Subconscious minds. The *chambers* (bedroom or private area) describe the desire for harmony with the Subconscious mind. There is nothing greater than practicing indifferent love and compassion for yourself, except giving the same to others. Appreciating and developing that love for yourself is the point of having the greatest love in the world for others also. This love is beyond any physical experience you may have. Indifferent love entails having respect for yourself even though you make a mistake. It also means learning from your mistakes so they are not repeated over and over. Indifferent love towards others means appreciating their right to learn, yet presenting truth when asked. It also means maintaining enough respect to not allow others to trample over you. In the *New Testament* of the Bible, Jesus drove the money changers out of the temple. He was strong and courageous. True indifferent love deals with respect, honor, and courage, rather than encouraging and promoting weakness and servitude.

Love's Boast verses 5 and 6. I am as dark-but lovely, O daughters of Jerusalem-As the tents of Kedar, as the curtains of Salma.

The Superconscious mind is the division of Mind closest to LIGHT. As I Am moved farther away from LIGHT first to Superconscious mind, then to Subconscious mind, and then to the Conscious mind, or physical environment, the I Am became obscured and dark. However the productive Conscious mind is very beautiful and attractive. The I Am moves all the way out into the

Conscious mind and becomes the conscious ego or a reflection of the higher I AM EGO, your individuality. For ego means I Am.

The *daughters of Jerusalem* are the daughters of Mind, the conscious aspects of the Self (see *woman* chapter 1.) *Dark* indicates a further moving away from your own I Am, your own individual light and true essence. *Light* indicates awareness while *darkness* is lack of awareness. The word Kedar means dirty or dusky or dark, dark skinned, obscure or overcast. Kedar was also the first son of Abraham by Abraham's servant, Hagar. Ishmael was the undisciplined son of Abraham while Isaac was the disciplined son. It was from Isaac that David and Solomon were descended. So *Kedar* indicates an undisciplined aspect as the son of Ishmael. *Kedar*, as used here, as a location or place, indicates a part of Mind that is undisciplined and since the *bride* is talking here we can be sure this is talking about the Conscious mind. The lack of discipline is what keeps our I Am obscured from each of us.

Tents are a *house* meaning Mind and more specifically *tents* indicate the Conscious mind. The *tents of Kedar* indicate the darkness and the movement away from light within Mind or the moving out and engrossment specifically into the physical Conscious mind. *Curtains of Salma* refer to the various veils (levels) of consciousness that were placed between the point where the attention is and the I Am. Salma means covering or garments or mantel or raiment and this is exactly what occurred as the individual moved outward, finally becoming entrapped within the physical level of consciousness.

Do not stare at me because I am swarthy, because the sun has burned me. My brothers have been angry with me; they charged me with the care of the vineyards: My own vineyard I have not cared for.

Being burned by the sun indicates a lack of use or misuse of the

Self awareness and awareness of your inner soul urge. The Conscious mind needs to use understandings to have a productive outer presentation *(garments and clothes.) Taking care of my own vineyard* entails adding to your subconscious mind. The *grapevines* indicate Subconscious experiences and growth. The *grapes* that come from the vineyard are the knowledge that can be taken in through the use of Mind. *Wine*, which is produced from grapes, is the further use of knowledge to produce wisdom. *Now Noah, a man of the soil, was the first to plant a vineyard. When he drank some of the wine, he became drunk and lay naked inside his tent (Gen. 9:20-21).* Noah and his sons lived through the *great flood* (engrossment), yet at the point of engrossment there was little experience in using physical existence. So when the first experiences were registered within, there was not enough reasoning built and understandings completed to be able to use the wine to develop wisdom, hence *Noah became drunk.*

Love's Inquiry verses seven and eight. Tell me, you whom my heart loves, where you pasture your flock, where you give them rest at midday, lest I be found wandering after the flocks of your companions.

The *true heart's love* is the Subconscious mind which is the soul. Forming the union that Adam and Eve achieved between the Conscious and Subconscious minds was the beginning of this love. *Midday* which is the time when the sun passes directly overhead indicates awareness. The Sun which shines brightly at midday indicates a desire to attune to Superconscious mind.

David said to Saul, "Let no one lose heart on account of this Philistine; your servant will go and fight him." Saul replied, "You are not able to go out against this Philistine and fight him; you are only a boy and he has been a fighting man from his youth." Then

David told Saul: "Your servant used to tend his father's sheep, and whenever a lion or bear came to carry off a sheep from the flock I would go after it and attack it, and rescue the prey from its mouth. If it attacked me, I would seize it by the jaw, strike it, and kill it. Your servant has killed both a lion and a bear, and this uncircumcised Philistine will be as one of them, because he has insulted the armies of the living God" (I Sam. 17:32-36).

The evolutionary movement forward of David to Solomon symbolizes the progressive expansion of consciousness from adolescence to adulthood within the evolution of the individual. This means productively applying the Self to the task of producing inner growth and being successful at this task.

Lambs or *sheep of the flock* are those aspects that desire to become harmonious with the Lord. In the *New Testament* of the Bible can be found numerous references to the lamb of God or the Lord. *Then David spoke to Saul: "Let your Majesty not lose courage. I Am at your service to go and fight this Philistine"* (Goliath). *But Saul answered David, "You cannot go up against this Philistine and fight with him, for you are only a youth;* David (reasoning) was a tender of the flocks and was willing to sacrifice anything to protect the *Israelites,* the teacher aspects of the Self. *A lamb of God* is anyone or any aspect of Self that is fully committed to living a Godly life, in alignment with their Creator. This is a person that is striving each day to gain in understanding, awareness, and spirituality.

There were shepherds in that region, living in the fields and keeping night watch by turns over their flocks. The angel of the Lord appeared to them as the glory of the Lord shone around them, and they were very much afraid. The angel said to them: "You have nothing to fear! I come to proclaim good news to you-tidings of great joy to be shared by the whole people. This day in David's city a savior has been born to you, the Messiah and Lord." (Luke 2:8-11)

So you can see that Jesus is an extension of the quality of *David* who represents reasoning. The word *David* means loved or beloved and the word *Solomon* (wisdom) means peace or peaceful one. We see these two qualities together in Jesus, reasoning and wisdom to produce intuitive man, actively expanding consciousness. *Shepherds* indicate the willingness to place all the attention upon using the whole Mind, to give up everything to gain all. The enlightened being is full of the Love of David and the peace that comes from a still mind.

Love and peace are built in the heart chakra when all experiences are used to build permanent understandings.

If you do not know, O most beautiful among women, follow the tracks of the flock and pasture the young ones near the shepherds' camps.

We have here the Subconscious mind's reply, saying if you do not know how to reach me, then follow the way of the lamb, of making a full commitment to yourself to learn from each experience and grow. Take care of the new awareness growing within yourself. Make it your holy goal to be true to yourself and to fulfill your assignment on earth of becoming an enlightened master teacher.

Love's Vision verses nine through eleven. To the steeds of Pharaoh's chariots would I liken you, my beloved; Your cheeks lovely in pendants, your neck in jewels. We will make pendants of gold for you and silver ornaments.

The *Egyptians* and *Egypt* symbolize engrossment into the physical existence. *Steeds* or *horses* indicate will. This passage presents the importance of using the will to move forward into the inner levels of Mind. *Pendants, jewels, gold,* and *silver* are giving us an indication of the value that is developed from using the will to learn to gain greater awareness and use of all Mind.

Love's Union verses twelve through seventeen. For the king's banquet my nard gives forth its fragrance. My lover is for me a sachet of myrrh to rest in my bosom. My lover is for me a cluster of henna from the vineyards of Engedi.

King symbolizes control. A banquet is where food is eaten. *Food* symbolizes knowledge. *Eating* symbolizes mental assimilation of knowledge. Knowledge is assimilated so the Conscious and Subconscious minds can be aligned and control of them taken. *Myrrh* symbolizes sacrificing to the higher self and aligning of the minds through the changing of the vibration, for it gives off a scent that rises to heaven, *the sky. Henna* was used to dye hair, which is therefore taking control of the conscious thoughts. Engedi means fountain of the kid or fountain of fortune. The fortune of Mind is built when there is application given toward gaining understandings thus causing growth as presented by the *vineyards.* The value is in the application, this causes the *vine to bear fruit.*

Ah, you are beautiful, my beloved, ah you are beautiful; your eyes are doves!

The Subconscious mind is beautiful. Much beauty is obtained for one whose perception and attention extends to the Subconscious mind. Beauty indicates the recognition in the Conscious mind of value, wholeness, and goodness in the soul of Self.

Ah, you are beautiful, my lover-yes, you are lovely. Our couch, too, is verdant; the beams of our house are cedars, our rafters, cypresses.

Furniture symbolizes tools of the Mind. A *verdant couch* or green bed is a place for growth and harmony that has been developed between the Conscious and Subconscious minds. The *house* is Mind. Cedar and cypresses are excellent wood and were used by Solomon in building the temple of the Lord. A strong or powerful Mind with a good foundation is presented here due to the harmony developed between the Conscious and Subconscious minds. This is the beginning of wisdom!

Chapter Two

Verses one through seven. I am a flower of Sharon, a lily of the valley.

The I AM, your own individuality is causing the opening up and flowering of consciousness. Even though we are entrapped in the physical behind *veils* (levels) of consciousness, still there is some degree of recognition of individuality, a unique personality. *Sharon* indicates fruitful, prosperous, righteous or just. The part of yourself that develops the righteous productive mental activity which is the correct way to reap understandings is the *most beautiful in all the valley* which symbolizes the productive Conscious mind. Even the Conscious mind, symbolized by the valley, has beauty and value. The goal for all humanity is to expand our consciousness into Superconscious awareness.

As a lily among thorns, so is my beloved among women.

In the previous verse the Conscious mind *(the Bride)* has described herself as a flower and a lily. In verse 2, the bride describes the Subconscious mind. Even though the Conscious mind is beautiful, the Subconscious mind is even more so. Thus, the Subconscious appears as a lily when compared to the Conscious mind *(thorns.) Thorns* also indicate desires, particularly unfulfilled desires. Unfulfilled desires can cause you much anguish. It is the duty of the Subconscious mind to fulfill all Conscious mind desires. If the Conscious mind keeps formulating desires and yet you do not initiate physical activity on those desires there will be much disappointment and pain within the conscious experience.

For example, let's suppose you want a new car. Your old car is rapidly deteriorating and there is a real need to replace the aging vehicle. Let us also suppose that this desire is not acted upon. There is no activity directed in looking for a new job, or a better paying job or an additional source of money with which to buy a new automobile. One day the old car wears out and would take a tremendous amount of money to repair to make it in runnable condition. Money which you do not possess. So there you are with an old car that does not run and a desire for a new car. But, you are without the means to purchase the new car merely because you did not act on your desire. The desire has become your *thorn.*

Weaving a crown out of thorns, they fixed it on his head, and stuck a reed in his right hand. (Matthew 27:29)

Crown indicates control and authority for crowns were worn by kings. *Crown of thorns* indicates control in fulfilling desires and in particular controlling the ability to create. The crown is located on the head, where the gland or chakra of interpretation is located, as well as the pineal gland, which is the gland of control of creation, the crown chakra.

As an apple tree among the trees of the woods, so is my lover among men.

With this verse the Conscious mind, the bride, is attempting to describe the bridegroom (*Solomon*) by comparing him with the other subconscious experience. In verse two the same thing was done except Solomon was compared with the Conscious aspect. The use of wisdom, which comes from teaching truth, produces the greatest aspect of Subconscious mind.

Trees indicate subconscious experience. Apple trees bear fruit that is palatable. An *apple tree* signifies the understandings and experiences that have been added to the Subconscious mind and are bearing the fruitful knowledge and understanding. Knowledge is being applied to build understandings. This use produces wisdom. *Men* are the physical aspects. Hence, the use of *wisdom* (Solomon) in the Conscious mind and in the physical is much more productive and valuable than operating from compulsion or even reasoning alone.

I delight to rest in his shadow, and his fruit is sweet to my mouth.

The bride is speaking of Solomon. The Conscious mind rests in the shadow of the Subconscious mind for with each succeeding veil of consciousness, each level of mind created, there is less light pouring through from the Creator. When there is harmony created between the Conscious and Subconscious mind, there is delight in the use of the Subconscious mind and the use of the understandings stored there. Knowledge (*fruit*), fills that yearning, the empty space inside each of us. *Mouth* indicates the ability to assimilate knowledge (*food*).

He brings me into the banquet hall and his emblem over me is love.

He, indicating the aggressive act, going into the *banquet hall*, or place of receiving knowledge, presents a picture for use of initiating activity on desires for the purpose of gaining knowledge. The Seal of Solomon is the six pointed star. The *six pointed star* symbolizes "as above, so below" which describes cause and effect. This is why the Seal of Solomon contains within it two triangles, one pointed upward, the other downward. When one begins to comprehend the

truth of this axiom, there is the beginning of the release from
engrossment in the physical. True indifferent love is experienced
through the complete awareness of yourself, and understanding
Mind and how it functions. The emblem is the key to the Seal of
Solomon. Thought is cause. When one lives this truth then you exist
in perfect love.

*Strengthen me with raisin cakes, refresh me with apples, for I am
faint with love.*

   Raisin cakes and *apples* represent knowledge. Raisin cakes are
prepared food while apples are raw fruit from the tree. Each of us
becomes strengthened by learning from our experiences to gain
knowledge. We are refreshed by opening up and receiving new
knowledge in its raw state. The Conscious mind's true desire is to
gain knowledge rather than belief or intellectualism. True knowledge feeds and refreshes the true Self, the inner Self as nothing else,
and quenches the desire to know. Knowledge is the offspring that
comes from building self respect and love.

His left hand is under my head and his right arm embraces me.
   For an interpretation of this verse I will quote from *Genesis 48:14.
But Israel, crossing his hands, put out his right hand and laid it on
the head of Ephraim, although he was the younger, and his left hand
on the head of Manasseh, although he was the first-born.* Joseph
responds in Vs. 17 to his father's conduct: *When Joseph saw that
his father had laid his right hand on Ephraim's head, this seemed
wrong to him; So he took hold of his father's hand, to remove it from
Ephraim's head to Manasseh's, saying: "That is not right, father:
The other one is the first born: Lay your right hand on his head!"
But his father resisted. "I know it, son," he said, "I know. That one
too shall be great. Nevertheless, his younger brother shall surpass
him and his descendents shall become a multitude of nations."*

Israel, even though he favored Ephraim over Manasseh, still gave purpose to Manasseh, by placing his left hand on Manasseh's head. The meaning of *left hand under my head* indicates that purpose (*hand*) is being gained in regards to working with Mind and perception in Mind (*head*). Purpose is used with perception and reasoning in the Conscious mind. Remember the right arm and hand were the ones favored by Israel. *Right* means righteous or correct way of using Mind. Since Manasseh was also blessed by Israel, I understand the left *hand* (purpose) to have value also. Together they form a picture of a very strong purpose developed for creating harmony between the Conscious and Subconscious minds (*Solomon and his bride*). Another point for you to consider in the development of Mind, is that Israel (Jacob) was an ancestor of Solomon.

I adjure you, daughters of Jerusalem, by the gazelles and hinds of the field, Do not arouse, do not stir up love before its own time.

Daughters of Jerusalem are the daughters of Mind, which are the aspects of the Conscious mind. *Gazelles* and *hinds of the field* are the habits or compulsive behavior each of us maintains. Do not move to new areas of development unless you have become responsible for what is already manifested within yourself and for those things you have created in your environment. Through responsibility comes freedom.

A Tryst in the Spring verses eight through seventeen. Hark! My lover-here he comes springing across the mountains, leaping across the hills.

The Conscious mind symbolized by woman is communicating to the Subconscious mind symbolized by the word *he*. The Conscious mind is speaking in regards to the action or motion of the Subconscious mind. Thus there is the Conscious mind's recognition or awareness of the response of the Subconscious mind. The movement of the Subconscious mind symbolized by *springing across the mountains and hills* connotes the lofty heights that the consciousness of the individual has attained.

My lover is like a gazelle or a young stag. Here he stands behind our wall, gazing through the windows, peering through the lattices.

The *wall* referred to is the wall between the Conscious and Subconscious minds. Each individual's subconscious mind is always giving to that same person's conscious mind. This is why dreams are so valuable to each one of us. Dreams are messages from the Subconscious to the Conscious mind. The Subconscious mind waits like an older brother or a lover to aid when given the opportunity to do so. *Windows* and *lattices* indicate the windows of the Mind or the ability to perceive from one level of Mind to another.

My lover speaks; he says to me, "Arise, my beloved, my beautiful one, and come! For see, the winter is past, the rains are over and gone.

Your soul which is your Subconscious mind is always beckoning for you to wake up, and cause yourself to be aware and increase your consciousness and knowledge that there is more to life than physical existence and that you are a mental being not a physical body. *Winter* is the beginning of a new cycle. This is the time when sprouted seeds begin to grow beneath the snowy crust of winter. It is the time to move into the next stage of growth which is adolescence and from there into adulthood. The *rains are over and gone*, indicates the time is past when there was no control over the conscious experience.

The flowers appear on the earth, the time of pruning the vines has come, and the song of the dove is heard in our land.

Flowers appearing on the earth indicates the beauty of the new growth within the Subconscious mind. *Pruning the vines* is the act of controlling the experiences so knowledge can be produced and from the knowledge and experiences can come the *wine* of wisdom. *Song* is harmony within and *dove* indicates controlled use of thoughts within the Subconscious mind or subconscious thoughts.

He waited seven days more and again sent the dove out from the ark; in the evening the dove came back to him: and there in its bill was a plucked-off olive leaf. So Noah knew that the waters had lessened on the earth; he waited still another seven days and then released the dove once more; and this time it did not come back. (Gen. 8:10-12).

Here *seven* indicates control. The control has been gained within the Conscious mind and the *dove being sent out* symbolizes the subconscious thoughts exploring and using the control that has been gained.

The fig tree puts forth its figs, and the vines, in bloom, give forth fragrance. Arise, my beloved, my beautiful one, and come.

Figs are the knowledge produced from the subconscious experiences. *Figs* are the fruits of understandings which have been absorbed into your subconscious mind from this lifetime and many others. This verse tells us there is a productive use of past understood experiences. *Figs from the vine* show the good return you have when there is an investment in Self. With the intention to learn from any situation created, the learning quickens. Arise Conscious mind, now is the time to be aware of your lover, your true love, your Subconscious mind, the other good part of self.

O my dove in the clefts of the rock, in the secret recesses of the cliff, let me see you, let me hear your voice, For your voice is sweet, and you are lovely.

Subconscious thoughts travel to all parts of Mind, to the most secret places. Yet all of those unused and secret places can be discovered and used by anyone willing to give the effort to know himself. To practice and develop the will and to control the attention and thoughts is a worthy goal for all of us. The person who develops these abilities will perceive the aspects and parts of the Subconscious mind and will know the wisdom of Solomon. There is no communication sweeter or more beautiful than the communication with Self. A beautiful romance to be gained and appreciated.

Shortly after I began the directed study of Self and Mind, I began to have an urge to write poetry. Now, I had written perhaps a total of 5 poems in my life. Yet, there came a time that I felt the urge to sit down and write and so I did. Since that day when I wrote that first poem of my inner growth, I have found it to be an exciting form of expression for me and a great way to express my growing creativity. And now I have expanded beyond even that. I do not use poetry to express my feelings because I share my thoughts and emotions with others every day in my interactions with others. When the attention is on self growth, the creativity must be enhanced for as we grow we become more like our mental parent, a creator.

Catch us the foxes, the little foxes that damage the vineyards; for our vineyards are in bloom!

Catch and control all habits, all experiences. For now is the time to produce. Do not nip this new growth in the bud, by allowing old limited concepts and attitudes to limit efforts to expand awareness of who you are and what you can be.

My lover belongs to me and I to him; he browses among the lilies.

The true beauty of this statement is that your conscious mind and subconscious mind truly do belong to you and to no one else. When each individual realizes this, there is a beautiful flowering of consciousness! Lilies grow in water yet are a plant. Together we have a beautiful picture of the conscious experience *(water)* and the subconscious experience *(lily)* forming a productive union. The water feeding and nourishing the lily and the lily adding beauty to the water. A fine picture of cooperation between Minds. Marriage between a man and woman is a physical manifestation of the cooperation of the aggressive and receptive principles. A good working marriage can be as beautiful as the lily on the water. Relationship between man and woman is a place to practice being *Solomon* and his *bride.*

Until the day breathes cool and the shadows lengthen, roam, my lover, Like a gazelle or a young stag upon the mountains of Bether.

The *cool part of the day* is the latter part of the daily cycle and therefore is the third part of that cycle which is adulthood. Adulthood indicates productivity and responsibility. Adulthood is producing more than you consume. At the time when an individual becomes mentally evolved, having an understanding of Mind, and cause and effect, he becomes responsible for words, thoughts, and actions. Then will the *lover* (Subconscious mind aspect) come down from the *mountains* (elevated levels of Mind). The individual will then be able to reach those places in the Subconscious mind from the starting point of the Conscious mind. *Bether* means house and the symbol for Mind is *house.* *In my father's house are many mansions* is saying in my mental parent's house *(Mind)* are many Minds. What an exciting manner to end chapter two! A picture of being able to expand your consciousness to all levels of Subconscious mind and to harmonize with those levels with the agility of a gazelle. Perhaps this verse will help anyone see how much control can be gained in that part of Mind which most people use only very slightly, the Subconscious mind.

Chapter Three

Loss and Discovery verses one through five. On my bed at night I sought him whom my heart loves—I sought him but I did not find him.

At night we go to bed, ceasing our physical activity and the Conscious mind shuts down. This is the time we enter the dreamland of Subconscious mind. The physical and material world is where our learning takes place so the sleeptime becomes a period of review of the previous day's experiences in order that assimilation of learning may occur. Night is a time of darkness. *Darkness* when used in the <u>Bible</u> indicates a need for awareness. Think of the times when you were in a darkened room or outdoors on a very dark night. You may recall stumbling over furniture or walking into a tree or wall. Sight is the sense on which we most heavily depend. Without the availability of the sense of sight we seem somewhat lost at times. So with a little reasoning you will see why the authors of the <u>Bible</u> would use *night time* and *darkness* as a symbol of lack of awareness. There is no way you will recognize your Subconscious mind and its aspects without the training of your Mind to reach beyond the simple physical sense awareness, until there is the direct seeing with the Mind which is direct mental perception. Most people are so caught up in the physical world and the physical senses they fail to realize the senses are merely crude tools which the Mind employs to perceive within the conscious experience. The five senses perform only within the Seventh Level of Mind, the physical environment, and do not suffice within the other six levels of Mind. The key is then to learn to see, hear, taste, touch, and smell with the Mind. This is the development of clairvoyant and intuitive abilities.

I will rise then and go about the city; in the streets and crossings I will seek Him whom my heart loves. I sought him but I did not find him.

You will not find your Subconscious mind and know it as you know your Conscious mind until there is a raising of your awareness, your consciousness. *City* indicates a grouping of many aspects of Mind. You will search long in many places outwardly and inwardly before there will be a union between the Conscious and Subconscious minds. Remember, by the quiet mind is the Real Self known.

The watchmen came upon me as they made their rounds of the city: Have you seen him whom my heart loves?

The *watchmen* are the guards of the Subconscious mind. The guards being the different qualities of energy of each of the four levels of the Subconscious mind. Anyone desirous of gaining harmony with their Subconscious mind will need to approach the guards. There must be a harmony, a communication and some control gained over the energies in the Subconscious mind. Each of us will need to learn to use the refined energy and substance of the Subconscious mind before final union is achieved.

Do you remember the first time you tried to swim? You probably got in the water and began splashing but had a hard time keeping your head above water. There was very little control. It was also very difficult to move in the direction you desired. The water was in effect, a form of energy with which you were not familiar. So it required many hours of practice to gain control in this form of energy. In a similar fashion you must practice and practice in order to gain control and be able to move within the energy of the Subconscious mind.

At first you experience your hearts desire, your inner love, your real soul mate. Then is required effort on your part to cause a permanent union with the soul mate of your heart which is your soul, your subconscious mind.

I had hardly left them when I found him whom my heart loves. I took hold of him and would not let him go till I should bring him to the home of my mother, to the room of my parent.

Remember your goal and keep it Holy. Your goal is to align Conscious and Subconscious minds, in order to attune both to Superconscious mind. By the time you have aligned Conscious and Subconscious minds there will quickly be an attunement to Superconscious mind as symbolized by the *mother's home.*

Upon finding your true love, your awareness of Subconscious mind, never let that go, never back off from the commitment you made to yourself, always follow through and make your goal Holy. *Home* of the Conscious Mind's mother is the Superconscious mind. The Superconscious mind contains the seed idea for each person to become enlightened. The seed idea of the creator that each individual can be, in other words, a whole functioning self. The picture presented here is one of returning home after a long absence, having had much learning and growth and being much the wiser and willing to do whatever it takes to be with the mental parent once again.

House is the symbol for Mind, for Mind is where you live. *In him we live and move and have our being,* as Paul put it. Man is not the physical body but actually a thinker, a mental being, so it makes sense that your home would be in Mind. Once there is a harmony built with the Subconscious mind and a bringing together of the Conscious and Subconscious minds, then further service to mankind and control of self and Mind will bring about the day when the next step will be taken. And that next step is to enter the Superconscious mind with awareness and control. This is the returning home of the *prodigal son.*

I adjure you, daughters of Jerusalem, by the gazelles and hinds of the field, Do not arouse, do not stir up love before its own time.
I'm going to let you in on a little secret. This secret has to do with time. Throughout the ages men have searched for the secret of youth. The secret of time has to do with speed, velocity and consciousness. Let's say you have a problem getting everything accomplished each day, you just don't seem to have enough time. No matter how hard you work, you get more and more frustrated, more worried and farther behind. Since you are working from sun up to sun down, there must be something lacking and it is not activity. Let's trace the problem back to its core, the center of the universe. Now, the center of the universe is you! This means there is something limiting within you or there would not be this time problem. The problem is your thought, your attitudes. The key to changing the center of the universe is to change you, the thinker. For change is growth and with each change, the inner motion of the individual is quickened. With this quickening, the gear ratio between you and your environment (universe), comes more and more into synchronization. You find somehow, and seemingly miraculously, there is now enough time to accomplish all the things you were only trying to complete before. Also there is time to do much more, even the things you always wanted to do but never "had" time for before. So here is a key to becoming a miracle worker. Change your inner universe, master your inner time, and

you become master of your outer universe "environment." You cannot force your way into the inner levels of Mind, for you must earn the right to be there and to earn this right you must change. So do not attempt to gain control of your Subconscious mind until you are willing to change your self and grow at an accelerated rate and expand your consciousness.

Regal State of the Bridegroom verses six through eleven. What is this coming up from the desert like a column of smoke, laden with myrrh, with frankincense, and with the perfume of every exotic dust?

In the King James version of the Bible the word wilderness is used in the place of the word desert. The *wilderness* or *desert* is telling you that reference is made to the physical level of Mind, the seventh level. The physical environment is the place where our learning takes place. It is the point from which we must move to understand the Subconscious and Superconscious minds. Smoke is the left-overs of fire. It is used energy returning to the sky. It is energy changed to another form, a lighter or finer form. *Sky* is the dome between the Subconscious and Superconscious minds. A *column of smoke* symbolizes the rising of awareness that comes after an expansion of Self. This means there has been a complete use of one form of expression and energy. *Myrrh* and *frankincense* are also odors that can rise and permeate the air as smoke does, yet they are pleasant to smell. *Dust* or *clay* or *earth* is the symbol for Subconscious mind substance *(see Gen. 2:7.)* Putting this together to form a picture that there is a change after the Conscious mind harmonizes, is connected to and aware of the Subconscious mind. For at this point the change, the result of this happening is reverberated throughout Mind all the way to the Superconscious mind. It affects the very stuff of which Mind consists. *Myrrh* and *frankincense* connote the sacrifice and the value given to yourself, the essence of which rises all the way to heaven.

Ah, it is the litter of Solomon; sixty valiant men surround it, of the valiant men of Israel;

I have presented earlier in this book what *Solomon* represents so you will need to see how this fits in again with this verse and this mental image. The *litter* is a type of vehicle and this is the vehicle used when causing motion and directing activity. *Six* is the number of service and *zero* indicates power. Power is the result of understanding. This verse explains that the value of service to the self is recognized. An immense amount of learning takes place when there is the intention to learn from every experience, whether pleasant or unpleasant. With the intention to learn, the understandings come at a more rapid rate. For anyone to gain the *wisdom of Solomon,* they must first practice sacred selfish service and learn from every experience. This is how you meet and get to know Solomon the great!!

Israel represents the aspects of yourself that are willing to give and teach. *Men* are the Conscious or physical aspects as presented earlier. Thus we see the value of movement forward with the intention of learning from each situation. The thinker recognizes that with each step of the learning there must be the consistent application of use of the information in the day-to-day, physical life, for it to be understood. Truth must be lived.

All of them expert with the sword, skilled in battle, Each with his sword at his side against danger in the watches of the night.

Sword indicates karma for it cuts two ways, always a balance. Karma is begun or initiated by intention. The physical aspects, at this point, have an understanding of cause and effect and hold the intention of learning or receiving understandings through each experience. This is why they support Solomon. For if wisdom is to be developed, it must have as its foundation learning which is fully received in order to become a part of yourself.

A battle is the place where death and killing occur. *Death* indicates change for death is change. *Skilled in battle*, therefore, indicates an understanding of how to cause change. Through my teaching I have found that very few people know how to consciously produce change within themselves. This is something that must be learned. When you have attained the point of awareness to be able to use Mind and align with Subconscious mind, at that point you begin to know how to consciously cause growth within self. *Sword at his side* symbolizes preparation to handle any situation that occurs. *Danger in the watches of the night* is the danger that comes from the times when you slip back into the old ways that were not productive, back into the old ways of lack of awareness. The *danger* is that the spiritual thinker will not continue to progress, but will revert to old ways, will not maintain his commitment but will backslide. Once you have learned something, use it. For there to be growth there must be change. If you would remain the same, you will stagnate, leaving in its wake, dissatisfaction and unhappiness.

King Solomon made himself a carriage of wood from Lebanon.
   King indicates control. Carriage is a vehicle. *Wood* indicates subconscious experience. The word Lebanon means white, clean, pure, brilliant. Lebanon is a range of mountains in northern Palestine, noted for its cedars. Here we have a picture of the control and experience being gained in all parts of the Subconscious mind. *White* and *brilliance* represent the high degree of awareness that has been gained. What a perfect place to obtain a vehicle for developing the whole Mind. Throughout the Bible *white* is used to symbolize pure thoughts, understanding, and wholeness.

He made its columns of silver, its roof of gold, Its seat of purple cloth, its framework inlaid with ivory.
   Columns are the supportive structure that rests on the founda-

tion. This is the value of the understood experiences and of the use of the Subconscious mind. You may want to refer back to the column of smoke referred to in Vs. 6 of this chapter. The *roof* is representative of the value that can be gained by moving through all levels of the Subconscious mind until the day comes when one is knocking at the dome between Subconscious and Superconscious mind. *Seat* is a place to sit as on a throne and indicates control. *Purple* was used for the clothes of royalty so here again we have an indication of control and value in working from the seat of Mind. The framework is what holds everything together and we see at this point that much value and beauty has been gained, in building the personal framework throughout Mind. You use a physical body to move in the physical. There is also the need for a vehicle in each level of Mind.

Daughters of Jerusalem, come forth and look upon King Solomon. In the crown with which his mother has crowned him on the day of his marriage, on the day of the joy of his heart.

Daughters, as have been related, indicate conscious aspects. This is an invitation for all conscious aspects to come forth and be aware of the wisdom and harmony that is being developed. *Crown* indicates control and this control has come from the Superconscious mind. On the day of the union between the Subconscious and Conscious minds there is the *marriage made in heaven.* This is your soul mate. Thus, on this day all parts of Mind are affected, all seven levels and all three divisions. On this day there is wisdom gained. There is *joy in the heart of Solomon.*

Chapter Four

Chapter four presents us with an image of Solomon communicating with his beautiful lover. This, is a response from the Subconscious mind. I have shown that in chapter three, the Conscious mind *(woman)* was speaking to and praising the Subconscious mind *(man.)* The communication in chapter four comes from Subconscious mind to Conscious mind where as in chapter 3 communication was from the Conscious mind to Subconscious mind. This chapter brings about a balance. It also shows there is complete communication.

The Charms of the Beloved verses one through eleven. Ah, you are beautiful, my beloved, ah you are beautiful! Your eyes are doves behind your veil. Your hair is like a flock of goats streaming down the mountains of Gilead.

When growth is occurring, the Subconscious mind then sings its praises to the Conscious mind. For they are two halves of a whole and when one part benefits, so does the other. If you watch people, you may notice that they are the most beautiful when they are growing, learning and improving themselves. No wonder there is beauty perceived here! The perception has been developed to this point when there is an awareness in all levels of Subconscious mind

and you are able to pierce through the veil of the Conscious mind.
Hair indicates conscious thoughts, showing control of thoughts affecting the highest parts of the Subconscious mind. *Goats* are very good at mountain climbing and this indicates a point of control and understanding of working with the Subconscious mind. *Mountains of Gilead* symbolize the use of will for a mountain is an obstacle or challenge until it is mounted through the use of the will. A mountain is also made of rock and *rock* indicates will. It is also seen that it was at Gilead that Joseph was sold into slavery *(loss of free will)*. *(Gen. 37:1-36)* Will is one's mental muscle. Will is the only means of motion or locomotion within Mind. We have here a picture of a highly developed will controlling the thoughts, thereby able to transfer awareness into the Subconscious mind. *Gileadites were descendants of Gilead of the tribe of Manasseh. (Num. 26:29.)*

Your teeth are like a flock of ewes to be shorn, which come up from the washing, All of them big with twins, none of them thin and barren.

The teeth in the mouth chew food which begins the process of digestion necessary for nourishment. This symbolizes the ability to process experiences into knowledge and wisdom. *Coming up from the washing (water)* is the movement of attention from the Conscious mind into the Subconscious mind after a period of purification has occurred. *Big with twins* indicates a balance of the aggressive and receptive principles, receiving knowledge, resulting in fertility or an abundance of productivity. Here is presented a picture of the ability to assimilate understandings from the experiences which are created. This *(birth of twins)* enables the individual to become a creator.

Your lips are like a scarlet strand; your mouth is lovely. Your cheek is like a half pomegranate behind your veil.

The lips and mouth are used to further elaborate on what was said regarding the teeth, now with the addition of beauty. Even behind the veil of the Conscious mind, there is much beauty and value in the physical life. Even though life seems at times to be all work, pain, and engrossment, still there is much to be said of the value that can be gained by using experiences to gain wisdom. You may be able to recall a time in your life that was not pleasant, yet looking back on that time you see a period of great learning and personal growth.

Your neck is like David's tower girt with battlements; A thousand bucklers hang upon it, all the shields of valiant men.

David, as presented earlier, represents reasoning. *Neck* symbolizes will. Reasoning is the ability to receive information and knowledge from experience and draw conclusions from it. The better the Conscious mind becomes at perceiving cause, the better conclusions it is able to draw from the information it receives. For cause is always mental and starts with a thought. Will is the ability to make more correct decisions than incorrect ones. When mistakes are made reasoning can then be used to see how to correct the mistake. Next, a decision needs to be made to change the mistake and last there needs to be follow through on the decision which is will power. Through this process learning and growth takes place. Better yet make a correct, productive decision the first time and avoid the mistakes! Will and reasoning are the weapons you will use to master all of Mind to gain control of your rightful heritage, your superconscious mind. The number *One* symbolizes an aggressive act. One thousand is one with three zeros behind it. The *zeros* indicate the use of reasoning to draw conclusions and thus gain power through understanding. The *shields* and *bucklers* are tools for change and the ability to protect oneself in any situation, in other words, responding to one's creations. This is a symbolic way to express will power, understandings, and the control of change. Be strong and the controller of your life.

Your breasts are like twin fawns, the young of a gazelle that browse among the lilies.

The Subconscious wisdom is communicating the value and beauty of the productive Conscious mind. *Two* or *twin* present the aggressive and receptive in balance. *Breasts* symbolize the nurturing quality. For a male can appreciate the beauty in the feminine expression that is never seen fully or understood until one begins to understand and appreciate the male expression. To be able to see the beauty in others, you must respect, appreciate, and value yourself. If you, the reader of this book have begun to see some of your beauty, you may very well appreciate the way in which the beauty of a woman (and also a man) is used to portray the value and peace of the Conscious and Subconscious minds.

Until the day breathes cool and the shadows lengthen, I will go to the mountain of myrrh, to the hill of incense. You are all-beautiful, my beloved, and there is no blemish in you.

The *cool part of the day* is adulthood within the cycle of growth. There are four parts to a day. They are, morning, afternoon, evening, and night. These parts of the day correspond to the divisions of a cycle we call infancy, adolescence, adulthood, and old age-wisdom. The *cool part of the day* is in the evening and indicates adulthood, which is a time of responsibility and productivity. Productivity comes when each physical experience is used to learn and grow. It includes teaching what you have found to be truth to others. There is no blemish in one who has the intention of learning from every situation that is created within the environment. There is no new karma created for the intention is to learn and all is productive.

Come from Lebanon, my bride, come from Lebanon, come! Descend from the top of Amana, From the top of Senir and Hermon, From the haunts of lions, from the leopards' mountains.

Lebanon has been described. Solomon had cedars from Lebanon brought to Israel, to build the temple of the Lord. Thus, is seen the value in using the experiences to know your "I AM", your individuality. *Lord* symbolizes your I AM, your individuality. For there to be a bride there must also be a bridegroom. Therefore, we have the union of the Conscious and Subconscious minds. *Amana, Senir,* and *Hermon* represent sacred or high mountains. Senir and Hermon, were all areas to the north or the northern area of the Promised Land. Mount Hermon marked the boundary of the land beyond the Jordan that the Israelites took from the Amorites. Solomon is imploring his bride to come to the place where he is so that the two may be together and complete the union of the Conscious and Subconscious minds. To maintain your commitment to become a creator is an act of devotion to yourself. This is what is sometimes called sacred selfishness or sacred service.

You have ravished my heart, my sister, my bride; You have ravished my heart with one glance of your eyes, with one bead of your necklace.

For an understanding of what heart is referring to you may turn to *(Matt. 5:8)*. You will find here *"single-hearted"* is referring to the singular ideal and purpose. With the single ideal and purpose maintained and tied in with the perception, there is the control of the Subconscious mind. *Bead of the necklace,* being around the neck indicates use of the will. Also refer to what was stated concerning the heart and Solomon.

How beautiful is your love, my sister, my bride, how much delightful is your love than wine, and the fragrance of your ointments than all spices!

Love unites. Love brings together. Love draws and joins. Brother and sister are about as close within a family as one can get. Yes, each thinker, each reasoning person is a part of the family of man and can truly call their Conscious and Subconscious minds, brother and sister. Love is what created the universe and what binds it together. To work in harmony with the universe one must practice first self love and following that, love for others. Even greater than wisdom is love. For even greater than Solomon's wisdom was the Christ's Love.

Your lips drip honey, my bride, sweetmeats and milk are under your tongue; And the fragrance of your garments is the fragrance of Lebanon.

Honey and milk are whole foods and sweetmeats are delightful to the palate. Your practice of receiving the learning in each experience is very palatable, very enjoyable and very good for the Subconscious mind. The outer expression is enticing and powerful because there are many understandings that are being used. They are productive and there is the intention to learn from each experience. (See *Gen. 3:10*)

The Lover and His Garden verses twelve through sixteen. You are an enclosed garden, my sister, my bride, an enclosed garden, a fountain sealed. You are a park that puts forth pomegranates, with all choice fruits; Nard and Saffron, Calamus and cinnamon, with all kinds of incense: Myrrh and aloes, with all the finest spices.

The Conscious mind is enclosed and limited. It is a division of Mind. All other divisions of Mind have more than one level. The *fountain* represents the conscious experience and the possibility of free flowing learning and growth. *Fruit* is the knowledge being produced from Conscious life experiences to be placed into the

Subconscious mind. The expansive beauty of these understandings goes all the way throughout Mind.

You are a garden fountain, a well of water flowing fresh from Lebanon.

A *garden fountain*, is a place where the conscious *(well of water)* and subconscious *(garden)* experiences come together in beauty and peace. Experience is being distributed throughout Mind as *Lebanon* indicates.

Arise north wind! Come, south wind! blow upon my garden that its perfumes may spread abroad. Let my lover come to his garden and eat its choice fruits.

Here we see command of some of the guards to direct and distribute energy *(wind)* throughout Mind. Now is the time for wisdom stored in the Subconscious mind to be used in the physical existence. *Wind* indicates the aggressive act of *Solomon* (Subconscious mind) once again–see *Genesis 1-2*. The Conscious mind in gaining the ability to move and gain awareness in the Subconscious mind with control. Yes, the two lovers come together!

Chapter Five

I have come to my garden, my sister, my bride; I gather my myrrh and my spices, I eat my honey and my sweetmeats, I drink my wine and my milk, Eat, friends, drink! Drink freely of love.

This is the time to reap the harvest of the investment in yourself. *Going to the garden to gather fine spices and good foods* symbolizes the full use of the knowledge and experience available to promote soul growth. This is the inner peace, satisfaction and contentment that comes from knowing you have made a real change and growth

has occurred. Here we have, once again, the wisdom of the Subconscious mind speaking to the Conscious mind, his bride, saying, develop wisdom, understandings. *All of my friends,* are aspects of the thinker. For *sweetmeats, honey,* and *milk* are knowledge, i.e: food for the soul, and *wine* is wisdom. You may look to *John 2:1 11* for there we see *Jesus* (the knower) changing *water* (conscious experience) into *wine* (wisdom) which comes from using the conscious experience. Also see *Isaiah 55* in regards to *honey* and *foods.*

A Fruitless Search verses two through eight. I was sleeping, but my heart kept vigil; I heard my lover knocking: "Open to me, my sister, my beloved, my dove, my perfect one! For my head is wet with dew, my locks with the moisture of the night."

Sleep is the time for assimilating the previous days experiences into Subconscious mind. *Sleeping* in this case, is a time of assimilation for the Conscious mind. However, even in a time of assimilation of experiences, it is possible to maintain a single heart, which is the singular ideal and purpose. The singular ideal and purpose is to become as the mental parent, in other words, a creator, and in the shorter run, to align the Conscious and Subconscious minds. The Subconscious mind is always knocking at the door of the Conscious mind asking to be let in, to commune, with the

Conscious mind. *Head* indicates identity and particularly within the Subconscious mind. The *dew* being *water* symbolizes conscious life experiences and the need to gain awareness through these. When the Subconscious mind extends itself into the Conscious mind, there is the opportunity to use those experiences to build identity and understanding of who you are as I AM.

I have taken off my robe, am I then to put it on? I have bathed my feet, am I then to soil them?

The Subconscious mind is saying, "I have become open to your awareness and I have placed my foundation *(feet)* in the conscious experiences so the two Minds may harmonize and function as one. Is the Subconscious mind then to back off from the commitment it has made, which is to fulfill the desires of the Conscious mind? Will the Conscious mind's activity and labor produce awareness and expansion of consciousness?

My lover put his hand through the opening; my heart trembled within me, and I grew faint when he spoke.

The Subconscious mind does its part to gain fulfillment. It fulfills all conscious desires and also acts as a storehouse of understood experiences. The Conscious mind is forever doubting itself and becomes unsure it is doing the correct thing and backs off from making a firm commitment to growth.

Have you ever been ready to take a risk, perhaps take a new position with a different company or move to another part of the country. Perhaps you have experienced doubts at these times about your ability to cope and create successes in the new area. Yet, there is always the inner desire for improvement that spurs men to accomplish great things. *Hand* indicates purpose. Thus we see here is the gaining of subconscious as well as conscious purpose. This occurs when we place soul learning and the development of direct knowing as a purpose above all else. *When he spoke* indicates communication from one part of Mind to the other.

I rose to open to my lover, with my hands dripping myrrh: With my fingers dropping choice myrrh upon the fittings of the lock. The time of assimilation is past, it is time for action. The purpose of the Conscious mind is aligned with the purpose of the Subconscious mind. The veil between levels of Mind is perceived and so it is time to open the door and to break the seal which separates the Conscious mind from the Subconscious mind.

I opened to my lover-but my lover had departed, gone. I sought him but I did not find him; I called to him but he did not answer me. There is an opening up of the Conscious mind to the Subconscious mind, yet the Conscious mind has not developed enough for there to be a full awareness, reception, and use of the Subconscious mind. Also being indicated is the lack of ability to listen to the inner voice, of the inner Self. When you hesitate you often lose the opportunity, and usually opportunity only knocks once.

The watchmen came upon me as they made their rounds of the city; They struck me, and wounded me, and took my mantle from me, the guardians of the walls. Since the watchmen have been explained prior to this, I need not cover this ground again. I will say that if you are to go into the Subconscious mind it must be with understanding of the qualities of the Subconscious mind or else there will be very little control. There needs to be harmony with the energies and the qualities of those levels of consciousness. There are four walls to a city, four sides to a square and there are four guards to the Subconscious mind *(see Numbers, Chapter 12)*. The King James version of the <u>Bible</u> says it this way:

Vs. 7, The watchmen that went about the city found me, they smote me, they wounded me: The keepers of the walls took away my veil from me.

The same picture, the same idea is being presented in this version. The *keepers of the walls* are the guardians of the Subconscious mind. Being *wounded* tells us that there will need to be further changes made. With this change the veil is being taken away. The *veil* is what keeps you from perceiving clearly beyond the five senses. When this change is completed there will be the ability to perceive in Mind more clearly. For reference you may remember that Jerusalem had four walls. They were the north, south, east and west walls.

I adjure you, daughters of Jerusalem, if you find my lover-what shall you tell him? -That I am faint with love.

The Conscious mind is addressing the conscious aspects of Self, asking for aid in comprehending and gaining control in the Subconscious mind. Why shouldn't one be honest in their love, in expounding on their desires, for that is a matter of self respect.

The Charms of the Lost Lover verses nine through sixteen. How does your lover differ from any other, O most beautiful among woman? How does your lover differ from any other, that you adjure us so?

The Conscious mind has charged the conscious aspects not to rouse love before its time *(Chap. 2),* and now is charging the conscious aspects to deliver a message. In this verse we find a reply from the conscious aspects. How does your lover or subconscious aspect differ from any other subconscious aspect? How is this one different? Remember, however, we are talking about Solomon as being the lover, the subconscious aspect and *Solomon* symbolizes wisdom. Of course, wisdom is the most valuable part of the

Subconscious mind-self that we can develop. Wisdom is the result of using those things which are understood, over and over. The ability to store understandings is part of the great power of the Subconscious mind. The most important love is your true, inner self, your soul mate, which is your soul.

My lover is radiant and ruddy; he stands out among thousands. His head is pure gold; his locks are palm fronds, black as the raven.

Solomon is so full of awareness *(Light)* that he is radiant with value *(gold)*. Obviously one cannot literally possess a head of pure gold, and live. Yet one can have developed the perception to a very high degree and to the point where it contains much value and much wisdom within it. There is such control of the conscious thought *(hair)* that there is control and growth within the Subconscious mind and the experiences thereof. In regards to the *raven* we can look to *Genesis 8:6-7*. It says: *At the end of forty days Noah opened the hatch he had made in the ark and he sent out a raven to see if the waters had lessened on the earth. It flew back and forth until the waters dried off from the earth.* So it is seen that the *raven* is a symbol of subconscious thoughts and how to use them. For *water* is conscious experience during our waking lives, and *earth* indicates the stuff of which the Subconscious mind is made.

His eyes are like doves beside running waters, His teeth would seem bathed in milk and are set like jewels. His cheeks are like beds of spice with ripening aromatic herbs. His lips are red blossoms; they drip choice myrrh.

Perception is so good as to enable the director to perceive both the subconscious thought in the conscious experience. This is the source of true creativity. The *teeth* are tools for assimilating knowledge *(food)*. *Milky* teeth indicate the healthy ability for assimilation of knowledge. See also *(Gen. 8)* for further information of the meaning of *doves*. The *jewels* indicate the value of the ability of ingesting knowledge. I have presented the meaning of spices.

His arms are rods of gold adorned with chrysolites. His body is a work of ivory covered with sapphires.

Arms are rods of gold says there is purpose and wisdom in the use of universal law. *Chrysolites* indicate the value of purpose within yourself. The body indicates the vehicle that gives the Subconscious mind mobility and has great value.

His legs are columns of marble resting on golden bases. His stature is like the trees on Lebanon, imposing as the cedars.

Two legs equals the aggressive and receptive, supportive factors working together within the Subconscious mind. *Trees* are subconscious experience and cedars were one of the most valuable and greatest trees available. Here they are used to convey the picture of great beauty, strength and control within the subconscious.

His mouth is sweetness itself; he is all delight. Such is my lover, and such my friend, O daughters of Jerusalem.

Getting to know the real self is a delightful and fulfilling pursuit. There is a sweet satisfaction that comes from growing in awareness. Thus, the beautiful bride ends her description of Solomon to the other women, the daughters of Jerusalem. I think most men would appreciate being described in such a powerful and handsome manner. Such is the beauty, strength, and power of the inner self.

Chapter Six

Discovery verses one through three. Where has your lover gone, O most beautiful among women? Where has your lover gone that we may seek him with you?

This is a continuation of the communication presented in Chapter 5 between the Conscious mind and its aspects. The bride has told the daughters of Jerusalem how her lover is different from any other and has done it in very descriptive and desirable terms. The daughters are responding that they would like to meet this very special *man* (aspect of the Subconscious mind). For the conscious aspects are beginning to perceive the value and worth of the inner Self and desire to know more.

My lover has come down to his garden, to the beds of spice, to browse in the garden and to gather lilies. My lover belongs to me and I to him; he browses among the lilies.

In *Nehemiah 3:15,* we see reference to the garden of Solomon and David in the repairing of Jerusalem's walls and gates. *The spring gate was repaired by Shallum, Son of Colhozeh, leader of the district of Mispah: He rebuilt it, roofed it over, and set up its doors, its bolts, and its bars. He also repaired the wall of the aqueduct pool near the King's garden as far as the steps that lead down from the city of David.* The city of David was Jerusalem. A *garden* is a place of subconscious experience. In *(Songs 5:7)* the bride was wounded as she searched for her lover. There was a need for further growth. The strong desire to know the Self remained and so after much searching, the lover (Solomon) was found once again. This time he is found in the *garden,* that means a place in Mind having to do with subconscious experience. So it can be seen there has been more experience, learning, and understanding gained. Lilies are very beautiful plants and grow on *water* (conscious experience). So *lilies* represent the coming together of subconscious and conscious experience. The place where these two divisions join is the emotional level of the Subconscious mind. The emotional level is the level in closest proximity to the Conscious mind yet it still remains a part of the Subconscious division of Mind. Each of us can recall situations where we were emotional or experienced some emotion. Perhaps anger or hatred, or fear, or emotional attachment. You can't physically touch emotions or sense them with any of the five senses, yet they are real. We are aware of them because of their close proximity to the Conscious, physical part of Mind.

Immediately after the reference to lilies there is the statement *my lover belongs to me and I to him.* This is saying the Conscious Mind belongs to the Subconscious mind and vice versa and the proper station for both of them is to work together in union and harmony as do the water lilies with the water.

The Charms of the Beloved verses four through ten. You are as beautiful as Tirzah, my beloved, as lovely as Jerusalem, as awe-inspiring as bannered troops.

It is interesting to note that the word David in Hebrew means: loved, or beloved, for *David* is the symbol used for reasoning. The Conscious mind is most beautiful and productive when it is using reasoning. By using reasoning, the Conscious mind is able to pump permanent and eternal understandings at a rapid rate into Subconscious mind. Tirzah was an ancient Canaanite city that was conquered by the Israelites. Later it became the royal city of Jeroboam and his successors. The Conscious mind is very beautiful when it is acting on its desires and using its will, for desire and will are the pushing and pulling factors needed for any creation. Salem was the place where Melchizedek was king *(Gen. 14:18, Heb. 7:1-2)* Melchizedek was a priest of the most high God. Even Abraham bowed down to him and showed him respect. Later Salem becomes Jerusalem *(Psalms 76:2-4)*. This is an indication of Mind energy working farther out toward the physical to become a more productive Conscious mind. You will only have peace and fulfillment when the Conscious mind and the Subconscious mind are aligned, symbolized by *Jerusalem* (peace). *Bannered troops* are disciplined aspects.

Turn your eyes from me, for they torment me. Your hair is like a flock of goats streaming down from Gilead.

Here again is the response of Subconscious mind to Conscious mind. When you feast your eyes on something you cannot yet have, there is torment until you lose the desire or you possess the object of your desire. Your Subconscious mind is tormented when it sees what is possible to develop between the two Minds and then sees that the Conscious mind is not quite ready for this harmony. *Hair* as has been presented is conscious thought, and here it is given that the Conscious mind has taken some control of the thoughts. *Gilead* means rock of time or enduring rock. This indicates a connection with will. Joseph was sold into slavery at Gilead and Jacob fled to the Gilead mountain. So there *Gilead* relates to the use of will or lack of use of it, as symbolized by being *sold into slavery*.

Your teeth are like a flock of ewes which come up from the washing, All of them big with twins, none of them thin and barren.

Lambs and *sheep* are referred to throughout the <u>Bible</u>. The lambs of God are referred to in the *New Testament*. Jesus uses this idea repeatedly. *Twins* are the aggressive and receptive principles about to be born and put into use. These are the principles that will be used to work into Mind as a lamb of God. For each of us will need to learn when to take action and when to listen, when to be strong and when to be tender. The book of *Ecclesiastes* said it very well in *(Ecclesiastes 3:1 8), There is an appointed time for everything, and a time for every affair under the heavens. A time to be born, and a time to die; a time to plant, and a time to uproot the plant. A time to kill, and a time to heal; a time to tear down, and a time to build. A time to weep, and a time to laugh, a time to mourn, and a time to dance. A time to scatter stones, and a time to gather them; a time to embrace, and a time to be far from embraces. A time to seek, and a time to lose; a time to keep, and a time to cast away. A time to rend, and a time to sew; a time to be silent, and a time to speak. A time to love, and a time to hate, a time of war, and a time of peace.*

Your cheek is like a half-pomegranate behind your veil.

Even behind the veil of not fully developed awareness, the beauty of the Conscious mind and its identity is apparent.

There are sixty queens, eighty concubines, and maidens without numbers-One alone is my dove, my perfect one, her mother's chosen, the dear one of her parent. The daughters saw her and declared her fortunate, the queens and concubines, and they sang her praises;

Queens indicate the power of receptivity to produce control, power, and authority. Sixty is made of the numbers 6 and 0. The *zero* of sixty indicates power. *Six* is the number of service. To come to know yourself there must be service to the whole self. This enables man to move from reasoning man to intuitive man. Eighty is 8 with a *zero* again indicating power. *Eight* indicates a new awareness, a new beginning of existence. The number 8 is formed by placing two squares on top of each other. Squares have four sides. Thus 8 represents the value gained from controlling both Conscious and Subconscious minds and bringing them into harmony.

Maidens without numbers indicates all the conscious aspects. The *bride*, the Conscious mind, is the one which will be able to harmonize with the conscious aspects. *Her mother* is the receptive principle of the Superconscious mind. The other conscious aspects are finally seeing the value and beauty of this harmony that is being built. Your Superconscious mind is your mental parent for it contains the blueprint that you will fulfill to become a creator. There is a dawning awareness of Superconscious mind and cosmic consciousness within the Self.

Who is this that comes forth like the dawn, as beautiful as the moon, as resplendent as the sun, as awe-inspiring as bannered troops?

Dawn is the beginning of a new cycle, a new day, a new point of awareness. This new and great awareness is also symbolized by the *sun* and *moon*. The *troops* connote mental discipline. The sun gives *light* (awareness) during the day and the moon provides a lesser, reflected light at night.

Love's Meeting verses eleven through twelve. I came down to the nut garden to look at the fresh growth of the valley, To see if the vines were in bloom, if the pomegranates had blossomed.

The Conscious Mind is speaking once again, saying I went to the Subconscious mind to look at all the new experiences I have added to it. I came to see the productivity and growth within the Subconscious mind.

Before I knew it, my heart had made me the blessed one of my kinswomen.

Heart symbolizes understanding and responsibility *(Solomon)*. The true heart's desire is to know the Subconscious mind. This makes the bride the blessed one for she alone knows Solomon. This verse shows the mastery of the Heart chakra by the individual. Such a one is a compassionate being. Such a one is expanding consciousness through giving and service.

Chapter Seven

The Beauty of the Bride verses one through six. Turn, turn, O Shulammite, turn, turn, that we may look at you! Why would you look at the Shulammite as at the dance of the two companies?

To find the meaning of the word "Shulammite," and the significance it connotes, we need to turn to the word "Shunem" which was one of the cities allotted to the tribe of Issachar *(Josh. 19:18)*. It was beside the native place of Abishag *(I Kings 1:3)*. It was at one time known as Sulem. *Now Abishag was a beautiful Shunammite, taken into David's harem to comfort him in his old age (I Kings 1:1-4).*

After David's death Adonijah talked Bathsheba, the queen mother, into asking Solomon to give Abishag to him in marriage. Solomon was so upset by this that he had Adonijah killed (I Kings

2:13), indicating that the only union or harmony for Conscious and Subconscious must be the uniting of the most wise, productive aspects of the two, and none other.

Since it seems to be Solomon talking in these passages, it is an interesting point for him to be talking to a Shulammite, when Abishag the Shulammite was the one he cared so dearly for. So we see the Conscious mind becoming more and more perfect as it grows, matures, and perfects reasoning. From this is seen the great love of the Subconscious mind. Also there is the impression of the great interconnectedness of the of the aggressive and receptive principles.

How beautiful, are your feet in sandals, O prince's daughter! Your rounded thighs are like jewels, the handiwork of an artist.

The *feet* (foundation) are very beautiful or becoming very strong and well built. A *prince's daughter* is one of authority and control. *Thighs* indicate the use of the kundalini and the value in the control of the creative energy *(see Gen. 32:23-32)*. *Work of an artist* means there has been much time and activity taken in building the understandings and putting them together to make a whole functioning self.

Your navel is a round bowl that should never lack for mixed wine. Your body is a heap of wheat encircled with lilies.

The full understanding of the solar plexus or navel chakra has been mastered. Wisdom in the use of this chakra has been gained. The *navel* indicates the solar plexus chakra which is the seat of the Conscious and Subconscious minds. The *round bowl* indicates the use and control of this chakra or energy for that area. *Wine* is the wisdom that has been built in using this energy and the qualities developed. *Wheat* indicates food which symbolizes knowledge. *Lilies* have been discussed previously. True permanent soul knowledge comes from the alignment of Conscious and Subconscious minds

Your breasts are like twin fawns, the young of a gazelle.

Twins have been presented previously pertaining to aggressive and receptive. This relates back to verse one of this chapter where the two companies are presented. For there the question is raised, why should we look at you the way we do at two companies? The Shulammite has brought into harmony the *twin breasts* or the aggressive and receptive principles of creation whereas the companies are separate. *Breasts* are also used to feed the young indicating preparation for the creation of a new part of the self, a new aspect. *Breasts* symbolize the nurturing quality.

Your neck is like a tower of ivory. Your eyes are like the pools in Heshbon by the gate of Bath-rabbim. Your nose is like the tower on Lebanon that looks toward Damascus.

Neck symbolizes the throat chakra the quality of which is will. *Tower of ivory* indicates the value of the will and the expansion of it from the Conscious mind. *Eyes* are perception as has been discussed prior. *Pools of water* represent the conscious life experience. *Heshbon* is indicative of reasoning. *Bath-rabbim* means daughter of many or daughter of the multitudes, indicating once again the many aspects of the Conscious mind. I have presented Lebanon previously. *Nose* indicates the identity. *Damascus* is talking about a place or quality of Superconscious mind.

You head rises like Carmel; your hair is like draperies of purple; a king is held captive in its tresses.

Carmel was a country in the hill country of Judah. Solomon was born into the tribe of Judah, one of the twelve tribes of Israel. Reasoning and awareness is rising above the Conscious mind, is what this verse is so poetically saying. Purple is the color of royalty and was highly prized. The value of controlling and directing the conscious thoughts is perceived. Even the points of maturity in the self have intelligent direction when the outer consciousness is controlled.

Love's Desires verses seven through ten. How beautiful you are, how pleasing, my love, my delight!
The Conscious mind has become pleasing to the Subconscious mind because there is rapid soul growth and spiritual development.

Your very figure is like a palm tree, Your breasts are like clusters.
The physical body and the Conscious mind are being used to add experience to the Subconscious mind. The Conscious mind has learned how to nurture learning and soul growth.

I said; I will climb the palm tree, I will take hold of its branches. Now let your breasts be like clusters of the vine and the fragrance of your breath like apples, And your mouth like an excellent wine-that flows smoothly for my lover, spreading over the lips and the teeth.
The individuality at this point is aligning with the Subconscious mind. The Subconscious mind will meet the Conscious mind together within the outer consciousness for productive use of aggressive and receptive once again. The *breath* and control of it indicates control of the life force. *"And your mouth like an excellent wine,"* is wisdom being used in receiving value from experiences.

Love's Union verses eleven through fourteen. I belong to my lover and for me he yearns.
The Conscious mind does belong to the Subconscious mind for it is stated in *Genesis 2:21* that *out of man* (Adam) *God created woman* (Eve). The Subconscious mind yearns to keep the two great

divisions of mind together and working in harmony, as the left hand works with the right hand or the hands and feet work together for the betterment of the whole body.

Come, my lover, let us go forth to the fields and spend the night among the villages.

This indicates a movement into Subconscious mind to gain experience. Spending night time in the villages also indicates there will be the need to assimilate all learning into the soul.

Let us go early to the vineyards, and see if the vines are in bloom, If the buds have opened if the pomegranates have blossomed; There will I give you my love.

At the place and time where there is productivity within the Conscious mind in adding understandings to the Subconscious mind, there will the Conscious mind find the Subconscious lover. And there will Solomon open to the Shulammite.

The mandrakes give forth fragrance, and at our doors are all choice fruits; Both fresh and mellowed fruits, my lover, I have kept in store for you.

Mandrakes were used by Leah in exchange for the right to sleep with Jacob, a right she obtained from Rachel. Through this union Leah bore a son and named him Issachar. Issachar became the patriarch of one of the twelve tribes *(Gen. 30:9-21)*. So *mandrakes* are plants of much value. *Plants* indicate the subconscious experience. *Doors* are the door-ways available for moving between different levels of Mind. Spiritual development can be enhanced by achieving the ability to move through different levels of Mind. The Subconscious mind is waiting with its knowledge and treasures for the Conscious mind to mature. For your Subconscious mind contains all your past understood experiences. The Subconscious mind, sometimes called Universal Mind contains a record of everything said, done, and thought by everyone. A vast treasure house is available for those who have earned the right to use the Subconscious mind, effectively.

Chapter Eight

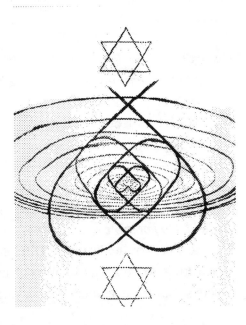

Oh, that you were my brother, nursed at my mother's breasts! If I met you out of doors, I would kiss you and none would taunt me.

Once again the Conscious mind is speaking to the Subconscious mind. Why would anyone wish for their lover to be their brother or sister? It doesn't make sense unless we interpret it symbolically, in the language of pictures, the language of Mind. If the bride has a brother of the same mother this would mean they came from the same mental parent and are kindred. The Subconscious mind is kindred to the Conscious mind, for out of the Subconscious mind, the Conscious mind was formed as has been presented. If the Conscious and Subconscious mind are in complete harmony then one is able to move through the doors of the Subconscious mind and neither the subconscious or conscious aspects of the individual can hold you back.

I would lead you, bring you in to the home of my mother. There you would teach me to give you spiced wine to drink, and pomegranate juice.

The *Home of my mother* symbolically is within the Superconscious mind. *Spiced wine* indicates the use of wisdom and *pomegranate juice* is the knowledge that can be assimilated if one uses the Subconscious mind as a teacher. I have referred to *spices* before.

His left hand is under my head and his right arm embraces me.

Left hand under my head is purpose being used with reasoning. It also indicates the understanding of purpose has been built through past experience. However, there is the need to build on reasoning and develop intuition. Thus we see the *right arm embracing, the whole person.*

I adjure you, daughters of Jerusalem, by the gazelles and hinds of the field, Do not arouse, do not stir up love, before its own time.

Use what you are learning. Discipline your Conscious mind. Teach truth so you may draw your understandings from your subconscious mind to your outer waking, conscious mind.

Homecoming verse five. Who is this coming up from the desert, leaning upon her lover? Under the apple tree I awakened you; it was there that your mother conceived you, it was there that your parent conceived.

Up from the desert or *wilderness* as in the King James version, indicates coming up to the Subconscious mind from the Conscious mind, so the bride meets Solomon. *Under the apple tree* shows productive subconscious experiences. The consciousness has expanded to include Subconscious mind. *Mother*, being an aspect of Superconscious mind, conceived of the idea of the Conscious mind and the use of physical existence to produce permanent understandings.

True Love verses six through seven. Set me as a seal on your heart, as a seal on your arm, For stern as death is love, relentless as the nether world is devotion: its flames are a blazing fire.

The *seal on the heart and arm* indicates singular ideal and purpose, which is to know thyself, placing this above all else. Once you have made the commitment to your whole Self the marriage in heaven occurs, at this point you can never be the same. For at this point you will know there is more to life than sensory experience and more than just the day to day living. You will realize man has a purpose. Therefore, you will never again be satisfied with anything less than learning the most from each situation. The practice of moving in Mind with control will become of utmost importance. The desire to know yourself will be as a blazing fire that keeps you moving toward your goal.

Deep waters cannot quench love, nor floods sweep it away. Were one to offer all he owns to purchase love, he would be roundly mocked.

Waters indicate the conscious experience, the 7th level of consciousness, the physical experiences. If you maintain and are true to yourself placing wisdom above all else, the Conscious mind and the physical cannot contain you. You can then move out of engrossment to true freedom. Remember your true love, your own *Solomon.*

For an understanding of the second part of this verse see *(Matthew 19:23-24). Jesus said to his disciples: "I assure you, only with difficulty will a rich man enter into the kingdom of God. I repeat what I said: it is easier for a rope to pass through a needle's eye than for a rich man to enter the kingdom of God."* And again in Matthew we see a reference to this same thing. *(Matt. 6:19-23). "Do not lay up for yourselves an earthly treasure. Moths and rust corrode; thieves break in and steal. Remember where you treasure is, there you heart is also. The eye is the body's lamp. If your eyes are good, your body will be filled with light, if your eyes are bad, your body will be in darkness. And if your light is darkness, how deep will the darkness be!"*

So it is clearly seen that you cannot purchase understandings nor wisdom. Neither can we enter the deeper and more expanded levels of Mind with control without earning it through committed effort to cause change and growth. Money, houses, possessions cannot be taken with you at the time of death, only permanent understandings.

Chastity and its Welcome verses eight through ten. Our sister is little and she has no breasts as yet. What shall we do for our sister when her courtship begins?

Here we see another aspect *(sister)* following in the footsteps of Solomon and his bride, desirous of gaining wisdom and understandings. This is the beginning of commanding armies and having nations bow unto you. By causing forward motion and soul growth new awarenesses of possibilities for soul growth become apparent.

If she is a wall, we will build upon it a silver parapet; If she is a door, we will reinforce it with a cedar plank.

King James versions has it thus, *If she be a wall, we will build upon her a palace of silver, and if she be a door, we will enclose her with boards of cedar.*

One wall is only one part of Mind having to do with only one level but a *palace* indicates all of Mind and its divisions. So we will teach this new aspect how to gain consciousness in all levels of Mind also. *Silver* indicates the value of movement. The door is the way in which one passes from one room to the next and so a *door* is the way to go from one level of Mind to another. Cedar planks make the doorway solid and strong.

I am a wall, and my breasts are like towers. So now in his eyes I have become one to be welcomed.
   The Conscious mind has become a force to be reckoned with. A very strong and sturdy structure, controlling the pathway to the Subconscious mind. For remember, Jerusalem had four walls. Through the use of the creativity and the receptive and aggressive principles there is the ability to perceive in many parts of Mind. Thus, the Conscious mind is welcomed by Solomon.

The Bride and Her Dowry verses eleven through twelve. Solomon had a vineyard at Baal-hamon; he gave over the vineyard to caretakers. For its fruit one would have to pay a thousand silver pieces.
   Baal was one of the foreign idols worshipped by the Israelites when they did not listen to the God of Abraham. *Ham*, the son of Noah, indicates the Conscious mind. Solomon gave the vineyard over to *caretakers* which are the conscious aspects. The conscious aspects must be productive in the physical to add knowledge *(grapes)* and wisdom *(wine)* to the Subconscious mind. Nothing is more valuable than understandings. When we became entrapped in the physical then the Conscious mind became the place where learning takes place. These understandings are then pumped into the Subconscious mind. This is how we, the caretakers, take care of the *vineyard* (Subconscious mind). There is nothing more valuable than understandings you achieve, for this is the only thing you take with you from lifetime to lifetime.

My vineyard is at my own disposal; the thousand pieces are for you, O Solomon, and two hundred for the caretakers of its fruit.

Use every day as an opportunity to gain in soul awareness and enlightenment. One thousand has been related. *Two hundred* is 2 with two zeros, which symbolizes the power of controlling the aggressive and receptive principles of creation.

Life Together verses thirteen through fourteen. O, garden-dweller, my friends are listening for your voice, let me hear it!

All conscious aspects are expectantly waiting and listening for the inner voice that indicates the full and complete harmony and union between Conscious and Subconscious minds. The *garden dweller* is one who is productively adding experience to the Subconscious mind.

Be swift, my lover, like a gazelle or a young stag on the mountains of spices!

The Conscious mind has as its top priority the quickening of soul growth and spiritual development. The aligning of the Conscious and Subconscious minds and the attunement of both to the Superconscious mind. The entire process of enlightenment is quickened 10 fold, 100 fold, and even 1000 fold!

So we come to the end of this book. If you have not read the *Song of Solomon* before, perhaps I have succeeded in exposing you to a very beautiful part of the <u>Bible</u>. If you have read the *Song of Solomon* then maybe you will consider the value this book can have for you when it is interpreted in the Universal Language of Mind. For the Universal Language of Mind is the language of the real Self, it is the language of the individual. I can think of nothing more important than developing a knowing of oneself, of using every learning situation to progress and grow and of teaching others to do the same. Reach out to build confidence, authority, love, respect, self-value, courage and pride, compassion and interconnectedness. These are understandings you can take with you when you withdraw from the physical.

Ultimately permanent understandings are the most important things you can gain. When you set a goal, have a purpose for it. The purpose is nothing more than what you personally receive from your actions to the goal. In the final analysis, purpose is the understandings you achieve for they are the ultimate thing you can gain for yourself.

One further thing about Solomon. His name is spelled with three O's. The numerical value of the letter O is 6. Therefore, three O's equal OOO equals 666, which is the number of the beast in Revelation. Sol-om-on: Sol is the name of the sun. Sol is the sun god. OM is the Universal vibration or creation as given in the Sanskrit writings of India. This shows a connection of Solomon to the universal religion and universal spiritual truth.

The Spirit of the Law

by Barbara Condron

from a <u>Bible</u> interpretation course given in 1984 in Tulsa, Oklahoma

In the Interfaith Church of Metaphysics we read and interpret the Holy Scriptures of the world in the Universal Language of Mind, the language used by the inner mind, the language that connects all of humanity. This is the language of your dreams. The more you understand what your dreams are telling you as an individual the easier it is to apply that knowledge and that wisdom to understanding the universal message in any Holy book.

We frequently draw upon the <u>Bible</u> because it is the Holy Work favored by most Americans. Most people in this hemisphere have been raised in the Christian religion that was founded, at its point of origin, upon this book called the <u>Bible</u>. The beauty of this Holy Work is how it reveals the steps that lead to enlightenment. From the creation of our world through all the evolutionary steps that lead to the second coming of Christ, it is all described here.

The word *bible* comes from the same root word as *bibliography*. This "book" is a collection of writings by many different authors, a library of books within one text. Each book has its own message, its own part, giving you the knowledge of where you come from, who you are, and where you are going. When read in the language of mind the <u>Bible</u> never contradicts itself and this is the essence of what we will explore today – man's capacity to understand himself and his world beyond materiality. It is within the realms of spirit that universal truths become known.

We begin in the book of *Matthew*, one of the four Gospels. Through describing the life of Jesus these books describe how we are to live as Reasoning Man. As is true in your dreams, each person in the <u>Bible</u> represents an aspect of the self or a stage of development the spirit experiences. *Jesus* represents the part of you who knows self as the "Son of Man." This is you, the outer thinker, beginning to reach inward so you can work from a point of knowing rather than just believing.

Matthew writes and describes the Universal Laws of mind in a way that gives you the ideal of how to be Human Man, how to think and how to act as Reasoning Man. He gives you the ideal. Mark gives you the purpose of being Reasoning Man, how to fulfill your purpose for existence. Both are essential elements in spiritual growth for they guide your actions. This consciousness is the essence of "The Spirit of the Law" taught by Jesus. Let us read and learn.

Jesus begins, "Do not think that I come to abolish the Law of the prophets. I have come not to abolish but to fulfill them." (Matthew 5:17) Remember, Jesus is the one who is talking at this point, so this is the part of you that's reaching toward that knowing. *"Of this much I assure you, until heaven and earth pass away, not the smallest letter of the Law, nor the smallest part of a letter shall be done away with until all comes true." (Matthew 5:18)* There are many prophets in the <u>Bible</u>. A prophet symbolizes your ability to see what's in front of you, to see what's ahead, to see where your life is going because you direct it, you cause it to go in that direction.

Most people live in a rather fretful state. If you ask someone where they'll be twenty years from now, most people can't tell you unless it's the same place where they are now. Life means more than just being and existing and staying the same. The nature of the physical, scientifically or philosophically, is change. You as a creative thinker — as an intelligent being — are responsible to cause whatever changes that will move you in the direction you want. Do this and you can be a prophet. When someone asks you, "Where will you be in five years? Where will you be in twenty years? Where will you be in fifty years? What will you think on your death bed?" you can give them a sound answer, because you have that much Self-knowledge, Self-awareness, and Self-possession of knowing how to cause the things in your life that you want that will produce a whole functioning Self. This is the *"Law"* that Jesus is talking about, the way that Mind works and why it works the way it does.

There are thirteen Laws that govern creation as we know it. Each one of us functions within those Laws. The Laws enable us to have the kind of life we want. These Laws are why we have the ability to think something and cause it to become a reality. Jesus is saying *until all the Laws have been used fully they will continue to govern our universe, our evolution as spirit.* In order to use something fully, you must understand what it is and how it works. When that occurs, then there will be no need for the Universal Laws. Now there is a need. The Laws governing our world are Universal. They exist for anyone, anytime, at any place. They have existed for thousands and thousands and thousands of years, and they will continue to exist as long as people like you and I are still striving to become compatible with the Creator who brought us into existence.

"That is why whoever breaks the least significant of these commands and teaches others to do so shall be called least in the Kingdom of God." Interpreting the commandments put forth in any Holy book is a rewarding challenge. It is very difficult to teach someone else how to use those timeless laws if you're working by the "letter of the law," by memory only. What this means is that you have learned certain things, as each one of us did as children, and yet to this day you do not understand why you do things in that particular way. There are certain boundaries that you have learned to abide by but do not understand.

Ralph Waldo Emerson said, "A foolish consistency is the hobgoblin of little minds." And so it is with those who possess reasoning skills but fail to exercise them thus leaving themselves scarcely better off than many animals. Jesus is constantly challenging us to do more, to think more, to *believe and know* through experience. He is constantly stirring up the belief systems of his own people, the Jews thus *Jews* are the Biblical symbol denoting *believing*. Think about it, certain beliefs most do not question — you only live once, God only created our world, life from other parts of the universe have never visited our planet, or when you flick a switch a light will come on. What happens when beliefs of reincarnation arise, or when science creates life through cloning, or evidence of alien life is discovered, or the lights fail to turn on? Our beliefs are challenged, our minds are stretched to consider something different from what we have known.

The thinker wants to know why beliefs exist, where they came from and where they are leading us. The thinker wants to know, in truth *has to know*. When you can add the "spirit" or the meaning behind those beliefs to your life, you nurture your own inner authority. You no longer have to blame someone else when things don't turn out right because it was them that made the rule, or taught you to believe that way. You begin to understand a code of ethics, a code of morality that you can live by, that adds meaning to your life. People who only teach what the Commandments are, only the rules, the beliefs with no understanding behind them, are the *least in the Kingdom of Heaven*. They know the least about why the Mind works and how.

The Kingdom of Heaven lives within you. Each one of us has experienced times of our own personal heaven and our own personal hell, right here now in this lifetime. But some of us tend to forget or have yet to learn that our choices create those states of mind. You are the one who creates the heaven or the hell.

"But the one whoever fulfills and teaches these Commands shall be great in the Kingdom of Heaven." When you know the meaning of your life, of your existence, you can describe it in words to someone else. Living it and being an example *fulfills the command*. Communicating means conveying it to others so they are inspired and stimulated to create changes, to bring out their best, to know themselves completely. Such a person is *teaching the commands*. Through this action of service, you understand more and more about yourself. In the process of teaching, you learn what you know. A teacher is one who recognizes that his authority rests within his competence as a student.

A teacher teaches because he wants to promote that learning in the Self as well as have the joy of sharing with others. It's exciting to come to a new revelation within yourself and to realize something that before was not apparent to you, but there is a special type of pride that wells up in a teacher when — from their efforts and the student's efforts combined — that student reaches a point of realizing something he or she did not know previously. This is that moment of enlightenment, the light bulb turning on over someone's head, the glow in someone's face. Every time you give of yourself, the time, the energy, the attention that it takes to teach something — just as a parent teaches a child — you are the one who benefits. You don't need to wonder if growth is going to happen, it does according to Law.

Jesus concludes, "I tell you, unless your holiness surpasses that of the scribes and pharisees, you shall not enter the Kingdom of God." In Biblical times the scribes copied the Bible, by hand. In the language of mind the *scribes* symbolize the times in our lives when we are only concerned with gaining information. They are the intellectual among us, those who rely upon the experience of others. Their beliefs come from someone else's research, someone else's life, someone else's efforts. The *Pharisees* were one sect of Jews. They lived by the letter of the law, following all the rules. They represent aspects of self that are aware of the truth, practicing it sporadically. The discipline is so little that the life does not measure up to the ideas expressed. Appearances are kept but the essence, the spirit, is missing. If you want to know the Kingdom of Heaven within you it's very important that your *holiness,* your attitude and ability to become whole, exceed the physical body and the brain. You won't find the Kingdom of Heaven in the physical plane and the Conscious mind. You can cause it to express itself in the physical or the Conscious Mind.

Both Matthew and Mark describe this next account of how to fulfill the law. We will interpret in dream symbols Mark's account, then at your leisure you can examine Matthew's in chapter 15 of his text. It begins: *The Pharisees and some of the experts in the Law, who had come from Jerusalem, gathered around him (Mark 7:1)*. *The experts in the Law* are the people who are supposed to know what they are talking about. *They gathered in Jerusalem. Jerusalem*, throughout the <u>Bible</u> indicates the material plane of existence, the seventh level of consciousness, or the physical world. We're talking about the activity of the Conscious mind, or the inactivity of it. Jesus is addressing the time when we are just keeping up appearances, functioning from beliefs based on the authority of something outside ourselves.

They had observed a few of his disciples eating meals without having purified, that is to say washed their hands. At the time this was written the Jewish custom was to never eat without scrupulously washing hands. *Hands* in a dream symbolize purpose. This is talking about knowing your purpose before you take any action, before you take any knowledge in, before you have any experience. Leading up to Jesus's time the Greek philosophers were exceptional in their thinking development but inept in being able to pass their concepts to the Roman civilization. The Romans were builders. They excelled at physical activity. The Greeks were very good at observing life and drawing conclusions. If the two could have come together, perhaps we would be farther in spiritual evolution by now. Going through the motions is not enough.

It's important to do more than just think about your life. To be in action, to be in motion, unveils our soul's purposes for being here. In action we begin to see what our true intentions are in any act. It's very difficult to do that honestly, if all we're doing is sitting back and thinking about it. It's very easy for our ego, our carnal ego, to color our perception, twisting the truth. That's the problem with the *Pharisee;* with those parts of ourselves there is the inaction and therefore the dishonesty.

So what's Jesus going to do with these people, what will the Knower do with these parts of Self? *Moreover,* it's still talking about the Pharisees, *they never eat anything from the market without first sprinkling it. There are many other traditions they observe, for example, the washing of cups and jugs and kettles.* The *Pharisee,* the part of ourselves that gives lip service, always adds something to what's already there. If you are to know your own Christ, then it's very important that you do one thing, and that one thing is that you present Truth as you see it. Not as your parents saw it. Not as your ancestors saw it. Not as a teacher saw it back in grade school. Not as your boss sees it. If you're in business, selling a product you don't believe in, then I suggest you get out of that business because you're not doing yourself any good, and you're not doing your company any good either. You're probably not doing too good at sales, but moreover every time you go out and try to sell this product, you're lying. You're practicing lying to yourself, to the customer, and to your employer. There's a lot of difficulty in businesses nowadays and much of it is because of what I've just given you. People are doing things out of something other than Truth.

You need to live your life investing in something you truly believe. You need to make your life worth something to yourself and others. When you truly believe in your life, in what you're doing with your life, you enjoy getting up in the morning. You enjoy meeting new people. You always learn. You grow daily, expanding your consciousness. The Pharisees aren't likely to do that. They're likely to sit back and analyze and make sure that they know what they can take out of the situation, out of this experience. It is very difficult to see everything an experience can produce in you, the profound effects it can have in you, until you've taken the initiative to create the experience. The more you reflect on experience and see how it changes you, then you

can become a prophet. You can become one who perceives
before it occurs what your benefits might be for the whole Self.
The Pharisees have a problem with that. *"So the Pharisees and the Scribes questioned Him: "Why do your disciples
not follow the traditions of our ancestors, but instead take food
without purifying their hands?"'* Why aren't you following the
rules? *He said to them,"How accurately Isaiah prophesied
about you hypocrites when he wrote: This people pays me lip
service, but their heart is far from me. Empty is the reverence
they do me because they teach us dogmas, mere human precepts.
You disregard God's commandments and cling to what is human
tradition."* What is human tradition? Human tradition is thinking that only the physical exists. The *Pharisee* parts of us rely
very heavily on someone else's authority, someone else's rules
and regulations, someone else's beliefs. Why? Because we
don't want to be responsible. We don't want to be the one who
is unpopular. Who is the bad guy. We don't want to be the
person who people envy, and so they won't be friends with us.
Each time we rely on "human tradition," each time we think
we're only physical beings, we break every commandment. The
commandments tell us that there's more to us than just the
physical part, and that it's those principles we are to abide by.
   *He went on to say, "You've made a fine art of setting
aside God's commandments in the interest of keeping your
tradition. For example, Moses said, Honor your father and your
mother, and in another place, whoever curses father and mother
shall be put to death. Yet you declare if a person says to his
father or mother, any support you might have had from me is
corban* (that is, dedicated to God). *you allow him to do nothing
for his father and mother. That is the way that you nullify God's
word in favor of the traditions you have handed on, and you
have many such other practices besides.* In the course of recog-

nizing the different parts of you, and we describe them as divisions of mind, you begin to recognize the *father* and *mother* represent the balance in the Superconscious mind that rests within you. This is where Heaven is found. It's also where your Christhood is found. *Honoring your father and mother* is remembering the point from which mind was created. Always remember that Heaven is within you, that it is real, it's alive. It's not a theory. It's not an idea. It's a state of being where your consciousness can thrive.

Each one of you has had moments that psychologists describe as peak experiences. A peak experience is a time in your life, usually short in duration, when everything is perfect. If you could make time stand still that moment you would do it, because everything is just right. It's Heaven! You know it's not by chance that we have those kinds of experiences. A thinker, who is alert, will begin to say, "If it happened once, then it must be able to happen again. I wonder how it happened? I wonder if I could cause it to happen? I wonder if I could live this way at all times." The Pharisees' part of each one of us says, "No it's not meant to be known. It's not meant to be discovered" or "I just did something good and I got rewarded for it by somebody else or something else." But is that really true? You've experienced enough events in your life to know that you can recreate an experience. Why would this type of experience –*Heaven* – be any different?

He summoned the crowd again and said to them, "Hear me all of you and try to understand. Nothing that enters a man from outside can make him impure. That which comes out of him and only that constitutes impurity. Let everyone heed what he hears." To take control of those Pharisee aspects of ourselves we need to entertain the idea that thoughts are things. They have substance. They use energy. They have a creative direction.

Thoughts are real in their own right. When you go to sleep at night and you have a dream, then you wake up and you remember it, you don't really think at that point whether that was real or not. I can remember waking as a child from nightmares. Mom would comfort me saying, "It's okay, honey, it was just a dream." I received her love, but even at that age, I knew that that dream was real. When I learned the dream language I understood what that dream meant.

When you can begin to recognize that thoughts are real, then you recognize that it's not what a man puts into himself — ideas, knowledge, whatever it is; food, bacteria, smoke - that makes him impure. It's not any of those things that you put into yourself as a mind or a body that poisons body and soul, it's what comes out of you. The quality of your thoughts produce truth or deceit, happiness or sorrow, heaven, or hell. This is something that the Pharisee tends to forget. In fact, the Pharisee practices forgetting that.

When He got home, away from the crowd, his disciples questioned Him about the proverb. The *disciples* are individuals who are attempting to be disciplined. There's a difference between people who followed Jesus, listening to his stories while thinking I'd never be able to do that, and the disciples. The disciples were people who said, "I want to be able to do that. Teach me how." Therefore the disciples symbolize the parts of self who are willing to be disciplined so they can move from believing to knowing.

"Are you too incapable of understanding?" He asked them. "Do you not see that nothing that enters a man from outside can make him impure. It does not penetrate his being, but enters his stomach only and passes into the latrine. Thus do we render all foods clean. What emerges from within a man, that and nothing else is what makes him impure." Interpreting

this physically, this says we can eat everything, anything available. There are some religious doctrines that have rules forbidding eating certain things, it's in most religions to protect people from eating harmful foods. That's an example of the "letter of the Law," without the spirit.

You have, in your world, a large schoolroom that offers you anything that you can imagine. It offers people. It offers places. It offers knowledge that you can put to work for you in your experiences to produce understandings that are going to be stored in your soul and you'll have them forever. Not just this lifetime, not just today, you'll have them forever. So any "food" is useful to you, any knowledge can be of use to you. It's what the thinker does with that information and knowledge that produces the cleanliness or the impurity. It's very easy to see the impure parts of your life because those are the parts that you're disgusted with, that you're miserable with, that you pout about. It doesn't take a lot of time, a lot of attention, a lot of Self-awareness to know when what's coming out of you is impure. The important part is: what are you going to do about it? How do you change it? Jesus gives an answer.

"Wicked designs come from the deep recesses of the heart." Heart represents the transforming energy of understanding and love. *The wicked designs come from the deep recesses of the heart.* When you're *wicked,* you're repeating mistakes. That's why those who sin are described as wicked. *Sin* in the Bible means to repeat the same mistakes, over and over and over again. We are thinkers. We can change. We are not destined or doomed to have the same experiences over and over again like an animal. Through reasoning we can take control of our lives bringing the light of understanding into our souls. Here Jesus teaches how.

Jesus lists these wicked designs that make us impure: *fornication, theft, murder, adulterous conduct, greed, maliciousness, sensuality, envy, blasphemy, deceit, arrogance, obtuse spirit.* Physically speaking, it looks like another long list of things not to do until you see the positive image in the language of mind. Here Jesus gives his disciples a detailed description of the understandings that will free the soul from material bondage. The first thought, or *design*, is the act of *fornication.* Fornication is having sex with a man or woman without the commitment of marriage. I'm not going to take a long time to take you through the train of thought of how I get to what this means, but I will tell you what I see that it does mean. In the language of mind, one who *fornicates* indicates the need to understand the purpose of physical existence. There's a desire to understand what the physical is and what it's for, because you don't know that.

Next is *theft.* Theft means stealing, taking without right or permission. Remember this <u>Bible</u> is talking about you. It's not talking about you stealing from someone else. It's talking about you stealing from you. There is a commandment that says, *Thou shall not steal,* and that means you recognize that you are a mental being. You are a thinker, using a physical body. You're not just a physical being, so no one can steal from you your existence. The body doesn't give you life, you the thinker gives you life. The true life is within you the individual.

Next is *murder.* Murder is unlawful killing. I looked up the word in the dictionary and it means "to mar or spoil by ineptness," and if I was ever taught that when I was growing up I've forgotten it. I always thought it just meant killing, but it means to mar or spoil by ineptness. That's murder. The way that we do that within ourselves is in thinking that we're incapable of living life. We allow somebody else to make our decisions for us. The answer is to know your life's goal. When

you know that and you live with awareness of the inner Self, you
don't murder parts of yourself. You don't spoil it by ineptness.
None of us at this point in evolution have any excuse for being
weak. We have absolutely everything we need to be strong.
The next is *adulterous conduct.* This is different from fornication. Adultery is sex between married people with someone
other than the lawful spouse. In terms of you the thinker what
you need to add to your storehouse of information at this point in
the *deep recesses of your heart* is willpower and understanding.
Doing so fulfills the duty of the Conscious Mind and the duty of
the Subconscious Mind.

Next is *greed.* Greed is a "rapacious desire for more
than one needs or deserves." Dictionaries precisely put the true
meaning of a word right in front of your mind;– *greed* is a
rapacious desire for more than one needs or deserves. If you fall
into greed in your conscious mind then you need to learn to use
what you have. To fully give of yourself for the fulfillment of
the soul, not the body.

Next we come across *maliciousness.* Maliciousness is
spite, it is "ill will with the desire to do harm." If you find you
are malicious towards someone in your environment or towards
something in your life, then you need to serve with love in order
to come to an understanding. The next thing we come across is
deceit. Deceit is deception, it's misrepresentation. The answer
to this is to know how your thoughts work. This is the part I was
talking about before, your thoughts are real. When you recognize that then you recognize what's important are your intentions
behind your acts. The next thing is *sensuality.* Sensuality is
"pertaining to, derived from or appealing to the senses." The
answer here is to be like *Arjuna* from the Bhagavad Gita, understanding how to control the body and the five senses.

The next design is *envy.* Envy is "discontent or resentment aroused by another's desirable possessions or qualities." If you find yourself envious then you might try changing that attitude to one of learning how to control your own mind. Within your mind is everything you could possibly want or need, to have the qualities and the possessions within mind as well as the physical if you will just learn to control it. Next is *blasphemy.* Blasphemy is "to speak irreverently or in an irreverent manner." And that means without esteem or concern, without respect. So if you find you tend to blaspheme, it would help you to know how creation works and why it works the way it does. It would also help you to know where your origin is, where your point of origin is. Did it begin as an egg and a sperm or did your point of origin begin somewhere else? When you know this you will uphold the second commandment.

Next is *arrogance.* Arrogance is being haughty and "an overbearing sense of pride." If you find you fall into arrogance then what you might want to do is to learn how to use your inner ego in each part of you, instead of relying so heavily upon the outer ego. I hope there can be more than one ego to you.

An obtuse spirit. Obtuse means "slow to apprehend or perceive." And *spirit* according to this dictionary means a "vital principle or animating force within living beings." As we work with the Bible, we talk about *spirit* being mind and mind being that principle that animating force within each living thing. If you have trouble being an obtuse spirit, if you are sluggish in your thinking then what you might want to do is to learn to quicken your total use of your mind. Develop concentration. Develop will power. Develop imagination. Develop memory. These are the cures for the impurity known as an obtuse spirit. It says quite a few times in the Gospel to *"come as little children."* That means open. When you hold an open perspective of your self to life then you are open to others. You find that you can begin to draw connections very quickly because you can take information very quickly. Your mind quickens in its ability to collect information, to put it together, to apply it to what you already know to be true. To what you understand to be true and apply it to your experiences that sometimes you know the truth of and some times you don't.

Each of these thoughts, listed by Mark in the distracting context, can draw us away from awareness of our purpose for existence. With each one, the knower in each of us, *Jesus,* elucidates the answer: there's a desire for something. No one gives you envy, no one gives you greed, no one makes you an obtuse spirit. In miserable or negative experiences look to see what understanding can be brought into your life. Cease reacting to life as if the physical is all that exists. Be more than a scribe or Pharisee, identify with what Jesus and the disciples symbolize. Knowing how to respond, how to be self-disciplined in the face of darkness, frees you.

Responding enables you to live the spirit of the law. You begin living the Truth, and the Pharisee parts begin to dwindle away. Your heart becomes pure. You are one step closer to claiming the Kingdom of Heaven within and being home.

The Book of Being

Discovering the Kingdom of Heaven

The Book of Being

Discovering the Kingdom of Heaven

by Gayle B. Matthes

first published in its entirety January 1983

Prologue

I want to tell you a story about a man who means a great deal to me. It is about a man who recognized his own importance and the importance of each other individual. It is about a man who reached great heights within himself and attempted to pass this on to others. It is about a very special man, special like you and me.

Now even though it is a story, it won't begin with "once upon a time..." though once upon a time he was born in a small village called Bethlehem. It won't proceed to tell you the kind of life he led, for he was only a carpenter at first, before he became a King. It won't go on to tell you of the many miracles he performed because, you see, he knew exactly what he was doing and so there were no miracles. And at the end it won't finish with "He lived happily ever after..." even though those who know the story and the man know that is precisely what did occur. It won't tell you that never before and never since has a man such as this existed. The reason is because such a statement is true. But it is also true of you and it is also true of me.

In fact you might miss the notion that it is a story at all. After all, would anyone think to write an account of your life? Yet that is what I am doing.

For some this will be obvious, for others only bits and pieces may fly off the pages and land in their laps. Still some of you may think "No, not a word makes sense to me!" while others cry, "She blasphemes." There are some who still allow others to control their thoughts and may be intimidated, never letting the bold truth of these pages cross the threshold of their thinking. But I take no offense at this, after all it's only a book, and books can be burned or banned.

So for those of you who have eyes that are willing to see, read on. Those of you who have ears to hear, listen closely. This might be the story or book you've been looking for.

Every story has a beginning and this is no exception. So I will begin, "Let there be Light..."

But before I truly begin, I want to give you some background on this story I'm planning to tell. I will tell you that it is about a man, but it could have been about a woman. This man discovered he had a kingdom. I say discovered not because he had newly received this kingdom — no, that is not the case. I say discovered because that is in fact what happened. The kingdom had been his all along waiting for his direction.

Now you can imagine what a kingdom would be like without a ruler to direct it. This was true of this kingdom as well. There was some food produced as there was fertile luscious ground and plants growing abundantly. But along with the plants were lots of weeds as well choking off much of this bounty.

There were guards as well but with no one to direct them they were doing only what they knew how to do. They were keeping guard over the many treasures in the palace. But not only were they keeping out thieves, they were also keeping out the ones who would be able to use the wealth to produce more wealth.

There was trouble in the palace because the water wheels that supplied power to the whole kingdom were collecting much and slowing down. Those people in the kingdom were doing their best but they could only do what they were trained to do and recently there had been very little training. So much of their days were spent lolling around and getting drunk. They stopped seeing reason to keeping things tidy and so the garbage started piling up. This brought in many animals who could manage very well on the scraps that were accumulating. Every once in a while someone would wake up from his slumbering and point an accusing finger at another and say "It is your fault we are in the state we are." Then fall back into complacency. At other times you would see a woman walking through the cluttered streets rubbing her hands together mumbling, "Why me, why me?"

A child, only occasionally (for there weren't many children), would cry, "Why doesn't somebody do something?" and a farmer would reply, "I'm trying, I'm trying" and scratch his head attempting to remember just what it was he was trying. This was the shape of the kingdom this man had discovered. And he grieved when he realized the beauty and abundance that was being hidden and unused because of his lack of command. He thought to himself, "If I could learn to rule this kingdom, I would be the richest man in the world. And if I could rule it with intelligence I would be the wisest man in the world." And so he began.

He began teaching the farmers to till the soil and remove the weeds and burn them. He taught them to store the good grain carefully so that it would not rot. He then taught them how to clear out the streams so that the life-giving water ran freely, supplying sources of power throughout the kingdom. He ordered the streets cleared and the animals contained. He taught them how to use the horses to help with the burdening work. He taught them how to prepare and eat good foods so that their bodies were healthy. He taught them how to pay attention to their tasks so that they would not have to repeat them, wasting valuable time. He taught them how to keep records and review those records so that they could learn how to produce more. He taught them how to listen to one another and himself so that their learning could be more complete. He commanded the guards and taught the money keepers how to multiply their holdings.

He did all this with love, determination, and a desire to fulfill his duty to himself and his kingdom. He found out in this process that this kingdom had been given to him by his Father and that this house had many mansions. Upon further investigation he found more riches than he had dreamed of. He found what he had been seeking and had become a king.

You have a kingdom as well that your Father has given you. You know the one I'm talking about – the one you've been searching for all your life. The one that will offer you happiness and security and most of all, peace. Why are you still looking for it? Stop for a moment and look closer, listen more intently, think. It is inside your own mind, that kingdom. What kind of shape is yours in? Is it still patiently waiting for its ruler?

This story could be about you, and in some ways it is. But I don't want to keep you in suspense any longer, so let us begin.

In the Beginning

Suppose you opened your eyes one day and looked around and found yourself standing on a foreign street in a land unknown to yourself. In your panic you reach out and attempt to gain the attention of passers-by only to discover that they do not understand what you are trying to say. They do not "speak" your language nor do you "speak" theirs. Your mind begins to whirl as you search for a way to communicate your distress. You begin waving your arms, and before you know it, your gestures are communicating a picture of your despair and those passers-by are beginning to respond to your questions. Perhaps you even take out a piece of paper and begin to draw an image of what you are trying to convey. In either case you find that you must use a language of pictures or images to make yourself understood. You might point to your stomach and mouth to indicate hunger, or point to your ear and shake your head to indicate that you do not hear or understand what is being said. But you would continue to gesture until your point had been made. It is this picture language that is the one sure means of communication that man can use to transfer his ideas to his world regardless of the language that is verbally spoken.

If you've been looking around you've found that pictures are being used currently to illustrate ideas previously related with words. These include "no parking," a P with a slash; "handicapped parking," a wheelchair; "no left turn," a directional line with a slash. There is also the old familiar skull and cross bones to indicate danger.

Yet pictures are not new! They have been used throughout the ages to tell a story, convey an idea, or teach values and morals, and to leave a history of events. We have mythology and fables, proverbs and Indian markings, as well as hieroglyphics, to mention only a few of the ways that pictures have illustrated our progression throughout the ages.

When you can understand that the Bible is also written in the picture language you will begin to see that it is written about you "the thinker," or the intelligence that travels through lifetimes growing and evolving. It takes you on the journey of your own evolution from the point of that first creation of light to the point where you now exist — human man, the reasoner — and further yet to that stage of intuitional or spiritual man.

The *Old Testament* begins with the first creation, that of light and life itself. *In the beginning, when God created the heavens and the earth, the earth was a formless wasteland, and darkness covered the abyss, while a mighty wind swept over the water (Gen.1:1)* . It in no way indicates that our world which we affectionately term earth was a globe spinning. The image that is conveyed, in fact, is the opposite, a *formless* (without form) *wasteland* (without substance) and *darkness* (without life of any kind), *covered the abyss* (an abyss refers to a nothingness and this has been illustrated). Yet a *mighty wind swept over the waters.* Have you ever watched water in its natural state? It has a certain quality of stillness yet it will respond to any action. It will mold itself to any container. It will move when a rock is thrown into it or when a wind sweeps across it. Consider if you will, then, *water* being a receptive state. The *wind* however is quite the opposite. As it moves through our environment it can be gentle enough to rustle the smallest blade of grass or tumultuous enough to uproot the sturdy oak. It, in fact, is aggressive in its very nature. Now for creation to occur in any form there must be the aggressive and receptive factors present. Look at the very creation of a child. There must be the father and the mother present. This time however the child is *light*.

Then God said, "Let there be Light" and there was Light. Now before you can say a single word there first must be the thought of that word. Creation itself was the result of a thought — a mental creation. And that creation was Light where before there was darkness. Life had begun. That *Light* was your beginning awareness.

Look at the ways we now use the word light: "I see the light," "that person is enlightened" or "let us shed some light on the subject." In all ways there is the indication that a different point of awareness is being reached. *Genesis* goes on at that point to talk about the *separation of light and darkness*, which is here indicating the individualization of that light, or your own individuality. This is as far as I will go at this point.

There is something of interest here however. In each of the Holy Books, creation always begins with Light. Even the scientific theories will agree with this. It is this Light and awareness that Jesus spoke of often in his teaching. That Light of your awareness is what we will be seeking to understand in this book. Now the *Old Testament* goes on to illustrate and use further pictures to denote the goal and purpose of that tiny particle of awareness and its great potential to become compatible to its Creator. It will open up to its reader the development of Light as the intelligence and the vehicles or lifeforms that were used by Light to gain experience up to the point of human man or reasoning man. The *New Testament* offers, in the teachings of Jesus, step by step instruction on how to fully utilize the reasoning abilities, how to cause growth in the individual and bring about the change from reasoning man to intuitive man or spiritual man. The steps include the recognition that you exist separate from the physical body you are inhabiting and thereby must have dominion over it. The *New Testament* also offers a set of laws or conditions for light to work with to reach its state of wholeness. There is one book, the *Book of Revelation*, that reveals in vivid pictures what man will need to do and understand in order to work in harmony with the goal of Light to become compatible to its Creator.

Let's investigate this compatibility a little further. Have you ever watched a small child at play? Notice how the little girl will dress herself up in her mother's clothing, walking awkwardly in those high-heeled shoes. She will preen herself in the mirror applying colors to her face in all the appropriate places. Or notice the young boy as he stretches his legs in walking while trying to match his father's footsteps. These children are attempting to imitate the parents or to be like an adult. They are practicing what grown-ups do. There is, in fact, evident a strong desire to be like the adult, and yet they are not yet compatible with the parents.

The child does not reach that stage of compatibility with its parents until he or she has had similar experiences of their own. You are not compatible to, or a companion to your parents until you have produced offspring of your own or been responsible in the ways they are.

This doesn't mean that you will get along any better with your parents just that you now can relate to the experiences that produce adulthood.

Now depending on your current attitudes towards your parents, you might begin to see that you too had the desire to become grown up or like them. You may have also had ideas of ways that you would do things that would be different. Just remember the statements you made back then, "If only I was grown up."

Consider then that you as an offspring or child of God, or a mental parent, had at one time a desire to be like your mental parent. I say at one time not because you no longer have the desire but only because you might have lost sight of that desire. If you will recall in the Bible it states that *man was created in the 'image and likeness' of the Creator. (Gen 1:26)* The *likeness of the Creator* would indicate that you are like the Creator with the same potential, to create. Just like a child has the potential to be a productive adult. Now it doesn't make sense to say that you were created "in the likeness and the likeness" but that is exactly what is assumed when there is only seen that we are made to be like our Creator.

Image — where have you heard that word before? Image maker? No? Well perhaps you're more familiar with the term imagination. In fact, I'll bet there have been times when you have discounted one of your most precious tools of creation. Your image maker. You were created in the image maker of your mental parent. You were created out of thought, the Creator's thought. You are a mental creation with the same capabilities as your Creator, to create with your mind. This is an important step to consider in your search for your own divinity.

I once knew a couple who were on their way to understanding their abilities to use their minds to create. They had already produced some very satisfying results in obtaining a new home that they had always dreamed of owning, and the husband had obtained a very prestigious and lucrative job. They had both decided that it was time to start the family that they too had always wanted.

Now there's one point about this couple that you will want to know. The fact is that physically they were both very homely people. Yes, I realize that beauty comes from within but right now we're talking about physical structure and attributes. The woman knew this and decided that she would put her creative abilities to work to give birth to a beautiful baby.

In her mind she began to imagine and celebrate the idea that she would have a beautiful baby. She did not merely want a lovely looking child but a healthy one as well — she was after all not a vain woman. She went so far as to put pictures of beautiful babies all around the nursery to reinforce her imaging. Now this was a woman full of love, and she would have responded to and loved any child, but she was practicing being a mental creator and knew that she was responsible to and for the child she carried inside of her. Needless to say, the couple delivered a very beautiful child. The child is starting in her teens now and is not only physically gorgeous but because of caring and wise parents, is also beautiful inside. Her parents do not chide her for using her imagination, they have taught her how to respect and use it responsibly. They understand the value of pictures as they are used in creating.

This demonstrates how to create with pictures, but there is another important step and that is understanding pictures that have previously been recorded. The Indians in their migrations left images drawn on walls of caves to indicate events that transpired while they resided in that area as well as information on the next movement of the tribe. Egyptians left great histories in pictures known as hieroglyphics. There are other races and nationalities that still use pictures to communicate. You only need to look at certain Oriental writings to see evidence of this. We spend hours, weeks, and years attempting to decipher these ancient pictures and oftentimes miss a book that is written in vivid pictures using each word as a brush stroke — The Bible.

When you interpret and unlock the pictures conveyed in the Bible, you can find the answer to three very important and exciting questions: "Who am I," "Where did I come from," "Where am I going." But it will take practice and a sincere desire to understand your part in your existence and development. It will require that you remember what you have read before and apply it to the picture you are currently building and wanting to understand. Now, when the stories and events in the Bible are read and taken literally you will find contradictions from cover to cover. When read in the "language of mind" (the picture language), the story is told through the use of symbols — symbols used to convey an idea of you as mind. There will be no contradictions.

In my studies I find that the Bible used people, places and circumstances to tell you a story about your own evolution and progression. Each person is referring to a part of you and each place is a place in your own mind. You will be going within to those parts of your mind to rediscover your past and find the kingdom of heaven that has been promised to you.

When you read the pictures of this book the insights become so exciting and rewarding. Keep in mind that I am not proposing to say that these events or people never happened. That would be quite presumptuous of me. But it might, perhaps, explain why only certain stories were presented and in a certain order. You will unlock the mystery of why Jesus continually told you that you will *reap what you sow.* You will also find that you can take these insights that you gain and apply it to every other holy book and it too will be talking about you as a thinker or intelligence moving toward mental maturity.

I will present to you, for your consideration, the pictures and stories that depict Jesus as part of you. It is that part that recognizes the Christ principle and desires to purposefully use this to produce knowing. *John* is that part of you that still only believes and therefore must precede Jesus as the harbinger or preparer of the way. With this I hope to give you a tool to enhance your use of this great book in your everyday life. I also hope to convey to you what practicing the teachings of Jesus represents to me.

In your quest for understanding and truth, you may have noticed that the Christ figure or master in each religion and holy book have been displayed as a man, or male figure that made it necessary to describe an action with the word "he." Is this coincidental or does it mean that if you are a woman you may as well forget about obtaining the state of Christ consciousness? No on both counts. Consider, however, it to mean that it will require you, the thinker, to become aggressive in your attempts to seek your kingdom of heaven. The Kingdom of Heaven lies within — within your own mind.

Remember the story of the woman and her child? She did not passively sit and let circumstances happen. She took action in a very responsible way. She changed something she saw as limiting or less than what she wanted and she created a change through her belief that she could. John the Baptizer, coming before Jesus, proclaimed, *"Repent, reform your lives. The reign of God is at hand."* *Repent* means to change your *sins,* or mistakes, into more productive attitudes and actions. *Reform* means to produce a change, you produce that change. *The reign of God is at hand*—not coming, but here now ready for your use.

The first step is to believe you can be different and then to determine the steps to take that will produce the results you desire. Belief is the first step — but it is only a step. Man was not meant to remain in the believing state. To remain in a state of belief is to allow others to rule your thoughts. When you cease to allow anyone to intimidate you and begin to initiate the action that will produce answers to your questions you will find ways to move from believing to knowing. It will require changes on your part and change is tricky and it is risky. But it is a necessary part of evolution. The first change will be you becoming aware of and responsible for your thoughts.

Let's talk about change for a bit. Changes occurred throughout the Bible in many different ways and at many different points. One of the things that indicates that a change is taking place is the number four. This is seen in the 40 days in the wilderness — the time of Jesus' temptation, the 40 years of exile, the 40 days and nights of flood. The *four* indicates stability resulting from carrying a change through four steps of development: infancy, adolescence, adulthood, and old age or wisdom. These are the four basic stages that you move through, or are in the process of moving through, in your own physiological existence.

Let's look at the infant. He or she relies upon others to care for him and to provide shelter and comfort as well as information or guidelines. His mind is like a sponge soaking up as much information or input from the senses as possible. Watch how a child in the beginning will shove everything in his mouth, relying on the sense of taste and touch to supply some of his learning. When the child cries someone reaches to comfort him by sticking a bottle or a breast in his mouth. As he cries again someone picks him up. He continues crying until someone notices his discomfort and remedies this by changing his diaper. Soon the baby learns that by crying he can gain attention. Even though there is information continually being absorbed, there is often a lack of discrimination about what is taken into the mind and brain and accepted as truth. It is a period of dependency.

The second stage, adolescence, provides a time of experimentation and sometimes rebelliousness. This rebelliousness results from mistakenly thinking you know more than the adult. Now if you've ever had a teenager or can remember being a teenager, you can remember also that this is the time when you think you know it all. There is not the immediate willingness to follow the dictates of others. The child wants to do all those things previously forbidden; like staying out late, smoking behind the bathroom door, skipping school. Anything that will prove he is an individual, or better yet, an adult. It is, though, a period of questioning and through this the experimentation arises. Sometimes there is anger directed towards those individuals or agencies that seem to want to control you with rules and regulations. Sometimes the anger is stimulated when you as the adolescent find that you were directed on the wrong course. So you might begin to lash out, sure that everything you were ever told was wrong. The cry of "Why is this happening to me?" is heard. There can be constant seeking for someone to blame for your discomfort (until you stop reacting and begin thinking). This takes us to adulthood.

The transition from adolescence to adulthood is often the most difficult. There is a desire to cling to that time when the only responsibility carried was being punished when we did something wrong and praised when we did something right. It is the beginning of letting go of blaming others for the situations and circumstances that befall you. It is the beginning of acknowledging that you are what you are because of your own personal choices and actions. You begin seeing all those things that used to make you angry as not nearly so important or nerve shattering. You begin seeing that perhaps you even learned some things that you can now put into practice. Instead of being angry with Mom for making you clean your room you are now finding ways to care for your own home, plus finance it. Instead of fretting over what dress to wear to the prom, you are planning a career that will be satisfying to you. In other words, you are beginning to produce and discover your own truths and your own answers as to what it is like being the adult.

The first recognition that you are responsible for yourself, your situations and circumstances, and your reactions to them can be a joyful experience or a painful one. It means blaming no one and giving credit to no one but yourself for who and what you are. It is a time to set goals and accomplish them. It takes practice and the willingness to learn from your mistakes.

The man Jesus gives us a clear picture to this effect *"If you live according to my teachings you are truly my disciples; then you will know the truth and the truth will set you free." (John 8:31)* When you can discipline yourself to learn from your mistakes instead of blaming others or condemning yourself, then you will discover truth. Truth can be painful when the discoverer is dwelling on the old attitudes, actions and comforts that are being left behind. When you become responsible for your successes and failures you will know freedom.

In order to truly understand and live according to the teachings of Jesus you must be willing to be decisive, determined, and cognizant of the true value of yourself as an individual. The man Jesus spoke from his own personal authority; he buckled under for no man. He recognized; the power of his own divinity, *The Father*, his own individuality, and responded to it. He encouraged others to do likewise. When he performed healings he would place the responsibility for action on the individual—*"Take up your mat and walk."* He did not say "Follow me as sheep or as a robot would." He taught man to be responsible to and for himself.

The fourth step in our progress through physiological life is old age and wisdom. Wisdom can occur when we are fully expressing all that we have accumulated in understanding and accomplished up to that point. It is a complete giving and teaching others what has been learned so that this can be passed on and used in future generations. For many years the United States has not taken advantage of this stage of growth. There has been a refusal to recognize the wisdom that is present in the elderly. You hear the phrase that experience is the best teacher and I heartily agree! So why not use the experience that is abundant in our senior citizens? We see evidence of these four stages of change in our seasons as well. Winter is often looked at as a dormant state or restful state. But those who have worked the land know this is not so. They can in fact appreciate the activity that occurs at this time. There are changes that are occurring constantly: absorption, regeneration, life. The substances that have exhausted themselves in the fall return to the earth, break down, and are eagerly absorbed and changed to make ready for the growth of new substance, new expressions. In our earth cycle this is the stage of infancy. Then there begins the pushing forth from the seed, young tender plants; the sap in the old tree rises again to push forth new blossoms, striving to reach for the sun. There is the evidence of awkwardness as the plants droop from side to side while gaining strength. In summer we see the results of what we have planted; it is a time of producing. In fall a full and final expression and a returning to the earth or a giving forth of the seeds to begin the new cycle is seen.

Man in his quest to understand God has likewise moved part way through these cycles. The dependency upon a deity to rule our lives and determine our decisions has exemplified this in the worshiping of fetishes, elements, and animals. It is demonstrated when we determine our course of action according to omens or apparent miracles. Look to your Old Testament for evidence of this.

God is portrayed as a vengeful, jealous, partial entity. One who dwelled in mountains spurting tongues of fire to indicate wrath. This picture of God was based on man's idea of himself; therefore it held the attributes and inconsistencies of man. Prayers that were offered were of a pleading nature and of a bargaining nature. Think of how the little child attempts to manipulate the parent into giving him what he wants. First a request, then tears and anger, and even a promise to be 'good if.....' This too is how man has often made his communication to God take form. We pray for God to step in and change the minds of nations so that they should see things the way we do. We pray for changes in nature (when nature is already in perfect balance), when it would merely take the responding ability of each individual to work peaceably with nature.

Yet Jesus demonstrated the command of someone who knew himself and his divine birthright. He did not plead with God to make Lazarus come alive. He did not bargain with God. Instead he spoke, *"Father I thank thee that thou hearest me always"* and then said with the conviction of those who know, *"Lazarus come forth."* He was demonstrating the need for man to begin taking responsibility for his actions. To be the adult.

As should be the case, before reaching adulthood one must move through adolescence. It can either be an enjoyable journey or an unpleasant one but needless to say it is a period of questioning and experimentation. We are in the middle of this at the present time. It can be heard in the cry that "God is dead." It can be heard in the statements that "God is mind, Supreme intelligence, Cosmic consciousness," etc. But in this time also are the statements regarding "God being within" and "I only do God's will" or "It is God's will moving through me." Nice as it sounds it is still demonstrating that

I am not a "child of God" but a puppet of God having no value or worth or real purpose for individual existence. There are beliefs cropping up that we are all One and that our prime objective is to return to that state of Oneness, that we will all unite back to being One. If that were the case then why was there a necessity for the individuality and awareness in the first place? Do you want the child you bear to go out in the world and experience, grow and produce only to be called back to your womb and lose its own right to life? Do you perceive that a Creator would want less for his Children than you?

This period of adolescence is good, it is healthy, and it is necessary. At first sign there is a tendency to feel as though we know it all and to become dogmatic in our thinking, only to realize that we have once again reached a point of stagnation and resistance. The rebellion of the masses has demonstrated this adolescence in cults, new religions, self-improvement courses, and "psychic phenomena." But it is still experimental and oftentimes creates the same types of dependencies previously experienced. It is, however, through this experimentation that man begins to look to himself and ask "How do I fit in? What is my responsibility for myself, my environment and my brother?"

In the adolescent stage there is a type of "over" learning that occurs. The "over" learning takes place when you see that a mistake has been made in your actions, attitudes, or values. There is the tendency to want to throw out everything, tear down what has been built before, and make everything new.

Sad to say, I've seen this demonstrated in groups that are sure the end of the world is coming whether through weather and earth changes or God's wrath. It is as though they are pleading with a deity to remove their responsibility for their life and their world. It is passivity at its greatest when you sit and expect someone else to determine your future or save you from future responsibility of correcting your previous errors.

I see the adolescence being portrayed in the environmentalists when they preach fear. There is fear of losing this and fear of losing that, but seldom is there seen the use of positive goals and greater uses of our environment. In the misunderstanding of evolution there is the frantic leap of saving lifeforms that are naturally dying out. There is fear of the use of power because of the lack of understanding of it. I am not saying that the environmentalists are all bad. I see these actions have served some valuable purpose in bringing the attention back to using our environment responsibly and productively. But it is the adolescent that is fearful of what he is leaving behind.

Adulthood is often approached with apprehension. It is a time of wondering what one will need to give up in order to become the productive and free person that he so desires to be. This is a stage some are currently striving to attain. It is when you begin to recognize that you have at your disposal everything necessary for discovering your own truth. Those who strive for this adulthood cease looking outside themselves for their answers to the question "Who am I?" That question is being answered. They cease looking for someone or something to blame for their circumstances. They no longer plead with a deity to make their life more comfortable because they know that they have everything necessary to create that peace and satisfaction within themselves.

The adult ceases to believe the edicts of others and the limitations others try to push on them. In fact he becomes tired and most frustrated with believing, period. There is a demand to know and so the adult moves willingly into creating experiences that will satisfy that hunger. He knows that there is nothing that is not meant for him to know.

When you begin to learn from your experiences, and begin to question the cause behind your circumstances then you can begin to create more productive and enriching experiences. Those who are reaching this adulthood are joyful, discovering that they are not merely mortal men but intelligences with an existence above and beyond that of the physical level of consciousness. They are beginning to discover that thought is cause and their physical world its manifested likeness. The adult has discovered David's key and has unlocked the mystery of its meaning. David's key consists of two triangles, one pointing up and one pointing down. The first is to indicate spirit into matter, the second is matter into spirit; as above so below. You see David knew that his thoughts manifested or became a real part of his world. He knew that everything in his world was first a thought. He knew how to reason.

As man begins to embrace the use of his mind and the responsibility that is his, he can and will produce the adult stage of the thinker.

Throughout the Bible and especially in the ministry of Jesus you will find descriptions of the laws of the mind and the truths that will explain these laws. It is through understanding the laws of the mind and harmonizing with these laws that man becomes the productive reasoning, intuitive thinker, and creator that he was designed to be. Jesus did not demonstrate a gift that was given to only himself nor a responsibility that was for only himself. He demonstrated what he had understood to be a most valuable truth for mankind: the realization that *"I and the Father are One."* He was here to save man from his sins but not in the way that had been expected of him. He was saving man from ignorance by teaching and demonstrating the way mind functions and the way to practice this. Because he was a teacher he used pictures to illustrate the workings of the mind. He taught people to reason according to their understandings. He did this in the form of parables, stories designed to cause man to think and come up with a way to apply these things in their own lives. To the masses he told stories, to the disciples he gave the meaning behind the stories. If you will begin to respect yourself as a thinker and will begin to examine the pictures that are portrayed in the Bible, you will begin to see a way to make your own existence more meaningful and purposeful.

Anyone can go through the Bible and pick out passages and verses much the same way that I am doing here and turn it around to justify his own truths. But after careful examination one will also be able to find parts of the Bible that will likewise appear to contradict what has been said before. This is where it is interpreted in the literal sense only. When the pictures in the Bible are interpreted with the idea that man is an intelligence with free will and imagination who has a goal and a purpose for his existence, then this book portrays the most vivid description of man's journey as a particle of light with an infant's desire to be like *(in the likeness of)* his mental parent or God to a completion of that evolvement there will be no contradictions.

In our journey we attempt first to shape God in our own image — to make him jealous, vengeful, manipulative, dependent, tyrannical, forgiving, and even loving at times, but always in our image. If we create him in our own image we can make him responsible for our successes and the devil responsible for our mistakes. Jesus did neither. He taught man how to become responsible to and for himself.

This is demonstrated in *John 14:12*. *"Believe me that I am in the Father and the Father is in me, or else believe because of the works I do. I solemnly assure you, the man who has faith in me will do the works I do and greater far than these."* Greater works than these. Now it is common to think, when reading this portion, that Jesus, because of your faith in him, will do the work for you and make it look like you did it. Does that make sense? I don't think so. But, if you will, remember when you saw an older brother or sister do something for the first time. Before you had seen someone do it there was not even the belief that you might be able to accomplish that very thing. Jesus offered you a challenge. If you can believe in the Christ part of yourself you can also accomplish the work he did and more. Jesus demonstrated ways for mankind to reach that state of enlightenment or awareness of who they are and where they came from for themselves.

God's only begotten son — the very first creation — do you remember what that was? Light. Is Jesus the only *"light of the world"*? He never made that claim. He told others over and over that *"You are the light of the world." (Matt. 5:14)* Remember *light* indicates awareness, and to have the awareness of where you came from, why you are here and where you are going truly will offer you eternal life and the full recognition of that eternal life. You have this now. It is up to you whether you will recognize this and respond to it.

With each change or reformation that you make in yourself you will find yourself experiencing the four stages of growth. You will start with believing you can accomplish it (whatever "it" is) but as you learn and struggle and aspire you too can produce the wisdom of knowing. Are you satisfied to only believe or will you claim the right to use your own kingdom?

Man's Divine Birthright

Jesus spoke of the divinity of man often. He was constantly affirming and reaffirming that the works he performed others could perform *(John 14:12)*, that the vision and perception he had others could accomplish if they would but make the effort. He offered up a challenge constantly, *"Those who have eyes will see and those who have ears will hear."* In effect he was saying, "Pay attention to what you see, pay attention to what you hear and reason and think."

So often man searches outside of himself for responsibility and even for truth. He looks in libraries, in churches, in self-improvement groups, in psychoanalysis, and even in friends, family and job. Man constantly is seeking validation as to the purpose of his existence.

I have not forgotten my own search in this regard. For most of my life I have been aware that there was more to life than met the eye. I had heard scientists report over and over that man used only about 4-20% of his mind and brain. My first question was, how did they know that? Did they have someone who used 100% of their mind and therefore measured everyone else by that standard? My second question was what was it possible to do with the other 80-90% of that power? I would ask the people around me and they didn't seem to have an answer either.

At the same time I was busy discovering a little trick I was able to do with my own mind. At night before I went to sleep I would decide that I wanted to dream about the next day and what was going to occur. As I would be dozing off I would put my attention on the place I wanted to go. Each time I did this I was able to see the people involved, what they would be wearing and what was going on as well as what was being discussed. I had done this repeatedly and I began mentioning it to my friends. I had assumed it was a natural phenomenon. Well, at first they didn't believe me and then they thought it was a little strange. So I kept my new found secret to myself. It wasn't until much later that I realized I was drawing on and using my subconscious mind.

I then began listening for others who had experienced similar things. I began to read a lot and began to see that others not only had similar experiences but they had similar ideas. I became satisfied with that. I lived in a world of ideas and spontaneous unexplained happenings within my own mind. Not for long though. In time my own urge to find out more took over. I began to see I had a kingdom at my finger tips that was waiting for some intelligent direction. I began to understand the other 80% of my mind.

I've watched others search as well. And I've seen them reach periods of a type of satisfaction. The satisfaction of reading about others' experiences; the satisfaction of finding someone who will tell them what to think or what to believe; or the satisfaction of finding something or someone outside of themselves to blame for their circumstances or give credit for their mistakes. I have seen others become satisfied in spontaneously causing results with their mind and with their situations, never once acknowledging that they could understand the causes behind this. I have seen people assume that positive thinking is the answer to their problems and watched them hold their minds frozen for fear a negative thought might enter uninvited.

For some that satisfaction has remained a life long condition and you might want to applaud them. I would too if I thought it brought them peace. Yet in each case there has still been present an unquenching thirst to know who they are and why they are.

I had a woman come to me one day saying that she had found the answer to all her problems. It was in her diet. She had then ceased to eat meat and many other things at which she now smugly turned up her nose. She began telling me how unhealthy, spiritually, it was to eat certain foods and that she was on her way to that spiritual enlightenment. I stopped her for a moment and asked her to tell me what was unholy about meat, or flour, or any other substance that she seemed to think was bad. She couldn't answer me. I proceeded to ask her, "Mary, how is this new diet changing your life?"

She gave me some examples that sounded pretty good at first hearing. She told me how the problems at work didn't bother her any more. But I began to probe a little deeper. I asked her why they didn't bother her and her basic response was that she just didn't care if "they" had problems. She would just smile and think of how much better off she was. But Mary was just experiencing a similar type of satisfaction I spoke of earlier. Mary was pretending everything was O.K. She had some more things to learn.

Well, a couple of months later Mary came by the school where I was teaching, rather down in the mouth. I was concerned and asked her what the problem was. "Dr. Matthes, I don't understand it but things seem to be worse than they were before."

"Before what?" I asked, fairly sure I knew "before what."

"Before I started my new diet!"

When someone is asking you for help it's certainly not the time to say, "I told you so," but I had a small suspicion that Mary might someday come to this conclusion, so we talked for awhile. I had been teaching a class that afternoon about the importance of thoughts and was using some reference where Jesus had taught the disciples this very thing. I brought out my <u>Bible</u> and asked her to listen for a moment as I read a passage from *Matthew 15 verse 11.* Perhaps you will recall it. Jesus is chastising the Pharisees for being so concerned with physical appearances only. *"It is not what goes into a man's mouth that makes him impure. It is what comes out of his mouth."*

She looked at me quizzically for a moment and then said quietly "O.K., it's not what I'm eating that's causing me problems, but what I'm saying?"

"Well, something like that but let's see what else it's saying, because, like you, his disciples wanted to know what he was talking about so they urged him to explain. He goes on, *"Do you not see that everything that enters the mouth passes into the stomach and is discharged into the latrine, but what comes out of the mouth originates in the mind? It is things like this that make a man impure."* Mary is a pretty sharp gal and her eyes began to light up at this. "It's my thinking that is giving me problems! Well I can do something about that!" Mary was on the way to discovering thought directed with intelligence is the most powerful force in the universe. It was a start.

She, like others who are learning about their own mind, will have much practicing to do because it will take more than just thinking about it. It will take being responsible for thoughts and actions.

Sound simple? It is. But it is not easy. From the time you are very young you learn how to try and think of or do many things at one time. In fact you learn how to scatter the attention so that it flits from one thing to another almost instantly. Many times so quickly that there isn't adequate attention given to the types of thoughts that you hold of yourself or your situations. Yet these same thoughts are continually affecting your attitudes, actions and circumstances. If you are constantly thinking thoughts of limitation, or of the things that you are not able to do for some reason or another, you will find life very difficult, hard, and dissatisfying. If you are constantly holding thoughts of doubt and indecision about one thing or the other, you will find that it seems like others are controlling your life. You're right, they are.

Upon hearing these words and possibly even accepting the idea that we can control our thoughts, we might begin to create more positive thoughts and a smiling expression. That is until something comes along to upset the apple cart of our new way of thinking. At that time our reactions begin and can take many outward expressions, from anger, frustration and grief to our own doubt and indecision. This is often followed by guilt or self pity because we have not achieved the goal of perfection in one easy lesson.

Not too long ago a man came barreling into the kitchen at the school I was currently visiting, excitedly exclaiming, "I did it, I did it!"

Getting excited with him regarding his accomplishment, whatever it might be, I curiously responded "That's neat Mark —

what was 'it' you did?"

He then began describing the scene of what had just
transpired. He had been happily on his way to the bus stop when he
had accidentally bumped up against a young guy. The fellow jerked
around and achieved a stance ready for battle. Seeing himself and
how he would have reacted similarly not too long ago, Mark looked
him in the eyes and said "I'm sorry for you. I love you just because
you are," and walked on. Needless to say the fellow was too stunned
to take any further action but just stood there with his mouth hanging
open. The thing that was so exciting to Mark at this time was
recognizing at previous points in his life he would have responded
to that particular situation by punching the guy out. He had finally
seen that he had a choice as to how he would respond to that situation
and that it needn't be based on another's actions or reactions. "I
really felt I did and could love him even though he did not act in a
way that was pleasing to me," was Mark's statement of pure
fascination with the whole event that had occurred. Mark was
learning the quality of compassion or turning the other cheek.

Now how does this story indicate the use of mind? Let me
explain further. When Mark first began to practice the developing
of his mind he recognized that he had held thoughts of himself as
being very short tempered and violent. He was actually imagining
himself as violent and thus causing situations and circumstances to
bring this out in his expression. His mind and his attention were very
scattered in the attempt to defend the image he held. Until he
decided to cease misusing his mind and start using it productively,
he would find himself reacting in the same old ways over and over
again. He could suppress the urge to be violent or angry but he
would still experience the mounting tension within himself that
would eventually erupt in an emotional outburst or a physical
disorder. It wasn't until he imagined himself as compassionate,
caring and in control, and took steps to practice this that he began

to notice the change occurring in himself. Mark had purposefully caused Mark to be responsible to himself and for his thought processes.

You might view this as "positive thinking." But it is so much more. It is, in fact, *using* the mind in a positive and productive manner. It wasn't until Mark was able to develop the use of undivided attention, placing his full attention at a single point or idea for as long as he desired, that he was able to develop the idea of what he wanted for himself and how he would put it into practice. Jesus was constantly teaching the Universal Laws and Truths of the mind and encouraging his disciples to do the same. He assured those whom he spoke to that thoughts really are things and that as you think you are, as your actions proclaim you to be, you will be this. *"If ye had faith the size of a mustard seed you could say to this sycamore 'be uprooted and transplanted into the sea' and it would obey you."* (*Luke 17:6*) This is not to say that God will move the mountain, or that Jesus would move the mountain, but that you would cause the movement of the mountain because of your own mental ability and divinity.

Another time, after demonstrating to his disciples what appeared to be a miracle in the withering of a fig tree, he was heard to say *"Believe me, if you trust and do not falter, not only will you do what I did to a fig tree, but if you say to this mountain 'Be lifted up and thrown into the sea' even that will happen. You will receive all that you pray for provided you have faith."* (*Matthew 21:21*)

The faith of a mustard seed. The tiny *seed* symbolizes your ideas. When you begin to see how much those ideas influence your life perhaps you will want to learn to control them. A wise man named Thoreau once wrote, "As a man thinketh in his heart, so is he."

Without controlling your thoughts you can still have the faith of a mustard seed. You will have faith that you can't accomplish certain things, you will have faith that you can't change, you will have faith that your fears will always be there holding you back — and *it will be so!* This faith works whether your thoughts are productive or nonproductive. There are certain mental laws that work whether you know about them or not. They are part of your kingdom. Faith carries a very important place in your evolution and your growth.

You will remember that John the Baptizer precedes Jesus in the Bible. In that same way believing must precede knowing. John baptized with water. He knew that a mightier baptism would occur, the baptism of the Holy Spirit and fire. Yet it is the baptism of water that begins the process of gaining control and rulership over your kingdom.

A *baptism* is a commitment that you make to yourself, a promise. *Water* is a symbol that has been used throughout the ages to denote your physical experiences. It is the place for you to practice and learn and grow. It is your schoolroom. Your physical world and your mental world are waiting to respond to your intelligent direction.

Whenever we begin to take action on something that is new, we start with an element of faith, a belief that we can accomplish it. It is not until the act is accomplished that we gain a sense of knowing. It is not until that act is accomplished again and again with repeated success that we gain any real security with the knowing. Yet it is not until we understand how we caused the success — mentally, emotionally, and physically — that we gain wisdom in our knowing. So often man chooses to misuse belief and therefore remains in a trapped and passive state.

The word *Jews* in the Bible refers to this type of belief. It is a belief that someone will come and solve all of our problems and bring us the peace we crave. It is a waiting, waiting for the Messiah to come. In many ways there is the same waiting currently happening. This waiting takes place in looking for the second coming of Christ, refusing to see that the second coming of Christ is upon us now. It will be a coming of the individual into his own awareness of the Christ principle within himself and the using of that principle. It will happen as man begins to recognize that his own kingdom is within his own mind and that he was meant to have rulership over it.

Our beliefs lack purpose until we begin applying them in our everyday lives. I refuse to acknowledge that there are things not meant to be known by man. I refuse to accept that idea of unworthiness and limitation. People have come to me over and over insisting that I cannot know certain things. As Henry Ford once said, "The word impossible is not in my mind."

St. Paul instructed the people in *Romans 12:12 Do not conform yourself by this age (believing) but be transformed by the renewing of your mind (knowing) so that you might judge what is God's will.* As long as man allows others to tell him what he can or cannot do, what he can or cannot think, what he can or cannot know, he will remain a believer, a thoughtless worshipper. Your dog worships you. He trusts you to feed him. In the process he loses any desire to try and feed himself. Man will also do this if he continues to hide from his greatest opportunity: the joy of knowing himself and his father.

I still find others trying to lay the responsibility on Jesus to be the Divine One who handles all of our problems, determines our desires and forgives us of our sins. And yet not once did he say, "Hey look at me, I'll do it all for you." Instead he showed man how to develop himself and how to seek for, find and govern that Kingdom of Heaven within himself. He never said "Here, let me hang myself on this cross so you don't have to be responsible for your mistakes *(sins)* or the mistakes of your ancestors." He instead urged each man to pick up their own cross and carry it themselves. Must you suffer to do this? Must responsibility be such a burden? Must you live in pain while you carry your cross? Yes, if you take this passage literally, a cross might be a pretty heavy burden.

Most people look at any form of responsibility as a burden but I'd like to present something for you to consider here.

The symbol of the *cross* in more ancient times was used much in the same way we use a skull and cross-bones today, or an X indicating a barrier. Jesus was instructing you to remove those barriers, your barriers. Those limited, unworthy attitudes that bar you from realizing and demonstrating your Christ potential. You are the only one who can remove your barriers to knowing the truth *"I and the Father are one."* Jesus was bringing the attention to the recognition that if you were created by a God, or a Mental Parent, and if you were created in the *image* (imagination) and *likeness* (same characteristics) of this Supreme Intelligence then you must also be divine with the same ability to create with thought. With this perhaps you can begin to see the joy responsibility can bring. It is, after all, merely the ability to respond in any way you choose to your creations.

I was talking to a woman a while back who was working to land a particular job with an advertising firm. This gal had studied and practiced night and day and she was a darn good artist, with a variety of skills that she had, with great effort, developed. She was mighty excited because she had landed the job at a good healthy salary.

I was congratulating her on her accomplishment and she refused my congratulations saying "Oh no, I did nothing, it was God's will that I got this job."

I inquired "Kathy, whose will would it have been, or whose fault would it have been if you hadn't got the job?"

"Well, mine of course!" Then she paused and said, "Or perhaps that would be God's will too — but I must have done something wrong." And she wrinkled her brow. I guess no one had asked her that before.

I then proceeded to ask her if she thought her time of practice and presentation had anything to do with it. Yes, she could see that it did.

This is not an uncommon predicament for many people. I remember a similar conversation with another woman who had been studying to become a minister for a particular church. She likewise had just passed a crucial determining factor in her getting the job that she wanted. In this case it involved an exam. Rebecca had been studying for six years and had put her heart and soul into her studies. So when it came time for the exams it was really no surprise to me that she did well. I was congratulating her also on her accomplishment as she excitedly told me she passed. Rather than accept the accomplishment, she too began telling me that it was God's will that she passed.

I asked her "If God was responsible for you passing then who would be responsible if you had failed?"

Well she didn't have too hard a time answering that, "Well me, of course," she instantly replied.

I said, "Rebecca do you think then perhaps you also might have had something to do with your success? I seem to recall that you chose to put a great amount of effort into your studies and practice."

"Yes, I guess I did." It took her awhile to think about that. "In fact it seems to me that you were continually making choices all along that would contribute to and insure your success."

She couldn't find argument with that, because it was true. She indeed had made the choices and paved the way for her own success. She in fact was using one of the greatest gifts and tools man has. The ability to choose what one will place their attention on and what one will do with their life. She was using her own free will.

This is not saying that there is no time to be thankful to your God for the many opportunities you have available but it is recognizing that the true thanks come when you are using the gifts you have fully.

Man does have this freedom to choose and with it goes the responsibility to exercise that right. Many have disagreed with me on this main point. Yet they cannot give me adequate reason why man would not have this right. In my mind, without free will, there would be absolutely no reason for man to exist. I think it would be a rotten joke to pull on humanity to give every indication of freedom of choice yet sit back and pull strings as though we were puppets. It also makes no sense that we as individuals should constantly live in fear because of our inability to second guess a God who will punish us if we step out of line. There would be no sense in our existence and no purpose for it. If there was no purpose, there would be no order in this Universe, thus chaos. Now we may sometimes believe our lives are somewhat chaotic, yet stop and look for just a moment. It only takes a brief glimpse around you to see the beauty and order and structure we live in. There is nothing that exists that does not have a purpose. This is true for man as well.

There is so much more that man is composed of than merely a physical body. His ability to think, choose, and act makes him different from any other species. His thoughts become reality as the invention of the lightbulb shows us. Man can create. So he not only lives with the physical order and structure but he has use of a most remarkable inner structure — His own mind. The physical order is, in fact, a reflection of the mind. If there is order in our physical world then there must be order in our mental world. Do you remember the kingdom described earlier? Do you remember the confusion and lack of direction? Do you remember the lack of productivity because there was no one there to take charge and govern things? This will happen with your own mind until you search for the keys to unlock its mysteries. Those keys are available to you if you will pay attention.

Our physical world is constantly striving to maintain balance. The laws of nature are working 24 hours a day to see that this does occur. The easiest way to see this is to take a bucket that is filled with water and scoop out a cupful. Watch what happens as the water (balance) surrounding the apparent void (imbalance) rushes in to recreate the state of balance that previously existed, even as the water level lowers. This balancing is present everywhere we look, including earthquakes and volcanic eruptions. The earth gathering pressure from the heat, forms an imbalance that must be released and relieved. It was true in the past when man created an imbalance by irresponsibly killing buffalo and failing to use the gains productively. Shortly after, there were plagues of locusts eating man's food in order to right this imbalance. It was not a punishment to man but a change that affected all life forms in that area.

We can and have seen imbalance occur in relation to the emotional system as well. After a continued period of suppression of the emotions or a lack of giving on our part occurs, there will be a type of eruption — a fit of anger or a physical disorder. This is one of the ways that your mind attempts to create a state of balance.

There is yet another way this balancing occurs. We've discussed several elements regarding man's potential. We've discussed his desire to become like his God and his use of free will or the ability to choose how to direct himself. We've talked about the idea that thoughts really do become a part of your physical world and are things, and of man's responsibility to and for himself. We've also discussed briefly that there is a type of order in the Universe. Now how does this fit in with man's free will and God's will?

Man must have a way to accomplish his goal. He must have a method that will guarantee he has every opportunity to learn who he is, where he came from and where he can go. Just like a child has guidelines so that he can become the mature adult, so Light also had and has guidelines which provide him with ways to learn and mature. If you did not hold some responsibility for your actions would you not do anything you pleased, never learning or maturing? Likewise if you were never responsible for the effects of your thoughts could you discover the ways to create productively? You do in fact get the opportunities to learn from your mistakes and successes as well. You have an operating structure within your own mind that guarantees you these opportunities. This structure is called mental law or Universal Law. When you discover these laws and cause yourself to work in harmony with them you truly are doing God's will. God's will is that you become all that you are capable of becoming. This takes *you* exercising *your* will. It takes you making decisions and following through on them. Recognizing your successes and correcting your mistakes is a part of this. So is uncovering the powers that are hidden but waiting for your direction.

Each time you have a desire or a fear stimulated in your own mind you establish a condition of imbalance. You have a wonderful device, a part of mind that immediately responds to this called the Subconscious mind. It's sole purpose is to fulfill those desires whether they take the form of love, hate, fear, want, it makes no difference. Your subconscious mind will go to great lengths to fulfill that imbalance with understanding. So you may find opportunities in the form of situations and circumstances that require your attention. These circumstances and situations may take you off guard if you are not paying attention to the thoughts and desires that you hold.

I had an interesting incident and realization occur for myself many years back that illustrated this quite well. I was experiencing great impatience with myself and with others. I had been praying, affirming, beseeching, and anything else I might do to cause myself to become a more patient person. I was walking up on my front porch one afternoon shortly after a business meeting at work, sighing to myself, "Why does this always happen to me?" It seemed like crises were coming at me from every direction possible. As I was muttering "Why me, why me?" this small voice went off inside my head saying "Well, how else do you think you acquire patience?" Voila, a light came on. This is true. How can one gain something whether it be patience or any other attribute if there is no place to practice it? I had been receiving the answers to my prayers and was able to practice patience to my heart's content. There is no magic element that will change you. But isn't it neat? You really do have the choice to become all you can be if you will simply look inside of yourself and listen very closely.

We have children for the love we can bestow upon them. They are an extension of our creative abilities and yet are unique and individual. There is the urge to shape them and mold them into what we want them to be, as to reflect our egos, yet at the same time we want them to have it so much better than we did. So in our overzealous attempts to give love we try to interfere with their expression of individuality and divinity. If this is done out of love can you imagine the immense love and mental concern our mental parent had when giving us the freedom to grow, expand and create on our own? This love is expressed in allowing us to make our own mistakes and be responsible for the correction of those mistakes. You give a child discipline, and guidelines. Mental law insures we have the opportunities to create with wisdom.

When we have a child do we really desire to keep them dependent and to keep drawing them back into our womb as the infant? Or are we secretly looking forward to the day when they are producing for themselves and can share in the compatible experience? Would it not be thrilling to see someone issued forth from your flesh produce something of beauty and radiance? Not just the pride but the sharing and the knowing that there was some effect evidenced in all your work. If we, upon creation, were created in the image and likeness as divine, then is it not our joyous duty to develop in every way that potentiality of Creatorship to exhibit and exemplify the Christ principle or Christ consciousness, or Buddha consciousness or Cosmic consciousness? Jesus was demonstrating the use of all parts of the mind in casting out demons, healing the sick, raising the dead, abundantly feeding thousands and effectively dealing with his own devil or ego. He was not saying "Look, see what I can do" but teaching others to respond to that divine part of themselves.

Jesus taught the masses using the form of parables or stories creating a picture that each one could use according to his own understandings and yet oftentimes he was most direct about his expectation of the thinker. *"He that believeth on me, the works I do shall he do also, and greater works than these shall he do." (John 14:12)* Does this sound like someone who sees the individual as helpless and hopeless? Or does it sound like someone who recognizes that those who have the eyes will see the truth and hear the message and take it to heart? Jesus truly did play the part of a savior but not in the sense that man often tried to lay upon him. He was teaching the principles of mind thus providing a means for the thinker to save himself from ignorance: the ignoring of his own divine birthright. You were given two great gifts that denote this divinity: life or awareness and free will, the ability to choose to function in harmony with Mental Law or out of harmony with it. The choice is yours.

Teachings

There was sitting at the side of the road, a very wise and a very old man. He'd been sitting there for a long while in contemplation, enjoying the birds of the air and the animals of the field that were close by. On this particular day the sun was shining brightly and the crickets were chirping most melodiously. The man looked up from some whittling he was doing and noticed a stranger in his midst. The stranger looked tired and weary and seemed to be looking for something. As he came alongside the old man he beseechingly inquired the old man to help him on his search.

"Can you tell me, old man, how may I reach Mount Olympus?"

The old man gave a simple reply with a twinkle in his eye, "Oh it's quite simple my son. Just make every step you take be in the direction of Mt. Olympus."

The old man's name was Socrates.

If we only knew the answers to the right way to live our lives so that we might reach that goal of becoming whole and complete. Yet if we had that answer would we recognize it?

In the *Old Testament* we are given a code to live by and to use for the betterment of ourselves and humanity. It is called the Ten Commandments. These were given as laws to be followed by the people of Israel. Jesus gives a description of these laws in a group of teachings called the *Beatitudes. (Matt 5:3)* Confucius gives the same description with different words in the Eight Paths of Confucius and Gautama gives another description of these same principles in the Nine Truths of Buddha. When you have discovered the way to look behind the words to the picture that is formed, you will find that these pictures indicate the same thing and that they are all referring to you, the thinker, and the journey you will make.

Before we go on to our discovery of the Beatitudes, there are some keys for you to begin to understand the pictures that are being presented. In *Genesis*, you will find that from the first chapter there is the description of how God created the heaven and the earth, but in the second chapter the title of the directing intelligence changes to Lord God. There is a change at this point of the intelligence and the power of that intelligence that is at work. If you will look at the *Lord God* as being a part of you, the rest of the <u>Bible</u> will begin to make more sense. It is the essence and power of your own individuality, that speck or particle of light with the recognition of its own individual existence. Your I Am.

It was through our desire to be like our mental parent, or God, that we began taking our attention away from that part of ourselves until the time came when we were so engrossed in our own creations that we forgot where we came from and why we are here. In other words we forgot about the goal of becoming compatible with our Creator.

Have you ever set a goal for yourself, perhaps of only walking to the supermarket, and become so involved in the walking and enjoying the scenery or talking to a friend, that you forgot or lost sight of your original goal of going to the supermarket? Think of how frustrating it would be to finish with your enjoyment and wonder what you were doing standing there in the middle of the block with nowhere to go. Well, this is also what has happened to mankind. They have lost sight of their purpose for existence and most importantly their goal. The Beatitudes give meaning to rediscovering that goal and the way to achieve it.

From this point look to the references to the *Lord God* and remember that this is the part of yourself that you are searching to rediscover and to build into maturity in the fulfillment of the goal.

The Beatitudes begin by Jesus saying, *"How blessed are the poor in spirit; the reign of God is theirs."* There is a specific word here I want you to notice — "Blessed." Now remember that when I told you about reading the <u>Bible</u> it would be important to remember where you have read something before. So with that in mind we must refer back to *Genesis Chapter 2* to uncover this. *God blessed the seventh day and made it holy, for on it he rested from all the work he had done in creation.* The creation of Light was good. It had all the necessary ingredients to become a full mature expression of its creator. But it was still an idea.

Have you ever given someone your blessings? You acknowledged the idea that they have presented to you, whether it be a marriage, a voyage, a new career, or a child. You bless it because you can see the idea is beneficial and yet you do not yet know all there is to know about that idea and it has not yet been accomplished. It is an intellectual idea but it is understood to hold in it the potential for success. *Blessed* is this realization that the idea is good, but it is still intellectual and it will require your efforts and understanding to bring about the full expression of that idea and to make it a part of yourself. *Blessing it* is recognizing that the idea is good and will work.

Making it *holy* is committing yourself to causing that goal to become a reality. It is a promise. If the creation of Light is to have a reason for existence, might it then be to become compatible with its creator? Remember the child and how its urge is to be like the adult. With this in mind let us examine how the Beatitudes can give us an idea of how to accomplish that goal with what we now have to work with.

Let's look at *the poor in spirit.* When do you know that you are poor in something? Isn't it after you become aware that there is something that you want that you do not have? You cannot recognize that you are poor unless you also recognize that you are without something. Think for a moment of watching someone play the piano. You become excited at the sound of the music pouring out of the instrument. You want to make that music yourself. So you immediately sit down in front of the piano and begin to play. After all, that is what the person did who was playing shortly before you. After a few attempts to make the same kind of music, you begin to realize that you do not understand the workings of the piano, nor the scales, nor the way to bring forth music. You have recognized that you are poor in piano playing. Now this is often translated to mean that one must be financially poor in order to gain God's good graces, but I think this is not the case. There have been many wealthy men, who have walked the way of God.

When a man recognizes he is *poor in Spirit* he then can begin the building process. It truly is the recognition that there is something that is not yet fully realized in one's self. *Spirit* is referring to that mental part of yourself, or your own divinity that Jesus spoke of. When you first become aware that there is something more to be known and used by your self you also become aware that you do not have this for your self. It is then if honesty is applied, that you can begin to see what it will be necessary for you to do to gain the peace and awareness that is rightfully yours.

Now what is the *reign of God?* Think of the word reign. In both spellings of reign or rein in Webster's dictionary this refers to some type of direction. If you are riding a horse then you must have something in order to direct the animal; thus the use of reins. Or another use of the word reign refers to rulership of a kingdom. But in either case it illustrates a need for direction and control. In the case of the horse for those of you who fancy yourselves as equestrians, the *horse* represents force without any intelligence. You, being the intelligence, must harness this force with the power of directing intelligence. The reins provide you with this power. There is a force in regard to mind as well. It is the laws that make up the operating structure of the working of mind. We know if we look around us that there is order in our world and in our universe. If this were not the case then all would be in a state of chaos. Now, sometimes it is easy to become so involved in our situations that we think that we are truly in a state of chaos but this is not true. Nothing exists that does not have a purpose in the scheme of things.

In physics, man can study the laws of nature and see how perfectly in tune these are, never faltering to man's whim. Yet with enough knowledge man can learn to harness and use these laws of nature for his own betterment. Look at space technology.

In metaphysics, the student studies the laws of mind and once again these laws are always constant and do not vary according to man's whim. Once these laws are understood man can harness the power of his own mind and realize not only his divinity but work towards having a greater understanding and companionship with his own creator. He would also be able to answer the question of "Who am I?" and "Where did I come from?" He would know his Father.

The *reign of God* is referring to the use and control of the Universal Laws and the responsibility to ourselves and our Universe to understand and use these with wisdom. The reign of God will be yours when you recognize its existence and begin to practice working in harmony with these laws. Do you recall the grief the man experienced upon discovering his bountiful fields in ruin?

As long as you are merely satisfied with collecting stimulating information and not putting it into practice in your daily lives you will stay ignorant of the reign of God and how it relates to yourself. Do not ignore this. If you want a greater understanding of this refer to *John 3*.

The Sower and the Seed

To truly begin to explore the Kingdom of Heaven you must first be willing to accept the responsibility of holding at your disposal your own mind. It will also be necessary for you to see that you are the intelligence who directs your own mind. The mind sees and thinks in pictures through the use of your imagination and your will. The better able you are to perceive in pictures (mentally see pictures) the more capable you will be in using your mind productively and knowing yourself.

You have heard the expression often that "a picture is worth a thousand words." A picture holds meaning and depth. Imagine yourself attempting to describe a Rembrandt to someone in such detail as to the brushstrokes, the brilliance of the colors and how they were blended to meet each other color, the depth and texture that occurred through use of the oils and reapplying them, even to the picture frame and how this complimented the work of art. Perhaps you would use even more than a thousand words and yet not convey the beauty and mystery that is held there. The more capable you were of using words to vividly bring to life that picture the clearer the person you are speaking to would see it. Each word that you use can become a brush stroke to a fine piece of art that will communicate exactly what you want it to communicate.

Jesus taught with parables or pictures; Confucius taught through using pictures, Gautama taught with pictures. All of these pictures were either in the form of stories or riddles with meaning behind them. They were used to illustrate a state of mind and the necessary ingredients or steps for producing results with your own mind. Jesus stated that those that have eyes will see and those that have ears will hear. You may now hear a similar expression when someone is attempting to communicate an idea to you in, "Do you get the picture?" or "Do you know where I'm coming from?"

I have a favorite story that I use often when people are starting to come to me with their own pictures of limitation, doubt or lack. Perhaps you will "get my picture." There was once an old sage with many students who were practicing to become adepts.

One balmy summer day one of the students came rushing up to the master and exclaimed "Master, master, I want to know the truth!! Give me truth." And so the old master who had gained much in the way of wisdom as his graying hair and twinkling eyes portrayed, said, "Go away and stop bothering me." So the disciple left. But on the morrow he returned saying once again, "Master, master, I must have truth!" You see the disciple suspected that the master would recognize his "determined" efforts. But this wise master was a bit wiser and said once again, "Go away and leave me alone." On the third day while the sage was taking his daily stroll along the shore of the river Ganges, the disciple once again frantically rushed up to him explaining his desire for truth. The sage then walked into the water and motioned for the overzealous disciple to follow him. Eagerly he ran to the master's side splashing in his haste. At this point the master took his head and forcefully pushed it under the water. Now it took great strength to hold the student's head under as he was writhing and flailing his arms in all directions. But finally, after an appropriate time the wise old fellow brought the student's head out of the water. Once his breath had been regained he looked puzzled at his teacher and his teacher inquired, "Tell me, Ramos, what did you think of while your head was under the water?" He cried "Air! Air! I wanted nothing but air!" "Did you not think of your family, or your wealth or what you had for breakfast?" asked the teacher with a twinkle in his eye. "No sir, I thought only of air!" "Well then," replied the sage, "when you can seek truth with the same fervency and attention, my son, you will have found it."

Is there any doubt then that this story is referring to the single pointed attention that is necessary for you to discover your own power and divinity? Is there any doubt that it will require a commitment on your part? It truly does indicate the value in the use of pictures.

The <u>Bible</u> is also written in pictures telling a story about you the thinker and intelligence that governs your physical body. And it is every bit as informative as the previous picture. Your own mind speaks to you in pictures and you call this a dream. You talk to yourself in pictures and sometimes call this a fantasy or daydream, while other times you might call it planning. You also hold pictures of what you expect from yourself whether these be in the form of desire or fears, or doubts and indecision. They are still pictures and it is communication to yourself.

If there could be one language that we could use to communicate with anyone on this earth or perhaps this universe it would be pictures. Jesus used pictures to teach man of his divinity and responsibility to become Christ-like or made perfect. He expected man to reason according to his own understandings and to follow through according to his own conclusions. We have been discussing some of the pictures that were presented to the people during Jesus' ministry and perhaps have shed some light on how this man was attempting to teach others of their own spirituality and the ways to reach for their own Kingdom of Heaven.

There are many instances in which Jesus described the need for goals and follow through. In teaching about the Sabbath and causing it to become holy, he indicated the value of resting upon completing a goal but not becoming complacent. You experience rest when you have passed through infancy, adolescence, adulthood, and old age in any activity you take on, any change you make in yourself. It is the time when you are producing as though it were second nature to you, your practicing is over. He told man that if he would but have the faith of a mustard seed he could accomplish what most thought to be miraculous. A tiny seed. Within mustard seed and within the acorn, even a kernel of corn, is a most intricate and beautiful blueprint of a full mature producing plant, bush, or tree. It will become that which the blueprint describes, nothing less, nothing more.

That seed is an idea. Your ideas can become your goals. You create constantly with your mind those ideas that become mature — the productive or non-productive things in your environment. Therefore what you sow in the form of seeds of expectancy you will reap in your harvest of life.

A most intriguing parable dealing with man's own responsibility to his own mental creations and the need to follow through on them becoming productive, is illustrated in the parable of the Sower. Remember that a *seed* is an idea just as the acorn is the idea that brings life to the oak tree.

"One day a farmer went out sowing," You are that *farmer sowing* your ideas. The idea here is in reference to God's reign, as you will see later on. The governing of mind and life as you know it is through working in harmony with Universal Law.

"Part of what he sowed landed on a footpath where birds came and ate it up." This is the point where your own thoughts of limitation keep you from embracing your birthright. You might see here that the footpath is your own compulsive thoughts. Thoughts you have had before, that you have practiced until you have actually built pathways in the brain. These habitual thoughts or habits of belief can keep you from understanding or perceiving truth. If you cater to thoughts of limitation and fear then your own subconscious mind will go to great lengths to fulfill this. You will continue to see evidence that will support your limited perspective. If you are attempting to cause a change in the manner in which you express because you have found that it is not productive, you will find those around you who will react and wonder what the devil is wrong with you, you seem so strange. So your good intentions go down the drain. It is sometimes easier to stay in a rut, whether in thought or action, than to do something different that might seem unsettling. Do you settle for wishing that things could be different, putting off your action that could produce that difference? Something for you

to think about. Notice how many ideas you have had and in your failure to take action on them someone comes along and does take action, thereby producing the very thing you were wanting to produce for yourself. This is misuse of your individuality. *"Part of it fell on rocky ground where it had little soil. It sprouted at once since the soil had no depth, but when the sun rose and scorched it, it began to wither for lack of roots."* Rocky ground is indicating some use of will power. *Roots* indicate a foundation. This was lacking. So it was no wonder the sun and its heat scorched this tender plant. It would seem to indicate that there are points in which you make resolutions to practice something — perhaps go on a diet — but you have no purpose for this nor have you developed enough will power to do it and follow through. So when the first hot fudge sundae comes along you falter. Your conviction is lacking because you have not made your goal holy.

I see that this is partially true but that there is even a greater message here. Upon studying *Genesis* I have discovered that *sun* refers to Superconscious mind or that God part within. I have observed many discover the idea of Universal Law and the idea of divinity within themselves. But there is not the understanding of what this means. There is not the recognition of cause and effect nor the understanding of responsibility in understanding and practicing creatorship. Therefore when a goal is set there is a type of faith alone that God or Subconscious mind or some internal power will make it happen. Again lack of personal responsibility. When it doesn't happen it "obviously wasn't meant to be" or "wasn't God's will." Even more disheartening is when there is a passivity in using the physical conditions to learn from and practice in and a reliance on mind-bound meditation. To say that because something didn't work out "I must not have wanted it" is a cop out on practicing to become a creator or building and developing your own Christhood.

Do you remember when Jesus spoke to Simon Peter? He said *"I shall call you Peter for on you my church shall be built."* *Peter* indicates rock. It indicates a foundation. The foundation which will enable you to use your mind is will power. When you can place your attention on what is productive, more often than not, you will begin to understand the development of will power. Undivided Attention is the ability to place all of the attention, that is normally scattered in the senses, at a single point. Concentration is your ability to hold your attention at that same point for as long as you desire and to move it to another point of your choosing.

We oftentimes accuse someone who is so involved in one point or one goal as absent-minded. They truly are absent-minded. They are absent from the surrounding distractions that might interfere or take time away from their goal. Develop your will power and you will find that there is much that you *can* do and *will* do that you thought impossible before.

"Again, part of the seed fell among thorns, which grew up and choked it." *Thorns* indicate desires. They prick you until they draw forth blood. *Blood* is life force and truth. Now in his description to the disciples of its meaning he refers to the interference of worldly anxiety and the lure of money. Choking off the ability to respond to the reign of God. It does not indicate that desires are bad and should be ignored. It is, however, your unfulfilled desires that cause you the greatest problem.

Desire is the most important facet of your development. Nowhere in the Bible does it state that *money* is the root of all evil. It does state that the love of money will cause you problems. The attachment to an idea that material wealth or power will bring you happiness is false, but fulfilled desires will.

You have a built in mechanism that insures you will be constantly stimulated and therefore constantly desiring. Its name is

Conscious ego (your *devil* or your *most beautiful fallen angel.*) As a child you experienced this stimulation in wanting to be like the adult. Remember wanting to cross the street? Or wash the dishes? Or stay up late? It was a desire you believed would bring you great happiness. Gone unfulfilled it would have left a lack in you as the adult. The lack of understanding and perspective.

This is what desires are all about. They are bringing to your attention something that is lacking. Something in you that wants to be filled. Think of that constant hunger you have experienced and in responding to it you put everything into your mouth possible to fill it until you began to see that food alone was not what the hunger was about. It was a soul hunger so you took another step to understanding that desire. When you try to side step or suppress desires you get all choked up. It takes so much effort to do anything.

You do not reach the desireless state by side-stepping your desires but in fulfilling them in the awareness of your goal and purpose as offspring of the creator. When you understand this you will pursue your desires with the recognition that this will aid in your soul growth. You will create with your mind, bring forth with your actions, and repeat this process over and over so that you can gain greater insight. You will establish a goal and follow it through to completion allowing nothing to distract you, being decisive and determined every step of the way. Through this action you will begin to produce knowing. When you set a goal one day and change it the next because you can see many other things that you desire you never fully give yourself the opportunity to gain confidence from seeing your mental creations materialize. Desire is healthy when it is used constructively and in conjunction with your idea to become in the image and likeness of your mental parent.

You can see this in the child who begins by saying "I want to do the dishes." Can you blame him? All of the important people in his world are doing things that seem to count. But oftentimes when the opportunity is presented to the child, he sees out of the corner of his curious little eyes the other things that look so enticing, like playing with the kids next door. So you as a parent bring the child's attention back to completing what was started. Wouldn't it be neat if you could remember the child's desire to begin with, so that you could begin to teach him the purpose for his following through?

This is the same thing you are attempting to teach your child mind — the conscious mind. It too may balk at discipline, may see that the grass on Tommy Joe's lawn sure looks more inviting than what I've got here. If you are to realize the truth that thoughts are things then it will be most important for you to see results in your life. You can believe these words but it will not provide the fruitful yield that is available to you.

"Part of it finally landed on good soil and yielded grain a hundred, or sixty, or thirty fold." The result of commitment! This is when you are causing your ideals or goals and purposes to be in alignment with the seventh day.

You are taking aggressive action *(1-00)*, you are fully expressing this, thus being of service to yourself and humanity *(6-0)* and practicing creation *(3-0)*. You now have the 3 steps that will insure your success — goal, purpose and activity. Open your eyes to your Light of life and creation. Set a goal for yourself today. You really can have anything you desire. You are worth it. If you don't believe me go look at yourself in the mirror. Study the individual who you find there. Introduce yourself. There is no one quite like you.

Beauty and the Beast

How often when you think of the word discipline do you find yourself associating it with the punishment you received as a child?

Or do you perhaps think of the many times you attempted to abstain from something and failed? Yet Webster defines discipline in this manner. "Training that corrects, molds, or perfects the mental faculties or moral character/orderly or prescribed conduct or pattern of behavior; to train or develop by instruction and exercise, especially in self control; to impose order upon." Discipline is to have order in your mind and in your life.

Even though everyone at some point in time has reacted to the idea of discipline, it is still easy to recognize the necessity for it. A musician knows the importance of practicing the discipline of scales in order to, at one time, produce beautiful music. The athlete knows that it requires discipline to cause the body to work correctly and in top performance. The dancer likewise. So you might begin to view discipline as hard work. After all, think of the effort required in staying away from that hot fudge sundae when you're on a diet.

Yet that very word and act is the keynote for understanding and using your own mind. Upon examining the word discipline you will find it resembles another word we have been discussing — to decide. Discipline is just that, to be decisive repeatedly to produce the results you want. It denotes that you, as a thinker, have a freedom of choice. But it is not until you have mastered discipline that you experience true freedom.

If the athlete did not practice daily governing and mastering his body with decisive action he would find that it would soon become uncooperative. If the musician did not practice the scales he would find certain restrictions in his ability to play music. Discipline provides a foundation.

You've heard the expression "spare the rod, spoil the child." There's been much debate as to the question of discipline in the rearing of our children. Yet sparing the rod of discipline does leave a child lacking in the foundation to be able to exercise choices that will be productive to his growth. This does not mean that it takes physical abuse to train a child but it does indicate that a child, just as an adult, needs to understand the effects of his actions.

I watched a father one day getting ready to change the oil in his car. He had a son who was most anxious to help. So he gave the child the responsibility of holding the pan that would catch the oil.

Now there was a cat in the neighborhood that this kid was very fond of. It happened to run by as the child was performing his job. He lost track of what he was doing and began to watch the cat playing with the ball and sure enough the oil began to run everywhere. The father yelled, "Bobby pay attention." Now in days gone by I can remember similar instances with parents and children and what the outcome would have been. Bobby would have been sent off with a swat on the butt.

This particular father was a little bit wiser. He took the pan and put it once again in Bobby's hands and instructed him on how to do it again. He also finished with giving Bobby the necessary ingredients to clean up his mistake, much to the child's chagrin. They finished their task by having a talk as to how important the goal had been and why the difficulty occurred in the first place. Bobby left with the idea that he could accomplish something and that if he did not succeed the first time he could certainly try again.

When you cease to think but merely act under compulsion because that is what others are doing you lose much of the ability to think. When you continue to make the same mistakes over and over it is difficult to think that there might be another way to do something. When you have continually used guilt and unworthiness to motivate yourself it is difficult to imagine the use of desire and follow through. Discipline is the key. It is not always comfortable to correct a mistake or to continue doing something when you feel awkward about it. Decisions enable you to do this. To decide: To decide what? To be able to decide indicates that you have free will. It is that will that sets into motion even the smallest movement — the blinking of an eyelash to achieving the impossible. There are degrees in which you exercise this will of yours. A wish is a helpless desire of the mind. It is the wanting of something but deciding you won't get it anyway. A desire is a bit stronger but carries very little potency if not backed up with your effort. An intention indicates you might make a fleeting attempt but if discouraged you will give up. But when you are using will power you will make every effort with determination, never ceasing, never yielding, until you have reached your goal. Remember the sower? So what is will power? It is your ability to make more correct choices than incorrect choices or more productive choices than non-productive choices. When you are decisive you cease to have problems and begin to have solutions and opportunities.

"So," you might wonder, "how decisive am I?" When you go out to lunch do you spend lots of time asking everyone else what they are having before you make your selection? In determining what movie to go to do you ask your spouse, lover, or friend what they want to see first? Do you change your wardrobe or hairdo according to the latest fashion? Do you refrain from answering questions truthfully because you don't want to offend someone? Do you change your opinion of things according to who you are talking to? If you've answered yes to most of these questions then you could use a little practice on being decisive.

Making a decision is not merely a mental process but it is one that is followed up by action. It is the dynamo that moves you forward toward your own evolution. You've heard the saying that to make no decision is a decision. I disagree heartedly. It is no more a decision than deciding not to *do* something. Both involve no motion and there must be motion for life. "To not decide" indicates that others are running your life. This is not living.

When you become decisive you begin to know where you stand on things and what you want for yourself. You begin to take steps toward achievement. There is no force involved. To know what you will do and can do is far more stimulating than what you can't do or won't do. Begin to practice discipline and will power instead of won't power. Won't power is nothing more than a type of obstinacy and stubbornness. Determination is much more fun. Take things that you have learned so far, that have made sense to you, and begin practicing them right now. Don't be satisfied with one attempt. Repeat your successes over and over. Learn how you made those successes happen. *Once you know all these things, blest will you be if you put them into practice. (John 13:17)*

Jesus taught the benefits of discipline in many instances. He had many followers. But he also had many leaders. He repeatedly let his disciples know that it would take practice, and practice is nothing more than the beauty of discipline. *"If you live according to my teachings, you are truly my disciples. Then you will know the truth and the truth will set you free." (John 8:31)*

You know if you have ever attempted a diet, that it does not involve one decision but a series of decisions. If you depend upon the one decision to abstain from all fattening foods you soon find yourself flat on your face the moment you falter. This faltering is followed by guilt and condemnation which is shortly followed by self pity. "Oh poor me, I do not have the will power to achieve what I desire." You continue to build this idea of yourself as weak, indecisive, and untrustworthy. What a sad picture to hold and so dishonest. Then something will come along again that stimulates you to "try" again but the same cycle occurs, ending with you more depressed than ever.

If you will recall, a decision involves action. It is something you practice and build upon. Determine where you are going, not what you are running from. In the case of the diet you are going toward thinness, not running away from fat. Will power is built through repeated decisions and repeated successes.

Will power is what is necessary to control the action of your mind as well as your body. It is the mental muscle that you will use to take your undivided attention and place it at a single point, holding it there for as long as you have chosen and moving your attention when and where you want it to be. It is the factor you will use in developing the ability to concentrate. It is this concentrated attention that will aid in moving you toward your goal.

Will power and attention will be the keys to unlocking the mysteries of your own mind, to parts you may not have known you had. It will provide you with the ability to heal your own body and that of others, it will aid in changing those negative limited ideas you have of yourself into positive productive aspects, it will aid in your ability to prepare your mind and body for your use of universal laws. Will power will give you the control you so desire, to become the kind of person you want to be. With the combination of will power and imagination you can learn to move mountains because you will have discovered the secret behind the faith of a mustard seed.

With the understanding of a disciplined mind you will experience the freedom of determining your own course of action under any circumstance. You will not be at the mercy of others' attitudes and actions. You will give love because you want to give and not be concerned with another's reactions to it.

There was a time in Kansas City that I had been appointed the task of training others in the same field as mine. I was doing just that one afternoon and was showing one of the newly hired women around the place. In the process I greeted several of the employees and did some introductions. There was an older woman working there and I walked up to her and said, "Good afternoon. Isn't it a beautiful day!"

She replied with a scowl, "Humph", and walked away.

The woman with me asked if she always replied in that manner. I answered "Yes, why?"

Well, you can imagine her shocked expression, "If she is continually rude to you why do you bother talking to her in the first place?"

I explained to her that it was not necessary for me to change my attitude about myself and the world around me because someone else chooses to see it as unpleasant. I did not need to become rude and step away from my goal of creating my own attitudes and embracing life just because she did not want to be pleasant. In other words I did not allow others to determine my attitudes or control them. I was also not going to judge her ability to receive my concern and love.

Now I could have told her that I was merely practicing to love others but this would not have been the entire truth or the complete picture of what I was accomplishing. I was accomplishing a goal I had established for myself and was allowing no one to interfere with it.

Now we have practiced the art of scattering the attention for a very long period of time. We have taught ourselves to attempt to do many things at one time and none of them well. There has been the tendency to involve our attention totally in matters of the senses until we are at the mercy of them. When the attention is engrossed in the senses it is most difficult to realize that you are not this physical body that you seem to exist in. You are subject only to heat, cold, taste, pain and pleasure. If you can't see it, it doesn't exist. It is through the act of undivided attention that you will begin to see you are a mental and spiritual being using a physical body. Now, had my attention been scattered while doing my job I would not only have forgotten my goal but I would have become involved in the attitudes of the others around me and lost sight of my own individuality.

Because you have practiced scattering your attention it will also take practice in focusing your attention to a single point. It will require willingness on your part to discover over and over again where your attention is and then put it where you want it to be. This involves discipline. When you have mastered this you can begin to see that you have also developed the complete and total freedom to put your attention where you want it to be. You won't be constantly saying "Why me, why is this always happening to me?"

It is the use of your attention that will heighten your awareness of who you are and why you are here. It will enable you to discover that your own mind is your servant and you its master. You will accomplish things you may have thought were impossible, because you won't be wasting precious time correcting or repeating your actions. You will uncover truths about yourself that will cause you to rejoice. You will begin to know yourself and your creator. The awareness that you seek is available to you. *"If thine eye be single, thy whole body shall be full of Light"* (awareness).

Law of Compensation

It is easy to look around and see with your physical eyes that all men are not equal. So how can our own Declaration of Independence give such a statement that all men are created equal? If we look to physical birth as being the creation of all men we will run into apparent contradictions. How can one man born with a healthy body be equal to that of the child born with immense deformities? How can the woman born into great wealth be equal to the rag-wearing child in the ghetto? We can pass this off to mean that we are all equal in the Creator's eyes but I think perhaps there is more.

I have presented to you the idea that thought is cause and effect its manifested likeness. Jesus relates it in another way *"You reap what you sow."* There is a Universal Law called the Law of Cause and Effect that insures that you do indeed reap what you sow. The Hindus refer to the physical evidence of this as the Law of

Karma. The Law of Karma denotes that anything set into motion in the physical must be completed or balanced out in the physical. This law has been likened to crime and punishment. The Hindus have often carried this to an extreme. Anyone experiencing any type of trial is thought to be experiencing the effects of their own Karma from a past life or present life. To aid that individual in any way is to interfere with his just punishments. If you followed this line of thought you would pass by a drowning man and leave him to drown rather than help him and interfere with this punishment. This is a rather negative and limited view of this law at work.

I have heard many references to there being "good" and "bad" Karma and this is another way man avoids seeing the beauty and perfection of this law at work. I prefer to view Karma as the law of opportunity. It is our opportunity to correct past actions that were incomplete with present actions. Karma is set into motion by intent, in other words your thoughts and motives.

For example, I might be passing you on the street and I don't like your expression. I then proceed to walk up to you and slap you to cause you pain. Now later on, perhaps the next day, you walk up to me with a large splinter in your hand asking if I will please remove it. Again I am going to cause you some amount of pain if I do remove it. In both instances the same amount of physical pain is inflicted but my intent is different in each case. Must I then be punished because I inflicted pain in both instances?

In the first act there is obviously a lack of understanding of something. That something is an imbalance in myself, something missing that needs to be filled with understanding. In the second act there is an understanding that to leave the splinter in will eventually destroy the entire body. Do you see the difference?

This difference is brought to light in the Sermon on the Mount. Jesus is indicating that he did not come to abolish the laws of Moses but to fulfill them. To demonstrate and teach mankind ways to do this as well was his intent. He gave a type of depth to the laws that Moses had laid down.

I spoke earlier of the different stages in our evolution and the understandings that accompany those states. Moses gave the laws in such a way that those individuals in the stages of infancy and adolescence might use those laws according to their understandings. It was the infancy and adolescence of reasoning. Rules or guidelines were provided in the same manner you provide rules and guidelines for your children. But there comes a point in your child's growth where you begin to expect more from him in the way of responsibility for his actions. You also expect him to begin to see the purposes for those rules. When the purposes are seen the child can then begin to expand his actions and develop perception. If this step is not taken then the child is liable to go to bed at 10:00 p.m. every night for the rest of his life because it was a rule. He is liable to never express his opinions or take a stance on anything because he has been taught not to talk back. So, no matter what the condition or circumstance, there does come a point in life where greater responsibility and decisiveness must be initiated in order to produce a sense of maturity.

Jesus demonstrates this in two ways in his talk on anger. *(Matt 5:21) "You have heard the commandment imposed on your forefathers. (Moses — Commandments) You shall not commit murder; every murderer shall be liable to judgement."* The law Moses laid down was, *"Thou shalt not kill."* Here in Jesus' words he is demonstrating responsibility. If you do murder, *"you will be liable to judgement."* You will be responsible for that action. Death refers to a change. There can be non-productive changes or productive changes. In either case you alone are responsible.

Now I spoke earlier of the idea you carry within of becoming a mental creator. If that is difficult for you to relate to merely think of the idea of perfection or wholeness. If that is a desire of yours then respond to it. You create a wholeness in yourself when you gain an understanding of creation and maturity. You will become your own judge. If you have practiced something that causes you to remain weak, or limited, would you not want to find some way to build a strength to replace that?

You experience desires and fears every day. This is the way you stimulate yourself to fill in those parts of yourself that are lacking. It is your ability to respond that determines how slow or how fast you will mature.

But there is more to this commandment that is equally exciting. He goes on to say, *"What I say to you is, everyone who grows angry with his brother shall be liable to judgement."* So it is not merely the action that will bring the effects of judgement, but the intent or thought as well. Thoughts really are things. If you are angry with someone on the inside but smiling on the outside you are no different than the Pharisees who find it more important to wash the outside of a cup than its insides. You are performing or pretending to be something you are not. Your judgement will be issued from your own self. You may receive temporary praise from your brother but inside you will be frustrated and resentful until you come to terms with your own imbalance.

I was doing a lecture once regarding thoughts and attitudes and how they affect the physical body. I had brought out the importance of expressing thoughts and emotions so that these could be met and understood. A woman tried to stump me with a question regarding expressing what you were thinking. She asked what she should do about this reoccurring desire she had about going to a particular person who continually upset her and "busting him in the mouth." She was severely taken aback by my reply. I told her to do it! Once she settled down a bit I went on to explain to her how she was destroying herself by repeatedly having this thought and not changing it but just suppressing it. I also reiterated the fact that thoughts are things and her mental attack on this person did have an effect on him, yet currently she had provided no means for him to defend himself. At least if she hit him she could see her thought expressed and see that hurting him did not change the way she felt. And he would have the opportunity to respond to it.

Jesus goes on to say, *"If you bring your gift to the altar and then recall that your brother has anything against you, leave your gift at the altar, go first to be reconciled with your brother and then come and offer your gift."* There are two things present here for you to note.

First that this is a story about you. So your *brother* is talking about a part of yourself that is inharmonious with the whole mind. It is difficult to give your undivided attention (this is your *altar*) to anything when you are condemning yourself or angry at yourself. It will interfere with your ability to communicate with your God. *Reconcile* yourself first.

We often think that God is on the lookout for sin. This is another way that we create God in our image. It would be the same as saying God is sinful. He makes mistakes. It is only in our limited conscious mind that we consider a mistake to be sinful or evil. Could you imagine thinking of a baby committing a sin because he fell down on his first attempt at walking? Doesn't make sense does it? You would be much more interested in seeing the act of walking and encourage that rather than instilling in the child to be careful or he's going to fall. Mistakes are our own business. The Creator is only interested in the fulfillment of his seed idea or only begotten son — Light.

The second note here on reconciliation with your brother has to do with your ability to practice this in your everyday life. More often than not when you are out of harmony with your brother is when you are out of harmony with yourself. If you are condemning yourself you will find that you will also be short tempered and condemning with others. If you will watch actions that others perform that irritate you, you may begin to find there are similarities present in yourself that need changing. Stop trying to change others and begin to change yourself. Don't pretend that you do not find others irritating—this only produces frustration. Find when you do become irritated and examine this.

I had a student once who had determined that she found very little to condemn in others even though there was much she found to condemn in herself. One time we were driving together to an event and had to pass through a highly congested part of the city. That gal must have had something rude to say about every driver on the road. It was the first time that Patricia became aware of her real attitudes towards others. Patricia began to see the specific things that others did that would set her off. Pat then began to see how short tempered she was with herself. She began to listen to her words and found that she was constantly berating others for their lack of respect. "Bingo." This is the very thing that was lacking in herself — a sense of self respect. Because of that lacking, Pat's attention was always being drawn to disrespectful conditions and actions of others. It would continue to occur until she began to bring a balance into herself. So she began concentrating on respect and listening to herself for ways to practice this. Pat is now paying her debt to herself. This doesn't mean that she condones disrespect in others but she does not lose control when this occurs. Pat now has something to give to others.

"Lose no time, settle with your opponent while on your way to court with him. Otherwise your opponent may hand you over to the judge who will hand you over to the guard who will throw you into prison (your own prison of restriction). *I warn you that you will not be released* (from your debt to yourself) *until you have paid the last penny"* (put out the effort to cause balance where there was imbalance in yourself).

There is another instance that reflects your debt to yourself. *(Matt 5:43) "You have heard the commandment 'you will love your countrymen but hate your enemies'* (sounds like an eye for an eye and a tooth for a tooth). *My commandment to you is, love your enemies, pray for your persecutors. This will prove that you are sons of your heavenly Father for his sun rises on the bad and the good, he rains on the just and unjust."* (consider rains here to possibly be indicating reigns — as the laws work whether you are in harmony with them or not.) *If you love those who love you what merit is there in that? Do not tax collectors do as much?"*

It is simple to love or be compatible with those who agree with us or who love us. Just like it is easy for us to be at peace with those parts of ourselves that are cooperative. It takes a disciplined mind to love and accept our shortcomings and to correct them rather than mire around in guilt or self pity.

"If you greet your brother only, what merit is there in that?" Could you imagine yourself saying "Hello" to everyone you pass?

"Do not pagans do as much? In a word, you must be made perfect as your heavenly Father is perfect." Look at the word *"made"*. You are not yet perfect for there is much for you to practice to become whole and compatible to your creator.

It takes effort to create your own attitudes. But much less effort than being buffeted around by the inconsistencies of those around you. Karma is talking about your indebtedness as an individual to yourself.

This brings to mind a question I will pose to you once again. It goes back to the first statement in this chapter; each man being created equal. It is also tied to the last statement of Jesus, *"Each man must be made perfect."* If you will look around your world you will see that everything nature provides us with has a purpose. There is beauty and balance in nature. Much thought must have gone into creating it. Doesn't it make sense then that the intelligence that is you also has a purpose? This has been discussed somewhat so far but what hasn't been discussed is how you are going to accomplish wholeness and perfection in the short time (70-100 years) that you are on this earth. It is no wonder that the man Jesus, or the man Gautama and other great masters are so revered. They seem to have accomplished miracles in themselves to have done what they did in such a short time. Were they so much different than you and me? And if they were, what made this difference?

What, for instance makes the difference that brings forth an Einstein, and Edison, or Leonardo da Vinci? I have asked others that same question and their reply has been quite quick and common — "Why, a loving God of course." "Then why," I ask, "would there be children born into poverty, sickness, and with deformities?" Their answers are still quick and sure but much quieter, "Why God's will also, I suppose." I've even been told that man has no right to know the answers to such questions. The question is not so hard to answer or discern. Perhaps you might want to open your mind to that possibility right now.

You have probably heard the idea that man has a soul and that this soul is immortal. Immortal to me means to live on after this physical body has ceased to function. But if the soul is the part of man that lives on and the body the part that dies wouldn't it make more sense to say man *IS* a soul and *HAS* a physical body?

I've said earlier that man has a tendency to create God in his image. When man assumes that he has only seventy plus years to be made perfect he paints a picture in my mind of a very wasteful God. I do not think my God is wasteful. It also paints a picture of a very impetuous and selfish God and I do not hold this to be truth either. When I can find no reason but whim to define why Johnny has a healthy body and Suzie a deformed one I am saddened indeed.

So in conjunction with the Law of Cause and Effect there is something else to consider. That something is reincarnation. Now this is not to be confused with transmigration. Reincarnation is the rebirth of the soul into a human body. Transmigration is where there is the rebirth but the vehicle being used could be anything from vegetable to animal. Reincarnation in its Latin translation is referring to being back "in the flesh again."

I present this as a theory for you to consider even though for me it is no theory. I have known reincarnation to be a truth for most of my life. It is now a part of my practice in developing compatibility with my Creator.

I say it is not a theory for me because as a very young child I had certain memories and ideas that I had been here before. I could in fact remember things that I had no way of knowing. You could attribute this to my parents talking, or TV, or any number of things but it would not explain my memories. I remembered being in England in huge ballrooms. I remembered how the men and women were dressed and how they danced. That is not so unusual, anyone reading Cinderella might do the same. But I also remembered how the clothing was made and stitched and formed to fit a certain way. Not so remarkable — but I was 3 or 4 at the time. But that is inconsequential.

I bring this up at this time to perhaps broaden your view of man's capabilities and his purpose. Reincarnation is not foreign to the Christian doctrine. There are many such references to it in the *Old* and *New Testament*. It was practiced widely in the early part of Christianity but removed from the teachings during the Council of Constantinople in 537 A.D. I believe at that time it was done because of a fear on the theologians part of losing their authority over the people.

Reincarnation does not offer one a means of procrastination. When coupled with the Law of Cause and Effect just the opposite is true.

It does however, offer the individual a means of practice and the freedom to learn from all types of experiences. You might compare it to school. If in going to the first grade you fail to give attention to the lessons that are provided you will find much to be desired on reaching the second grade. If you have failed to learn your A B C's in the first grade you will have the opportunity again in second grade but you will also be learning the second grade lessons as well.

Neither does it provide the means to sit back and rest on your laurels. I had a lady once boast to me about the high stations she believed she held in other lifetimes and how glorious she was at those times. I asked her quite bluntly to demonstrate a point, "So Charlene, what happened between now and then that you hold such a lowly station?" I was teasing but it certainly got my point across. If reincarnation is to have a part in the scheme of things then its part is infinitely more meaningful than whether you were rich or famous or beautiful. It has to do with what you accomplished and did with yourself and for humanity.

If man has a goal to become like his Creator then he must have the means to practice this. He must have a way to correct his mistakes and build the wisdom and maturity necessary to become the mental adult. He must have a way to develop the Christ within himself.

Earlier I told you the duty of the Subconscious mind — to fulfill the Conscious mind's desires. The Subconscious mind also has a purpose. It is to store those things that you have made a permanent part of yourself, that are in accordance with your maturity as a mental creator. It would be that part of man that moves on from incarnation to incarnation.

The Conscious mind is created new each lifetime. It is the part of mind you use to build those understandings with. It is the part that we tend to see as the personality of man. This Conscious mind works directly with the brain, collecting and storing information to be drawn upon as needed. Now if we only had a Conscious mind then there would not be seen the differences that are so apparent in siblings. There would be no way for a genius to be born into a family that contained no other geniuses. It is the Subconscious mind that determines the uniqueness for it holds the sum total of all the previous understood experiences: those things you've carried over lifetime after lifetime.

Now when I refer to things that are understood this is not talking about things that you have stored in the brain, nor things that you have merely realized. It is referring to things that you have made such a part of yourself that they are second nature to you. For instance, take the driving of an automobile. Remember the first time that you got in to drive? Your attention went all over, to the pedals and which ones you would use for what, the steering wheel, the mirrors and so on. It took persistent continued effort to learn how to drive that car. Now, however, if you have been doing it for many years, you now can get in the car, turn on the ignition and you are on your way. It is second nature to you.

With reincarnation and the Law of Cause and Effect, if I were to perform deeds that were harmful to others and to myself, it would be necessary for me to have the opportunity to correct my mistakes. Likewise if I had spent a lifetime of service there would need to be a way for me to receive from that as well. Reincarnation provides that way. It offers a means for man to gain the mastery of his mind that is so necessary for him to become compatible to his Creator.

I mentioned there were many references to reincarnation in the *New Testament*. Over and over there is mention made of John being Elijah reborn: *"And the wife Elizabeth shall bear a son and thou shalt call his name John. He shall go before Him in the spirit and power of Elijah." (Luke 1:3-17)* The spirit or soul that was once Elijah is now John the Baptist. Another example is in *Matt. 11:13-*

14. In talking about the violence the kingdom of God has suffered up until the time of John, *"All the prophets as well as the law spoken prophetically. If you are prepared to accept it he is Elijah, the one who was certain to come."*

Still another time in *Matthew 17:10-13*, *"The disciples put this question to him, 'Why do the scribes claim that Elijah must come first?' In reply he said 'Elijah is indeed coming and he will restore everything. I assure you Elijah has already come but they did not know him and they did as they pleased with him....' The disciples then realized that he had been speaking to them about John the Baptist."* This is clear that Jesus knew John was Elijah.

It is indicating something else you might want to look further into — that is what Elijah symbolizes. He came before Elisha in the *Old Testament.* You might consider then who Elisha might have become. Elisha followed Elijah. You will find similar references throughout the four Gospels regarding John and Elijah. Look for them.

There are other references to reincarnation. In *John 9:1-3,* *"As he walked along he saw a man who had been blind from birth. His disciples asked him 'Rabbi was it his sin* (how can an unborn baby sin?) *or that of his parents* (would a loving God punish an innocent child for his parents' sin) *that caused him to be born blind?' 'Neither' answered Jesus, 'It was no sin* (mistake) *either of this man or of his parents. Rather it was to let God's works show forth in him!'"*

You have been given the ability to choose. This does not cease between lifetimes. You have the opportunities to determine conditions that avail you any type of learning opportunity. In this case there was no mistake but the choice made to experience in this condition.

There is a subtler demonstration of reincarnation in beautiful pictures in *Matthew 9:17.* *"People do not pour new wine into old wineskins. If they do the skins burst and the wine spills out and the skins are ruined. No, they pour new wine into new wineskins and in that way both are preserved."* The *bottles* or *skins* symbolize the physical body of man, and the *wine* the life force or creative intelligence that inhabits the body. You don't, upon death, seek out a body that is already in use by another. Each new lifetime begins with a fresh body and brand new conscious mind with the new experiences available to you.

When you go to sleep at night you rest. You wake up refreshed with a new day ahead. You have the opportunity to create many things in this new day and you will also reap the effects of the previous days. But your choices of how to learn and respond can be many. If you put off your choices or procrastinate then those same choices diminish. You know that if you procrastinate you soon reach a point of feeling overwhelmed. Reincarnation offers you a new day, not a way out. I see God as a most loving parent, to have provided this means for man's maturity.

When you understand reincarnation and its place in your growth it will become evident that your responsibility starts with yourself and fans out to include humanity as well. Each day I look to what I can practice and build in myself. I look to see my responsibility to my environment and humanity. I pass on what I find to be truth to others. I give service to humanity for I know that as mankind becomes more aware then this will increase my avenues for experiencing in my future lifetimes as well as right now. We each really do have some say in our future.

The Prodigal Son

*Jesus said to them, "A man had two sons. The younger of them said
to his father, 'Father, give me the share of the estate that is coming
to me.' So the father divided up the property. Some days later this
younger son collected all his belongings and went off to a distant
land where he squandered his money on dissolute living. After he
had spent everything, a great famine broke out in that country and
he was in dire need. So he attached himself to one of the propertied
class of the place who sent him to his farm to take care of the pigs.
He longed to fill his belly with the husks that were fodder for the pigs,
but no one made a move to give him anything. Coming to his senses
at last, he said, 'How many hired hands at my father's place have
more than enough to eat, while here I am starving! I will break away
and return to my Father and say to him Father I have sinned against
God and against you; I no longer deserve to be called your son.
Treat me like one of your hired hands.' With that he set off for his
father's house. While he was still a long way off, his father caught
sight of him and was deeply moved. He ran out to meet him, threw
his arms around his neck and kissed him. The son said to him,
'Father, I have sinned against God and against you; I no longer
deserve to be called your son.' The father said to his servants,
'Quick, bring out the finest robe and put it on him and put a ring on
his finger and shoes on his feet. Take the fatted calf and kill it. Let
us eat and celebrate because this son of mine was dead and has
come back to life. He was lost and is found.' Then the celebration
began.*

*"Meanwhile the elder son was out on the land. As he neared
the house on his way home, he heard the sound of music and
dancing. He called one of the servants and asked him the reason for
the dancing and the music. The servant answered, 'Your brother is
home, and your father has killed the fatted calf because he has him*

back in good health.' The son grew angry at this and would not go in; but his father came out and began to plead with him.

"He said to his father in reply 'For years now I have slaved for you. I never disobeyed one of your orders, yet you never gave me so much as a kid goat to celebrate with my friends. Then when this son of yours returns after having gone through your property with loose women, you kill the fatted calf for him.'

"'My son,' replied the father, 'You are with me always, and everything I have is yours. But we had to celebrate and rejoice! This brother of yours was dead and has come back to life. He was lost and is found.'"

This truly is a story of love and compassion. It is the story of a son turning away from his Father to find his own way in the world, to find satisfaction and comforts. It wasn't until the son had become tired, hungry, and desolate that he began to look toward his home, where he had come from. He recognized what he had lost. But instead of finding a Father that was vengeful and spiteful, he found one that welcomed in joy his return.

You too have a father that is awaiting your return. You are that lost son squandering your time and your attention on that which fails to satisfy your inner growing urge. You have, perhaps, lost sight of your purpose for existence and are not quite sure which way to turn.

I hope this book has been some aid in giving you a start on your journey home to your Father. Jesus knew his Father and he gave you ways to meet and know yours. Abraham knew his Father. He worshipped the one living God for he knew that as long as he was living, his God was living. He worshipped his own individuality.

I must warn you however that upon returning to the presence of your Lord you will also find at your disposal a kingdom — a kingdom that you must rule wisely. There are parts of you that you know not, as Isaiah so wisely put it. *"So shall you summon a*

*nation you knew not and nations that you knew not shall run to
you." (Isaiah 55:5)* Those *nations* are your own mind, waiting for
you to awaken.

As long as you wander, wander, continually scattering your
attention in matters of the senses only, you will find yourself at the
mercy of those senses. You will be constantly wondering why
conditions and circumstances befall you. You will forget what
makes you miserable therefore continue to create misery producing
actions. You will cease to listen to that innermost voice that can
answer questions you have not before felt worthy to ask.

Jesus said, *"Seek ye first the Kingdom of Heaven and all else
will be added unto you."* In our foolishness we seek to find a place
to be for our happiness and contentment. He even told us where to
look for that Kingdom — within our own minds. He also told us
how to recognize that Kingdom — to come as little children —
innocent, receptive, and expectant. His whole life described how to
use that Kingdom while we exist here on earth.

As you understand your own mind, your origin, and your
goal and purpose, you can begin to add the Light of your awareness
to your daily activity.

I know that Jesus was trying to tell us something in his
encouragement to seek that Kingdom and if you are prepared to hear
it he was stating very simply to seek ye first the *power. . .* of the
Kingdom of Heaven. With your use of that power you shall want
for nothing.

Amen.

We Are All
Connected in Superconscious Mind

by Dr. Daniel Condron

> *from a Bible study originally given in 1997*
> *on the campus of the College of Metaphysics*

The Bible is based on a secret code. That secret code has been deciphered. It is called the Universal Language of Mind. You can begin to learn the Universal Language of Mind by writing down your dreams in a dream notebook. The Universal Language of Mind is the language your inner Mind, your subconscious mind uses to communicate with your outer mind, your conscious mind. The Conscious mind uses the five senses for communication. Form and structure enable the senses to perceive. Therefore, the languages of the physical world are based on physical form and structure we can see, hear, taste, touch and smell.

The language of the Subconscious Mind is based on function and use. Therefore, until you learn the Universal Language of Mind your dreams seem to be nonsensical because you are attempting to understand them literally in the physical

language of form. What you really need to be doing is interpreting those dreams in the language of function and use which is a
symbolical language. We call this symbolical language, this
universal translator, the Universal Language of Mind.

The Bible was also written in this Universal Language of
the inner Mind. In order for you to understand the deeper
meanings of the Bible or any other Holy Work you must begin to
comprehend the secret code. You must be able to interpret from
one language to another. Suppose, you are from an English
speaking country and you hear two people speaking Japanese.
Now, suppose you have never heard the Japanese language
spoken prior to this. You, of course, find what is being spoken to
be nonsensical. It just doesn't make sense. In other words, your
senses cannot or do not know how to interpret what is being
communicated. So it is with most people and the Bible. They
do not understand the deeper language it was written in.

It is an immense source of fulfillment when you begin to
understand the Bible on a deeper and much more expansive
level. You find the wisdom of the ancients available to you. It is
as if you are seated at the feet of the Master listening to him
speak right to you. It is more than a sermon because sermons are
for the masses. Sermons are given so that people who do not
know the Universal Language of Mind can gain a valuable
concept to use in their lives for the betterment of themselves and
others. After his sermons Jesus would retire with his disciples
away from the crowds. Then he would teach his disciples the
inner meaning of what he had just taught to the masses. This
inner or secret meaning is the Universal Language of Mind.

One of the most wonderful things about the Universal
Language of Mind is you can apply it to the Holy Scriptures of
ancient Egypt, to Babylon, to Chaldea, or to the Druids and
Celtics or to the Hindus or to China. This is because what makes

a work Holy is its connection with and explanation of the whole Mind. This is what the Universal Language of Mind does, it connects with, interprets, and explains the whole Mind. The Universal Language of Mind can be used universally to interpret the Bible, the Vedas, the Bhagavad Gita, the Tao Te Ching, the Upanishads, the Koran etc.

The earliest languages were written in pictures. Nowadays, we write using an alphabet. We use individual letters to form words. We use words to form sentences and sentences to form paragraphs. The ancient languages used pictures to convey words or ideas. Therefore, theirs was a picture language. The Universal Language of Mind is the way of understanding the picture language even when it is written in words. If you will, consider that all communication is based on pictures. For example, I have a thought of a green tree. I say the words green tree to you. You hear the words green tree and form the image in your mind of a green tree. You may be thinking of a green maple tree while I had in mind an image of a green walnut tree. So our communication was effective but incomplete. The Universal Language of Mind permits us to understand what the ancient enlightened beings throughout history were saying to us and to understand it on a deeper, a more complete and thorough level.

The ancients' world was very advanced scientifically. The priesthood was more advanced scientifically than we are today in many ways. They did, after all, build the great pyramids of Egypt. A feat of which we are today, with our mighty technology, incapable of repeating or reproducing. The idea that the ancients were primitive is egotistical and was begun after Western Europe began to come out of the dark ages having forgotten or destroyed all of the High Science and Technology that the ancients had passed on and added to for tens of thousands of years. Western Europe was so primitive that they could not even begin to understand the magnificent explanations of the Universal Laws and the structure of the Universe given in the Holy temples of the world such as the great pyramid at Giza, Egypt until the late 1800's! It took the finding of the Rosetta stone in the early 1800's before modern man could begin to understand the High Wisdom and science of the ancients. The Rosetta stone is a carved stone found in Egypt with characters or letters given in three languages. The message on the rock was saying the same things in three different languages. So if you understand just one language you can learn to interpret the other two based on correspondences.

In the same way, when I was growing up in the 1960's, nobody knew how to interpret the writings of the Mayans. Scientists weren't even sure that the Mayans even knew how to write. Well, along came the 1970's and 1980's and all of a sudden the pictures on temples are interpreted, because they figured out that it was the picture language. It was based on pictures. When I was growing up, they said the Aztecs had no written language and the only written language of the Incas was the Quipu which is knotted cords, used for bookkeeping and accounting. Now we have figured out that the Aztecs did have writing after all. Someday the writing of the Incas will be understood also.

Mankind had become so immersed in seeing everything physically, during the Dark Ages and during Kali Yuga. We are now coming out of the Kali Yuga and on the upswing in our own evolution. Everything has been viewed as separate, because this is the nature of physical experience. Everything is viewed as separate. You are sitting over there in your physical body, and I am sitting over here in my physical body. You live in Chicago. You live in Indianapolis. You live in Tulsa. You live in Kansas

City. I live here. We are all separated by distance and by time because it takes time to physically travel from one place to another. Although a phone call shortens that time quite a lot. So that is what our civilization and life has become. Everything is based on separating everything out.

Sir Isaac Newton's laws of physics are a step by step process of explaining how the physical environment functions by breaking it down into all its constituent parts. It helped move our mechanistic civilization forward because it said 'here is how the parts work and what all the parts do.' So then people said, 'Oh this is what all the parts do. I can put all the parts together and make them perform functions and work for us.' This is called technology. We have built a technology in western civilization based on this premise. We tend to think that we are the first ones to do this, a once only civilization that just progresses steadily in one direction. But the ancients knew technology too. Most of the inventions that were so called invented after the 1700 and 1800's and up to our present time had already been invented by the ancients. This science was lost during the Dark Ages. The electric battery was already known and used. Electric lights were already known and used. The steam engine was already known and used before the time of Christ. The technology was available, it may not have been used as much, but the steam engine and other great inventions were known.

If you just develop technology alone, you see everything as separate. You can have lots of technology, but nothing will be fulfilling. It won't add to your soul growth. That is when technology becomes destructive. Wars become more and more destructive, because the evolution of the people is not occurring as the technology increases.

The Universal Language of the Mind comes from the inner levels of Mind, therefore it unites rather than separates.

The farther you move outward, from the first level of mind outward, towards physical existence the more separation there is. The deeper you go into the inner levels of mind, to Superconscious Mind, the less separation there is. The less separation there is, the more awareness you have of who you are, and where you are.

The Universal Language of Mind is a way for us to comprehend while still physically engrossed or entrapped in the physical. It is a way to understand the whole mind. To understand ourselves is a benefit of knowing Mind. The Universal Language of Mind becomes a tool in quickening our soul growth and spiritual evolution. Dreams are an important tool that you can use to receive messages from your subconscious mind every night. What do those messages tell you? They give you insight as to how to unite your whole Self, all aspects of yourself. They tell you how to do it by being productive and using your mind while involved in activity.

When you remember a dream you receive a picture, a mental image. You write it down. You translate it into words. You write it down on paper and interpret the meaning often with the help of your teacher. When using the Universal Language of Mind, the words are already there. Somebody has already translated the picture and put it into words. Now, it is up to us to reform the words into the picture. That is the exciting part of the study of the Bible because then you see and perceive and understand the Universal Language of Mind from both sides, the inner and outer, the Conscious and Subconscious minds. We can use the Universal Language of Mind to understand all Holy Books.

It is much more fun, exciting, satisfying, and fulfilling to operate from, to experience from, to think and to reason from, and to use your mind from the point of universals rather than separateness. Universals lead us to our interconnectedness. If something is universal it is everywhere. Universalness means that all is connected. In Superconscious Mind we are all connected. Superconscious Mind has a plan for us. The plan or grand design is for each one of us to become a whole functioning self. It is our duty to expand our consciousness, first beyond our physical body which is identified with our conscious ego and conscious mind, to others in our environment. To deepen that expansion of consciousness to family, friends, classmates, and to your community, to your city, to your county, to your state, going beyond that to the United States your country, and to the world, and from that throughout the universe. That is your goal for your consciousness. It will occur. The quicker the better. Because all deserve to have happiness, joy, fulfillment, peace, bliss, love, contentment. Sooner or later you will come to know that you are not alone, you are never alone, and that you are always with others. The Creator is always with you and you are always with the Creator. It is important that you experience these truths so that you know they are true. Not just know it from one experience, but so it is a permanent part of your expanded consciousness. Then you will experience in the eternal now, and be with the omnipresent Creator at all times. The Universal Language of Mind helps you know your connectedness to the Creator and your connectedness to all of creation.

I like to teach from *Matthew* and the four gospels in the Bible, because they form the centerpiece around the rest of the Bible. The appearance of Jesus, who became the Christ is the example given in the Bible of the potential for every one of you, of what you can be and what you can achieve. Jesus said, *"Even greater things than I do, you shall do also because I go to the Father."* Stating quite plainly the example he gave of cosmic consciousness is a possibility for you also.

It has been 2000 years since the man, born on the physical earth, named Joshua of Nazareth, that is Jesus, walked the earth. It's been 2500 years since Gautama the Buddha walked the earth. The time of Zarathustra, Lao Tzu, and Pythagoras was about 2500 years ago also. This means that you and I have had over 2000 years to catch up and evolve to be enlightened like those masters just named. We are in a better position now than we were then to know the truth, and the truth will set us free to expand our consciousness.

This lifetime is a very important life ime to each of you. Not every lifetime does one awaken to the idea of quickening their soul growth. Not everyone has the opportunity. The School of Metaphysics hasn't always been here. Prior to the present time period it had been pretty hard to get into the secret societies and priesthoods. From our Past Life Profiles we know of a person who in a past time period was female, and her father knew how to meditate. He knew the inner secrets, of the Mind. She wanted to learn those things, but her father would refuse to teach her. So she would sneak around the corner of the temple or the grove of trees, or where ever they were teaching, and listen in and watch and try to learn as much as she could about the inner secrets.

That's something very special about the School of Metaphysics, this organization that you are in because it's for anybody. Anybody that's willing to put forth the effort, to give enough effort and time to apply what is being taught and used.

Rome wasn't built in a day. You didn't learn to ride a bicycle the first time you got on it. Neither will you be a master of meditation the first time you meditate. Every day you meditate your meditation will improve. The truth seeps into you a little bit each day, you get a little bit more disciplined and you get a little bit better at it. The alignment received in meditation pervades your consciousness more and more. You allow your

soul awareness to come into your conscious mind. Every day
you are transformed bit by bit, aspect by aspect. In a few short
months or a few short years, you are transformed. You will
never be the same and you are fulfilled because your consciousness is expanded.

Jesus in the Bible represents the knower. What is the
knower? One who has had direct experience with truth, and can
cause the experience over and over again. For example whatever
skill you have, whatever job you do you have learned and can
repeat. Knowledge which leads to permanent understanding is
much more than a skill. In order to achieve knowing, you must
teach the truth you have learned, experienced, and that you have
been taught.

The universe is designed according to certain principles,
truths, and laws. One of these is you must give in order that you
can receive, and you give more so that you can receive more. So
when somebody gives you something that is permanent and
lasting, then you treasure it as the greatest gift of all. The greatest thanks you can give for such a gift is that you use it, apply it,
and are transformed, and then teach it to at least ten more people.
That is the greatest thanks. True gratitude is using truth, and
applying it, and changing. Great thanks is teaching the truth you
have learned to others. *Jesus* the knower was a teacher. People
would come to him and say "Teacher." They would call him
Rabbi which means teacher.

The second class I ever taught in metaphysics I had a
man in that class who was in his seventies, and at the time I was
in my twenties, so he was close to 50 years older than me. He
started calling me Rabbi. He said "Well Rabbi means teacher
(he was Jewish by the way) and he said we always call the
teacher 'Rabbi.'" He said, "The understanding of Mind and the
Universal Language of Mind are the things I have been wanting

to know all my life. Where have you been and why doesn't anybody else know about them?" Of course, the School of Metaphysics was just a few years old at the time.

Jesus, the Knower in the <u>Bible</u> came to give all of his learning, wisdom, and understandings. He gathered around him a group of disciples, who later became known as the Apostles. Twelve of them in fact. They represent the twelve major aspects of yourself. Most importantly, they signal the willingness on the part of the Knower to teach and give of all parts of the Self through all the understanding that have been and are being developed.

There was a man that came before Jesus, he was called John the Baptist. He baptized with water. *John* symbolizes the quality of believing. Before you can know something, before you can become a Knower, before you can build knowing in yourself, you must first believe. Before you can know how to ride a bicycle, you first believe you can ride. Usually a child sees somebody else riding a bicycle and they say, "Wow! He does it, so I can do it." They believe they can ride, without any doubt. They practice, they may fall off a lot of times, but after awhile, sure enough, they can ride a bicycle.

Believing precedes knowing. That is why *John the Baptist* comes before *Jesus* in the <u>Bible</u>. *John* represents believing. John baptized with water. He would immerse people in the water and then bring them out. Jesus came down where John was baptizing in the river Jordan. He said, "Baptize me." And John said, "No, I can't do it because you're greater than me. You should baptize me." In other words, the one who is the greater should be the teacher. But Jesus said, "No, do it this way so the Father's will will be done." In other words, so that we can have a dramatic example according to the Universal Language of Mind that believing precedes knowing. Baptizing in water, precedes baptizing in fire or spirit. What is baptizing in water? *Water* represents in dream symbols, conscious life experience. Which is the day to day experiences you have in physical waking life. So what does baptism by water indicate? It indicates the commitment to use your day to day experiences productively and usefully to know God.

What does *baptism with spirit* indicate? Sometimes this is translated as spirit sometimes fire, usually as fire. *Fire* in dream symbols will indicate expansion. Expansion of what? Expansion of consciousness.

When I was in the first series of lessons, in the School of Metaphysics, I had a very special dream. Actually I had this dream a couple of times. The first time was when I was in the first series of lessons. In the dream I was in my father's house. I grew up on a farm and my father and mother had a big farm house, so my brother and I shared a room on the second floor. In this dream the house was on fire and I was on the second floor. I was on the second floor and it was on fire, I realized that it was OK because I had plenty of time to move or get the things out that were really important to me in the house. The *house* represents Mind. The *second floor* symbolizes Subconscious mind. This fire was indicating expansion of consciousness that was going on in my mind. The Bible says "In my Father's house are many mansions." The dream was indicating that to me, through the symbols that the tools of mind, being the *furniture*, what I had that was good and productive, I would still be able to use. It wasn't taking away anything from me. The expansion of consciousness was going to expand and cause everything I had that was good and productive to still be there, and to add more to it.

Baptism by fire means you've made a commitment to use the physical to cause an expansion of consciousness this lifetime. John baptized Jesus. After which Jesus came up out of the water. *A dove descended from heaven, and a voice from God said, "This is my son, in whom I am well pleased."* The Superconscious mind is well pleased when you make the full commitment to know the whole Self, and expand your consciousness to the whole universe. Since you become connected through Superconscious mind with everyone, you will give to everyone as if they are yourself. As long as you are alone, as long as you operate or exist from your conscious ego and do not surrender your conscious ego, then you are limited to your physical body. You are alone. Your giving is somewhat limited. You tend to give with some kind of hook. You give and you expect something in return. The *dove* represents subconscious thoughts.

This whole *baptism experience* is an image of the Knower in the physical body being fully committed. The minds are aligned with subconscious thoughts and with the Creator is coming through Superconscious mind. It shows the whole alignment, existing in the physical, symbolized by the *water*. But no longer entrapped. After that, Jesus the Knower, begins his mission of teaching.

The story of Jesus then continues with his choosing his 12 disciples. *Disciples* indicate discipline. Showing discipline in all parts of Self, all aspects of Self is necessary for rapid soul growth. Discipline is the directed continuous use of the will. *Jesus* the Knower went out to the wilderness or desert and fasted, and then the devil came to him to tempt him. *Devil* in the Bible represents your conscious ego. There's three major ways that your conscious ego shows up in the Bible. The *snake* in the first part of *Genesis* is the first way. The snake tempts Eve to eat of the fruit of the tree of good and evil. Then the *devil* or *Satan* or *Lucifer* in the *Gospels* tempts Jesus in the desert. Then the *snake* gets really big and becomes a *dragon* in the *Book of Revelation.* These symbols of the conscious ego show the maturation and the building in strength of the conscious ego.

As your consciousness grows you gain more awareness of yourself, your identity, and your individuality. It also always shows the need to be honest. Honest with yourself. True honesty is recognizing that you are connected with everyone else. You are not isolated. When you look at life as being separate and isolated, then you tend to just think of me, me, me, me, me, I, I, I, I, I. Being alone, you take care of yourself, alone. You don't think you have anything else to give to anyone else because whatever resources you have, you have to take care of, and protect yourself. So you see that ego getting stronger and stronger. In *Genesis*, the *snake* is using words in order to manipulate. In *Matthew Chapter 4* the devil makes all kinds of promises. "Jump down off this building and I'll cause my angels to catch you," the devil said, "and you can turn these stones into bread and eat them, you don't have to be hungry," he said. Of course the Knower, *Jesus*, who is committed to the whole Self, and therefore is connected with all, knows that being selfish and thinking in those terms will not be really satisfying or fulfilling, nor would it accomplish the whole mission of the Self. Jesus rejected them. He does more than reject them. He says, *"Scripture says that man shall not live by bread alone but by the word of God."* So when there is the temptation to think physical, think separate, think alone, think selfishly, think limited consciousness, Jesus operates from the expansive Superconscious mind. He used his lifetime to the fullest. Everything will come to the one who is productive. Each person needs to be doing what's important for their soul and for the soul growth of others in order to fulfill your assignment for this lifetime.

Jesus carried on his mission of teaching. Crowds begin

to gather around. He has great big crowds come to him because
he could heal the sick, the lame, and the blind. They wanted to
be healed, but more importantly they wanted to hear the truth
that he had to say because it had been a long time since they
heard the truth. So they come from far and wide. They are
mostly what would be called the common people. They are not
the world's wealthiest people, or they are not the most powerful
people on earth. They are not Caesar the Emperor. They know
that there are other things important in life. That is why they are
not the world's richest people or the world's most powerful
people, because they didn't place those things as their top priority. So they hear truth easier. So that's who Jesus preaches to
around Galilee. He has big crowds, thousands. He taught on a
mount and gave the sermon on the mount. Then the people were
hungry and Jesus fed them.

    People in dream symbols represent aspects of yourself.
In the Bible *people* also represent aspects of yourself. We can
receive a clear definition of what those aspects represent in the
Bible from their number which was 5000. Five is the number of
reasoning. That passage is discussing the quality of reasoning.
Jesus the Knower asks, *"How much food do we have here?"*
And his disciples say, *"Well we've got some fish, and some
bread."* There were 7 fish and a couple loaves of bread. He tore
them up and he put them in a whole bunch of baskets, and just
kept making more and more. He fed all those 5000 men plus all
the women. 5000 men, plus all the women and children, and still
has more food than they started out with. People were pretty
impressed with that, naturally.

    Food represents knowledge in the Bible. This shows that
the one who is fully aligned in their Conscious, Subconscious,
and Superconscious minds and has expanded their consciousness
knows no limit, therefore has no limitations, therefore has no

want. Whatever is needed is always provided. Because you are capable of creating what you need at any time through the Universal Laws. Not only that, it means you have all the opportunity to gain all the knowledge of the universe. Not all the details of the physical, but all the knowledge.

The true knowledge of creation is important knowledge because with the High Wisdom you can create rapid soul growth. *Fish* represent spiritual awareness in the <u>Bible</u>. By *multiplying the fish,* the Knower, *Jesus,* is showing that there is no end to spiritual awareness You can always create more without limitation when you are aligned with Superconscious mind, and therefore committed to soul growth and spiritual development. Jesus had *12 disciples* which shows that he is totally disciplined. It means the Knower does his spiritual exercises every day. Twelve is a master number. Twelve plus Jesus equals thirteen. Thirteen is the top master number. It shows the complete mastery and the complete use of all the major aspects of the Self, which the knower has.

Jesus after preaching in the areas of Galilee decided it was time to finish up his mission, so he went down to Jerusalem. I say down because he went South. If you know the present state of Israel you know it is not a very big country. You can walk from one end to the other in a few days, a couple days, or weeks. He walked down there and started preaching. He had already preached in the temple once. The Pharisees and Sadducees were the people who were running the temple and in charge there. They worked directly under the Romans to keep control of the people. Jesus had already run the money changers out of the temple. So he had made enemies with the Pharisees and Sadducees. They are very egotistical. They've got important positions. But they are positions in name only, not in spirit. So when Jesus came in, he is the true authority and they are not.

Because Jesus speaks from the whole mind, and they are just from the physically engrossed self. They don't like it. So they start plotting against Jesus.

Pharisees represent the hypocritical part of yourself that says one thing and does another, that thinks one thing and says a different thing. They pretend to be one thing to one person, and a different thing to another person so that the real Self never shows. The Pharisees' real Self never showed. That is why Jesus would call them vipers, because he could see what they were really like inside. They did not like being exposed to the Light of truth. He made enemies because he spoke the truth. You never make enemies with people by speaking the truth with people that want to learn and grow. But when people are really invested in being dishonest or physically engrossed, and don't want to change, then they don't want to hear the truth.

Being a teacher was a part of Jesus' mission. A good teacher always shares truth. The Pharisees plotted against him. They had Judas, one of the disciples, betray him by pointing out who Jesus was to the Pharisees and Romans. They already knew who he was anyway. They could have figured it out, he was around all the time everyday in Jerusalem.

Judas, the betrayer, symbolizes the motivator because he was motivating Jesus to perform his assignment. Physically looking at Judas it would seem that he is a bad person. However in the symbolical Language of Mind he is really not bad. He is just one of the aspects that produces motivation so that the plan of creation can be fulfilled.

Jesus is brought before a trial of the Sanhedrin and then before Pilate. He was tried and convicted and taken out to Calvary, Golgotha, which means "Place of the Skull," and put on the cross between two thieves. He didn't hang there for three days. Besides being very painful it took a long time for the person to die on the cross. During crucifixion the arms are spread out. Usually nails were driven into the feet and hands. The hands and arms are stretched out and the nails are driven into the hands making it impossible to let them down to the sides of the body. He could never let them down and he could never really rest and sit down and move. After awhile, the blood in the body will not circulate right and it will plug up your heart and you die from lack of blood circulation. It's a very, very painful way to go and that is why the Romans used it. To teach a lesson to the subjugated people. The lesson was, do as we say.

But it didn't happen with Jesus that way. He died within about three hours. Everybody was kind of surprised he died so quickly including the Romans. One soldier came up and stuck a sword in his side to make sure he was dead. Then Joseph of Aramathea dressed Jesus' wounds and placed him in a burial cave. The *cross* that Jesus was crucified on symbolizes the intersection point of physical time (linear or horizontal) and mental time (vertical time). Mental or vertical time is the time that aligns with the inner mind. So *being hung on a cross* represents the mastery, the control and the understanding of both physical-horizontal and mental-vertical time. Therefore, you are a master of time. Once you place your attention on your learning and growth in the expansion of consciousness as your number one priority, physical time is compressed. You can cause rapid learning and soul growth ten times more rapidly, 100 times more, 1000 times more rapidly than if you had just went on with the natural scheme of things. The cross shows the mastery of that process of quickened enlightenment.

Jesus is raised from the dead, came out of the tomb, moved the rock back and scared the people that see him first. They don't believe that it is really Jesus. Later they realize it is Jesus. Doubting Thomas said, "I don't believe it is Jesus raised from the dead." Jesus said, "Stick your hand in my side Doubting Thomas, you can see this is where I was stabbed with the sword." So they come to believe, indicating that the disciples have now moved another step farther in knowing themselves, the truth that you are not a physical body, that this physical earth is temporary and that you exist eternally, above and beyond physical time and space. This is an example to all of us. We all exist beyond physical time and space but we don't know it. We accept Maya, which is the illusion that the physical is permanent. We are in fact unlimited, because we are eternal, and that is the example set at the end of *Matthew*.

That is a general overview of the book of *Matthew*. I have just given you the major symbols. There is a lot more detail. In a weekly <u>Bible</u> class we would go through the different people and then discuss, *Now this is how the birth of Jesus Christ came about, when his mother, Mary was engaged to Joseph, but before they lived together she was found with child through the power of the Holy Spirit.* And then I would explain what the mental image is — sentence by sentence or paragraph by paragraph. Any time you see the word *spirit* in the <u>Bible</u>, it can also be translated and interpreted as Mind. *Holy* means whole. So *Holy Spirit* means the whole Mind. The phrase *found with child through the Holy Spirit* means this new idea, symbolized by the *child*, concerns the use of the Whole Mind. That is what we are teaching in the School of Metaphysics, to use the Whole Mind. Not just the Conscious mind, but the other two divisions of Mind, Subconscious and Superconscious Minds.

First of all we teach you to use the Conscious Mind very productively. This is what is symbolized by *Jesus being born, and educated early to be productive* so that he could go into the temple at age 12 and teach the Rabbis, and astonish them with what he knew. First you build the conscious mind, and use it productively and wisely by disciplining your mind to build concentration, memory, listening, attention, reasoning, honesty, goal-setting, motivation, ideal, purpose, and activity. All of these are learned in order to use the Conscious mind productively. This is what prepares *Jesus* to be the authority, the knower.

The Genealogy that comes right before the birth of Jesus is telling you every thing that you have accomplished as a soul up to the point of this lifetime, to get ready for this lifetime. Everything from the family record of Jesus Christ, the son of David, the son of Abraham explains the steps to become a Christ an enlightened being. Abraham was the father of Isaac, Isaac the father of Jacob, Jacob the father of Judas and his brothers. It tells all the different people from Abraham to Jesus, which is the whole story of everything you've done up to this lifetime to get ready for this lifetime. This lifetime is very special to you so that you can increase your soul growth and spiritual awareness in this lifetime at a much more rapid, accelerated rate.

Joseph her husband, an upright man, unwilling to expose Mary to the law decided to divorce her quietly. Such was his intention when suddenly the angel of the Lord appeared in a dream and said to him, "Joseph, son of David, have no fear about taking Mary as your wife. It is by the Holy Spirit that she has conceived this child. She is to have a son, and you are to name him Jesus, because he will save his people from their sins. All this happened to fulfill what the Lord had said to the prophet that the virgin shall be with child and give birth to a son and they shall call him Emmanuel. A name which means God is within us." When Joseph awoke he did as the Angel of the Lord had directed him and received her into his home as his wife. He had no relations with her at anytime before she bore his son who he named, Jesus. (Matt 1:19-25)

We have got two different names here. The angel said *to call him Emmanuel*. But Joseph, his father, named him Jesus. *Joseph* represents perception, and perception always precedes knowing and leads to knowing. Before you accept a truth you have to hear it. Before you can see the truth of anything, before you accept the truth of anything you have to see it. You may have heard the same thing a hundred times before you really receive it into yourself.

When you combine the five senses, you create perception. Then you are capable of building knowing. Until you have perception, you are not very capable of building knowing. From perception comes the capability of building knowing.

Perception symbolized by *Joseph* called the child *Jesus*, the knower. *Jesus* is the *child,* the new idea of knowing. All the other aspects called the new idea, *Emmanuel,* which means God is within us. The new idea of having an awareness of the God within us and our Godhood or ourselves as being creators. Also within the word *Emmanuel* is the word man. *Man* comes from the Sanskrit, *'manu'* which means thinker. From the time you start doing your spiritual exercises such as meditation and concentration and combine the senses to build knowing and perception, you are in the process of becoming an enlightened being.

Consider how you looked at life before you entered the School of Metaphysics, and consider how you look at life now. I think you'll agree that you are more of a thinker. You understand yourself better. You understand life better. You understand physical existence better. You understand your purpose. You understand creation. You understand your associations, friendships, relationships, and interconnectedness with other people to a higher degree. Those are all qualities and aspects of being a thinker which is symbolized by *Emmanuel.*

Mary indicates the quality of love. It's great to have the power of perception. We need to combine perception with that quality of love. What does love do? Unite! What does hate do? Separate! Love is very much akin to interconnectedness and universalness and oneness. Jesus the Christ commanded us to, *"Love your neighbor as yourself."* Do unto others as you would have them do unto you. That is love. All the qualities that make for the Christ are given in the first and second chapters of *Matthew*. Jesus becomes the Christ. Christ in the original title.

Jesus was never called the Christ when he was on earth. He was called the Messiah, or referred to as the Messiah, because Christ is a Greek word. But as the *New Testament* was translated into the Greek or written in the Greek Language they used the Greek word. Christ means enlightened. Messiah means anointed. The meaning of the word Buddha also is enlightened. *Jesus* is the Christ, who is the knower who has become enlightened. What does enlightened mean? Enlightened means full of Light or in Light. What is light? Awareness! So to be fully in Light or enlightened, is to cause your awareness to expand to all of creation. Enlightenment is to know your Creator and therefore all of creation since the Creator is in all of creation. The Creator created creation out of himself.

That is the meaning of the crucifixion, the resurrection, and ascension. The resurrection shows the overcoming of death. Have you noticed in Western culture a preoccupation with death. The idea now is that you create a cloned body of yourself and then every time you need a spare part, cut it off the cloned body and have somebody replace your ailing parts so that you can live longer. Where does that idea come from? It comes from the idea that you are only a physical body, you are not a soul, and you'll never get another chance. So you've got to hang on to this physical form as long as you can. If you know you're a soul and know about reincarnation, you know you'll have another opportunity to learn. If you know that you are here to use this lifetime to the fullest, to fulfill your purpose then you'll do the best that you know how.

When you have an illness you attempt to heal that area of the body, and you'll hopefully look at the attitude that's causing it, and do something about that attitude instead of just staying the same. "No, I want another body part so I can stay the same, and not have to change." In our society, we have a fear of death, and it comes from thinking we are just physical beings. The example of *Jesus overcoming death* shows that the consciousness has expanded to fill all of Mind so that there is no cessation of consciousness whether you are in a physical body or not in a physical body. There is no cessation of consciousness. You are you regardless of whether you are in a physical body or not. In other words, you are not a physical personality anymore. You are the eternal soul, and that's how you act.

Each one of you is unique. Everyone has a personality that they have adopted this life time. But you won't take your personality with you at the end of this lifetime into the next lifetime. It will be sloughed off, and you will be raised in a different sex, race, time period, country. You'll adopt a different personality each lifetime. The more enlightened you become, the less that personality and its limitations affect you, the more you become like the Creator. Therefore we become more alike instead of more different.

Celebration of Unity in diversity is opposite of enlightenment. That's saying, "Separateness is great." Individuality is great when the individuality is together with others. I say unity in individuality, not unity in diversity, unity in interconnectedness. The *resurrection* shows that the individual can have eternal consciousness whether you are in a physical

body or not. The *ascension* shows that there is the full awareness and existing in Superconscious mind. Because *Jesus
ascended to heaven,* and *heaven* is Superconscious mind.
Heaven, represents Superconscious mind. It shows that there is a
full alignment with Superconscious mind. You deserve to exist
at your highest level of being which is Superconscious mind.
You may lower yourself to other people's levels in the sense that
you will put yourself in situations that you don't have to do,
because you have already gone beyond that learning. It's a
matter of wanting to give to all humanity, and wanting to give to
others. It's a recognition that we are all part of God's creation
and that it is our duty to everyone else in creation to lift everyone
else up to our level of awareness and beyond. It is our eternal
duty to ourselves and to others. That's the *resurrection* and the
ascension.

    Genesis represents the beginning of your being, the
essence of where you came from – light. It describes your
countless millennia of evolution and growth for you as a mental
and spiritual being. It also describes the development of the
physical body. The *Old Testament* continued all the way
through back to the point of entrapment. And yes, you can take
individual passages out of the *Old Testament* and glean tremendous amount of good and insight. That's because the plan of
Creation is outlined in *Genesis*. Then you go through *Matthew*
and the *New Testament,* all the way to *Revelation.*

    The book of *Revelation*, explains the stages of becoming
Spiritual Intuitive Man. It will give you the step-by-step proce-
dures and processes. It gives you insights and awareness into the
qualities of the seven major chakras. These are the energy
transformers that transform your thoughts and attitudes and
physical energy into mental energy and recycles it back into the
Subconscious mind, and Superconscious mind where you can

use it again. It gives you insight into the Superconscious mind.
It gives you insight, understanding, and knowledge of your
conscious ego. The *Book of Revelation* describes the steps you
must take to direct the ego productively. The more powerful you
get mentally, the more directed and focused you will be in
building understandings rather than trying to getting more things
or power in the physical. It shows you how to be productive
with your ego all along the way. It shows you how to use the
levels of Mind. It shows you the final stages of using the whole
Mind, and what it is to become enlightened. That is the *Book of
Revelation.*

There is nothing bad in anything in *Revelation.* It
concerns using the stages of growth and the reactions you may
go through, or the way you fight the change. That is the difficulties and the battles portrayed. But in the end, you face them all,
go through the difficulties, and expand your consciousness. You
are the victor. You achieve the tree of life, and the river of life
giving water. You have eternal life which is eternal, unceasing,
expanded universal consciousness.

Someone once asked me, "Why did the writers of the
Holy Books write in the Universal Language of Mind, when so
few could understand them?" Because mankind, in those days,
we as souls had not progressed to that point of evolution where
the average entrapped soul could understand the inner mysteries.
The optimal way it was supposed to work, was the most enlightened beings were accepted into the priesthood. They were
taught the Universal Language of Mind, because they were the
ones that were capable of receiving it and understanding it. They
were taught according to their level of attainment of soul growth
and spiritual development. And if they got to a point where they
couldn't or wouldn't learn any more, that's the point where their
learning would stop.

Only a very few went all the way through and achieved the highest initiation, and they were called Christs, or Buddhas, or Zarathustras, or Pythagoras. It had to do with the point of evolution of humanity. Humanity has evolved during the past 2500 years. The masses or most of the people are ready to hear the truth. That was not true 2000 years ago.

The Book of Realization

The **REVELATION** *of* **JOHN**

The Book of Realization
The *REVELATION* of *JOHN*
by *Barbara Condron*

first published in Thresholds Quarterly beginning in May of 1993

In the vast array of literature available to mankind, there are recorded thoughts which capture the universal needs and desires of every man. These pieces become part of classical literature. They stand the test of time, yielding their wisdom to generation after generation, because they embody Universal Truth. From Prometheus Bound by Aeschylus to The Divine Comedy by Dante, from Frankenstein by Mary Shelley to The Time Machine by H.G. Wells, from the plays of Shakespeare to the works of Mark Twain, our world is filled with profound thoughts waiting to impress our consciousness. All we need do is read.

Classical literature is rich in allegory and imagery, and so can be interpreted on many levels of awareness. Jonathan Swift's Travels of Gulliver was viewed by many contemporaries as a social commentary on the class structures of the time and area thus giving it a physically oriented interpretation. Those reading the text now might see the work in light of man's own search for identity and the struggle with his own ego and many aspects of self thus lending a more spiritual orientation to the story.

We can readily see the wide scope of interpretive possibilities in the following passage from Shakespeare's *Hamlet*:

"What a piece of work is man! how noble in reason! how infinite in faculties! in form and moving how express and admirable! in action how like an angel! in apprehension how like a god! the beauty of the world! the paragon of animals!"

Upon first reading this passage some may believe Shakespeare is mocking man; the animal filled with potential often wasted or misused. Yet many interpretations can be derived from this soliloquy. The ecologically-minded individual might read this passage as extolling the responsibility and need for man to care for the environment since he alone displays the ability to have dominion over other life forms. Upon closer reflection, he might see the passage as a commentary on the need for man to set himself apart from all other animals by using his God-given abilities. With another examination, he might discover the purpose for this separation is rooted in man's faculty for reasoning, imagination, Self expression and determination. He might birth realizations of the duality of man, being both spiritual as angels and god, and physical as animals. This piece might speak to an inner urge to know his Creator and become like his Creator.

A great part of what makes literature classical is its ability to stimulate the thinking of the reader. The fact that these pieces can be read and interpreted on an infinite number of levels gives them their timeless quality insuring their longevity. The same is true with what has become known as the Holy Scriptures of the world.

For thousands of years, as individual cultures developed a means of recording their thoughts for posterity, physical records of metaphysical insights have thrived. From the Hindu <u>Mahabarata</u>, the world's longest poem, to the Islamic <u>Koran</u>, from the <u>Analects</u>

of Confucius to the Zend Avesta of Zarathustra, the world is filled with literature devoted to the expansion of man's consciousness, his relationship to creation, and the reason for his existence. This intention of Holy writings — to serve as a means to bring the heart and mind of man to his God — is what separates these texts from other classical literature. Because Holy Scriptures center upon man's divinity and spiritual nature, they are whole and complete in the insights they afford. They are also written with an expanded awareness characteristic of the inner self and thus are penned in the Universal Language of Mind; the same language used in man's dreamstates.

Dreams and visions abound throughout Holy scriptures. The first mention of dreams in the *Old Testament* of the Bible occurs in the first book, *Genesis.* The *Lord,* representing the highest expression of individual creation, appears to *Abimelech,* a righteous man symbolizing the willingness to cooperate with goodness and law. The Lord informs Abimelech that his house guest Abram has lied to him by presenting his wife Sarah as a sister. Abram had offered Sarah to Abimelech, and the Lord warns Abimelech against taking Abram's wife as his own consort. When Abimelech heeds the dream message he is able to maintain his integrity and Abram is confronted with his own dishonesty. A deeper awareness in the commitment of the conscious, waking mind symbolized by *Abram* is achieved. In studying our own dreams, we find an honest perspective of who we are just as Abram did, for our dreams originate in the inner levels of consciousness apart from our physical and finite world. We sometimes find deception in our outer mind and life, and by heeding messages from our inner mind we can become free of these lies or deceits.

The dreams of the Bible also reveal the inner Self's ability to assess conditions of our lives and propose productive action. *Jacob,* representative of Superconscious awareness, receives much guidance and insight from his dreams, including the well-known episode of the *ladder reaching to Heaven* which symbolizes the movement of thought and energy throughout all levels of consciousness. Having journeyed to Syria where he fathered many offspring including Joseph, the angel of the Lord appears to Jacob in a dream instructing him to leave that land and return to the land of his father, Canaan. Later that son will find his ability to interpret the dreams of the Pharaoh is the key to his freedom. In the *New Testament,* Joseph, the earthly father of Jesus, is instructed through a dream to take Mary and the newborn to Egypt to escape Herod's slaughter of newborns. As you become attentive to your dream messages you will also find instruction and guidance toward a whole and more complete existence during your waking hours. By learning to exist in your dream states with awareness you release yourself from bondage to the physical plane.

Moses is another Biblical figure who receives guidance through dreams. When there is jealousy among the people of Israel concerning Moses' singular ability for communication with the Lord, the Lord speaks to Moses, Aaron, and Miriam saying, *"Hear now my words: If there be a prophet among you, I the Lord will make myself known unto him in a vision, and will speak unto him in a dream."* Moses, like the Biblical prophets who follow him, represents reasoning man's capability for foresight. Only man displays the inherent ability for imagination, and it is this capability which separates him from the rest of creation. The developed use of imaging gives us the talent for creating the experiences in our lives, and perhaps more importantly it serves to promote the spiritual development of intuitive thinking. As it was in Biblical times, it remains a truth today that those who heed the communications from the inner, Subconscious Self receive guidance from their nighttime dreams and experience daytime visions as their consciousness reaches toward enlightenment.

Of the many prophets who received visions recorded in the Bible, from Abraham to Isaiah to Daniel to the disciples of Jesus, perhaps the most well-known and most worthy of our attention is the apostle John who penned the *Book of Revelation* in 95 A.D. while he was exiled on the isle of Patmos. The rich imagery of his writing elevates his work beyond the limits of physical existence for it describes that which does not exist in physical form, only in the imagination of the reader. From the *beast with eyes inside and out* to the *dragon with seven heads and ten horns* to the *great Babylonian harlot,* symbolic language flourishes in John's allegory. When interpreted in the same language your dreams speak, you discover a text which instructs the spiritual development of mankind from Animal man to Spiritual man.

Here are images in the language of mind revealing the inner spiritual Truths found in what is perhaps the most confusing, horrifying, controversial and unequivocally the most profound piece of spiritual literature ever written: *The Book of Revelation.*

Written by an apostle named John in the year 95, it is described as the record of a vision he received while exiled on the isle of Patmos located in the Mediterranean Sea between present day Turkey and Greece.

For centuries, *Revelation* has endured as the Biblical book provoking the most discussion and argument by theologians throughout the world. Its words paint pictures of people, places, and things beyond the realm of physical reality. This rich use of imagery demands investigation by the reader for it requires the expansion of thought and imagination in order to discern its theme of spiritual enlightenment.

Still, many approach *Revelation* in a very physical sense, giving its words a literal interpretation. Taking the words on face value only, they fall short of grasping the Truths revealed that will transform the heart and mind. By moving beyond the physical senses and the limitations they impose, we can begin to perceive the imagery in *Revelation* with a spiritual sense and enter the transcendent worlds of omniscience. To fulfill this quest for understanding, we will endeavor to reach for a deeper and more expansive interpretation of these scriptures by translating them in what is known as the Universal Language of Mind.

Physically, the words of *Revelation* are believed to have been written in the Aramaic language. Many scholars have made translations available in the common languages spoken throughout today's world. These translations make John's words accessible to anyone who has learned how to read. As with any literature written about man's divine nature and reason for existence, the words stimulate the reader toward understanding of his whole Self.

One of the best ways to grasp the inner meaning of *Revelation*, is to interpret its passages in another language, a universal language often described as pictures.   This picture language is actually a combination of people, places, and events which hold significance no matter who you are, when or where you live, or what language you use for physical communication. This is the language your inner, subconscious mind uses for communication to the outer, conscious mind or to other subconscious minds. It is comprised of images which convey perceptions and you are probably most familiar with this language through your nighttime dreams.   In this series on the *Book of Revelation,* we will be translating John's vision in a fashion similar to how dreams can be interpreted. By using the language of mind, we can more easily identify the meaning of the symbology used and discern the Universal Truths conveyed in this text.

ChapterOne *Prologue*

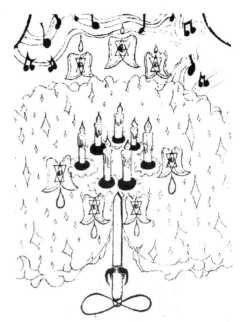

Verses one through three: This is the revelation God gave to Jesus Christ that he may show his servants what must happen very soon. He made it known by sending his angel to his servant John. Who in reporting all he saw bears witness to the word of God. Happy is the man who reads this prophetic message. And happy are those who hear it and heed what is written in it for the appointed time is near.

    Revelation is portrayed as John's vision. Characters named John, or similar name derivatives such as Joshua, appear several times in the <u>Bible</u>. In the language of mind, *John* represents the whole-hearted belief in the inherent creative ability of man, the thinker. John the Baptist prepared the way for the man known as Jesus. *John the Baptist* refers to the intelligent use of the Universal Law of Believing and Knowing which prepares the thinker's awareness for the birth of Christ consciousness signified by *Jesus*.

    The *Book of Revelation* describes the opening and development of man's spirituality from the dawning of awareness of the Christ consciousness to its full manifestation as a state of being. For anyone who pursues the study and understanding of the *Revelation*, the "appointed time" is near. John's vision is how this spiritual evolution is revealed to anyone who experiences the Christ consciousness. When you can understand what *Revelation* is conveying, you are ready to make the transition from Reasoning Man into Intuitive Man, from Human Man into Spiritual Man.

Revelation begins with the dream of one individual, an individual who believes in more than just physical existence. The dream is a hope for a future filled with the control born from understanding the nature of man and his destiny to be like God. It speaks to and about each of us.

The vision paints a picture of man, the thinker, in an enlightened state using the Master known as Jesus as the recipient of this revelation. Although John is the one recording the vision, it is Jesus who is credited with receiving the vision from God. Of all Biblical characters, it is Jesus who finally attains the Christ consciousness. The word Christ is from the Greek *Kristos* meaning "anointed one" or "one who is devoted to a great duty." This state of awareness is available to all of mankind and is the personal quest for each individual experiencing the fifth day of creation, Reasoning Man, as given in the book of *Genesis* in the <u>Bible</u>.

Letters to the Churches of Asia
Verses four through six: Greeting To the seven churches in the province of Asia; John wishes you grace and peace—from him who is and who was and who is to come, and from the seven spirits before his throne, and from Jesus Christ the faithful witness, the first-born from the dead and ruler of the kings of the earth. To him who loves us and freed us from our sins by his own blood, who has made us a royal nation of priests in the service of his God and Father—to him be glory and power forever and ever. Amen.

Greeting describes man in the sixth day of creation, Intuitive or Spiritual Man. This man has at his disposal *seven churches:* seven major energy transformers, often referred to in esoteric literature as the chakras, to use for transforming his thoughts into physical reality. He is committed to believing in the spiritual nature of Self and is willing to use every part of his intelligence *(spirits)* to know that spirituality. This man has experienced the inner levels of mind having gained control of the five physical senses *(kings of the earth)* by using them to attain higher states of awareness. He is committed to accelerating spiritual growth and development through seeking Truth so productive change can occur.

Verses seven through eight: See he comes amid the clouds. Every eye shall see him. Even those who pierced him. All the peoples of the earth; shall lament him bitterly. So it is to be! Amen. The Lord God says, "I am the Alpha and the Omega, the One who is and who was and who is to come, the Almighty."

The man knows where he came from, why he exists, and where he is going. He uses the Universal Laws of Relativity and Infinity *(Alpha and Omega).* He has understood the awesome power entrusted to humanity, the creative power of thought and accepts full responsibility for all aspects of Self.

Verses nine through sixteen: First Vision I, John, your brother, who share with you the distress and the kingly reign and the endurance we have in Jesus, found myself on the island called Patmos because I proclaimed God's word and bore witness to Jesus.

Believing completely in the destiny of Spiritual Man and having gained control of any doubt, this man is prepared to know the inner levels of consciousness.

On the Lord's day I was caught up in ecstasy, and I heard behind me a piercing voice like the sound of a trumpet which said "Write on a scroll what you now see and send it to the seven churches: to

Ephesus, Smyrna, Pergamum, Thyatira, Sardis, Philadelphia, and Laodicea."

The *Lord's day* represents the dawning of awareness of the true Self. Knowing who you are causes the Kundalini energy to be stimulated resulting in mystical experiences often described as *ecstasy*. This stimulates the inner intelligence and energy signified by the *seven churches*.

I turned around to see whose voice it was that spoke to me. When I did so I saw seven lampstands of gold, And among the lampstands One like a Son of Man wearing an ankle-length robe, with a sash of gold about his breast.

Produced from the disciplined expansion of awareness in the Conscious mind of all levels of consciousness, this Spiritual Man stands before us in our dream of what can be. This man represents anyone who is prepared to accelerate his evolution beyond what already exists. The description of this man reveals the preparation necessary to pursue the state of enlightenment.

The hair of his head was as white as snow-white wool and his eyes blazed like fire. His feet gleamed like polished brass refined in a furnace, and his voice sounded like the roar of rushing waters. In his right hand he held seven stars. A sharp, two-edged sword came out of his mouth, and his face shone like the sun at its brightest.

His thoughts and expression are pure having gained full understanding of physical existence. His perception is expansive because his spiritual foundation is strong. His thoughts are directed by the righteous use of awareness in the seven inner levels of consciousness. Knowing who He is produces control of Karma, the cycles of rebirth.

Verses seventeen through twenty: When I caught sight of him I fell down at his feet as though dead. He touched me with his right hand and said: "There is nothing to fear. I am the First and the Last....and the One who lives. Once I was dead but now I live forever and ever. I hold the keys of death and the nether world,"

Having gained these insights, the individual assesses his place in evolution, recognizing the need for change and the need for developing his spiritual foundation. By purposefully using what he has made a part of Self, he can begin moving beyond the entrapment in those things of the physical and reach toward the freedom of enlightenment. By using the Universal Laws, he realizes the secrets of life, the continuity of consciousness beyond the physical, and is no longer a slave to the inaction and stagnation symbolized by *death*. The limitations of the physical or *netherworld* are accepted for what they are: temporary and transient. They no longer blind the consciousness of the Self.

"Write this down, therefore, whatever you see in visions - what you see now and will see in time to come. This is the secret meaning of the seven stars you saw in my right hand, and of the seven lampstands of gold: the seven stars are the presiding spirits of the seven churches. The seven lampstands are the seven churches."

Through experience, the development of Spiritual Man becomes the understanding of Self. With righteous and productive use of consciousness, awareness expands in every inner level of mind. The way the individual uses his intelligence and energy is quickened and his realizations are heightened. Full respect is given to the spiritual and physical parts of Self because we now understand thought is cause and the physical is its manifest likeness.

Our journey toward Christ consciousness and enlightenment has begun. This vision, the dream, the hope, are impressed in the mind of the believer. Full intention of knowing and therefore living the vision of being Spiritual Man is born.

Chapter Two

To Ephesus. To the presiding spirit of the church in Ephesus, write this: The One who holds the seven stars in his right hand and walks among the seven lampstands of gold has this to say: I know your deeds, your labors, and your patient endurance. I know you cannot tolerate wicked men; you have tested those self-styled apostles, who are nothing of the sort, and discovered that they are impostors. You are patient and endure hardship for my cause. Moreover, you do not become discouraged.

The first church, *Ephesus,* addresses man's existence as a physical being. Here, we discover the learning gained in the physical plane of existence is what has produced the evolutionary development apparent in our present state of awareness. The thinker continues to incarn into physical experiencing in response to an inner urge for spiritual maturity. In each incarnation, we find the opportunity to discover Truth, leaving behind the errors of ignorance and embracing the righteousness of awareness. Challenges arise when mistakes are made — errors in judgement born from a misunderstood sense of Self. This false egotism is rooted in identifying only with the physical part of Self. As long as we experience for the sake of ego and sense gratification only, the need for incarnation continues.

I hold this against you, though: you have turned aside from your early love. Keep firmly in mind the heights from which you have fallen. Repent, and return to your former deeds. If you do not repent I will come to you and remove your lampstand from its place.

The constant rebirth in the physical plane is caused by spiritual forgetfulness. Upon incarning, the physical mind relinquishes knowledge of the purpose for its existence. This promotes physical ways of thinking which deny our existence as soul and spirit. We find ourselves engrossed in experiences rather than the creator of those experience. *The early love is first described in Genesis, that is why a man leaves his mother and father, and clings to his wife, and the two become one flesh.* For enlightenment, the Conscious mind must release its preoccupation with transient physical experiences and seek wholeness through harmony with the Subconscious mind. The first step along our journey is awakening the awareness in the Conscious, physical mind to the Subconscious, inner mind. It is time to return our attention to our early love by consciously creating each experience for the purpose of gaining understandings which will be permanently stored in our subconscious minds. As this change occurs, awareness is expanded of who we are.

But you have this much in your favor: you detest the practices of the Nicolaitans, just as I do. Let him who has ears heed the Spirit's word to the churches! I will see to it that the victor eats from the tree of life which grows in the garden of God."

By harmonizing the Conscious and Subconscious minds, we experience direct knowledge of Truth. We think and act in alignment with our purpose for existence, and awareness of Spiritual, Intuitive Man is born. This will lead to constant awareness of who we are and why we exist, the Truth of the mystery of life.

Verses eight through eleven: To Smyrna. To the presiding spirit of the church in Smyrna, write this: The First and the Last who once died but now lives has this to say: I know of your tribulation and your poverty even though you are rich.

With expanded conscious awareness, we begin to acknowledge the inner levels of consciousness. The first of these is the Emotional Level. Described in *Genesis* as the *rib taken from the*

man and used to build up the *woman,* this level of consciousness is
the connecting link between the Subconscious and Conscious
minds. The emotions act in the Subconscious mind to push desires
outward into physical manifestation, and they react in the Conscious
mind as desires are received. When the Conscious mind fails to
cooperate with this natural functioning, it seems that what we want
does not manifest. What we desire does not come about in our lives
and we are poor in spirit, away from the presence of our own divine
nature.

*I know the slander you endure from self-styled Jews who are nothing
other than members of Satan's assembly. Have no fear of the
sufferings to come. The devil will indeed cast some of you into
prison to put you to the test; you will be tried over a period of ten
days. Remain faithful until death and I will give you the crown of
life. Let him who has ears heed the Spirit's word to the churches!
The victor shall never be harmed by the second death.*

Internal conflict arises from conflicting beliefs which damage
our spirituality. When we believe only in the physical part of self,
discounting the inner realms of our existence, we are entrapped in
limitation. It is the ego that will motivate our consciousness beyond
what has already occurred into new awarenesses which will bring
understanding of the emotional level, eventually leading to freedom
from entrapment and the cycle of rebirth. By focusing the attention
upon Spiritual growth, we can more readily accept the manifestation of desires with joy and create new desires that reflect expanded
awareness. Cooperating with the inner Self deepens identification
with the soul and supports the transformations yet to come.

*Verses twelve through seventeen: To Pergamum. To the presiding
spirit of the church of Pergamum, write this: "The One with the
sharp, two-edged sword has this to say: I know you live in the very*

*place where Satan's throne is erected; and I know you hold fast to
my name and have not denied the faith you have in me, not even at
the time when Antipas, my faithful witness, was martyred in your city
where Satan has his home.*

Pergamum is the next inner level termed the Lower Spiritual
Level of Consciousness. Here karmic obligations begin to make
themselves known so that we may experience inner equilibrium and
wholeness. As we become aware of the debts we owe to the whole
Self, we can guide our evolution as Spiritual Man. We become
aware of our individual responsibility for enlightenment—aligning
the ego with the desire to be like our Creator.

*Nevertheless, I hold a few matters against you: there are some
among you who follow the teaching of Balaam, who instructed
Balak to throw a stumbling block in the way of the Israelites by
tempting them to eat food sacrificed to idols and to practice
fornication. Yes, you too have those among you who hold to the
teaching of the Nicolaitans. Therefore repent! If you do not, I will
come to you soon and fight against them with the sword of my mouth.
Let him who has ears heed the Spirit's words to the churches! To
the victor I will give the hidden manna; I will also give him a white
stone upon which is inscribed a new name, to be known only by him
who receives it.*"

The key to karma lies not in the physical action which
causes imbalance or harm to self or others, but rather in the thought
or intention motivating the action. The aspirant no longer dedicates
his life to the pursuit of physical satisfaction, but transforms his
consciousness into the spirit of service to his Creator and his
fellowman. The Self aware individual knows his responsibility to
develop spiritual thinking thus freeing the mind from that which is
temporal and its illusionary rewards. He is willing to cause change
through illuminating thought, will, and action, thus becoming the

architect of his own Karma. His identity is transformed through the use of will power, and knowledge of the Spirit is his.

Verses eighteen through twenty-nine: To Thyatira. To the presiding spirit of the church in Thyatira, write this: "The Son of God, whose eyes blaze like fire and whose feet gleam like polished brass, has this to say: I know your deeds — your love and faith and service — as well as your patient endurance; I know also that your efforts of recent times are greater than ever.

Thyatira is the next inner level, the Higher Spiritual which is the realm of thought reaching toward manifestation. The quality of this level is expansion and all thoughts are touched by its power which we identify as love. As our awareness of who we are grows, our devotion to Spiritual development increases. The labor of gaining understanding quickens as we come to know our Self apart from the physical form.

Nevertheless, I hold this against you: you tolerate a Jezebel — that self-styled prophetess who seduces my servants by teaching them to practice lewdness and to eat food sacrificed to idols. I have given her a chance to repent but she refuses to turn from her lewdness. I mean to cast her down on a bed of pain; her companions in sin I will plunge into intense suffering unless they repent of their sins with her. I mean to cast her down on a bed of pain, and her children I will put to death. Thus shall all the churches come to know that I am the searcher of hearts and minds, and that I will give each of you what your conduct deserves.

The commitment between the Conscious and Subconscious minds for accelerated growth will be tested each time the attention is distracted from the path of enlightenment. Challenges that have previously been ignored or denied reoccur, tempting the Spirit away from its Spiritual nature and destiny. Each time the same mistake is repeated, an opportunity for greater awareness arises. These opportunities must be acknowledged and utilized for the aspirant's growth. As his intelligence births illumined consciousness, productive change occurs and the meaning of life is made known.

And now I address myself to you others in Thyatira who do not uphold this teaching and know nothing of the so-called 'deep secrets' of Satan; on you I place no further burden. In any case, hold fast to what you have until I come.

As the commitment to Spiritual progression becomes all-consuming, the identity of Self transcends limited thinking. The physical is seen for what it is, a place for the soul to learn. The ego is directed by desire-motivation, and the attention is freed from carnal temptations. Responsibility is now known as freedom, and growth is accelerated by using understandings previously gained toward Self awareness and service to mankind.

To the one who wins the victory, who keeps my ways till the end, I will give authority over the nations—the same authority I received from my Father. He shall rule them with a rod of iron and shatter them like crockery; and I will give him the morning star. Let him who has ears heed the Spirit's word to the churches!"

With the birth of Self realization in the inner levels symbolized by these four *churches,* the Spiritual aspirant holds the keys to the cycle of rebirth. He is well-acquainted with the Universal Laws governing evolution, and uses them wisely. This brings authority which only comes from personal experience and understanding. It is the authority that arises from knowing who you are, why you are here and where you are going. This authority is one of the indications of the consciousness becoming illumined.

Chapter Three

Verses one through six: To Sardis. To the presiding spirit of the church in Sardis, write this: The One who holds the seven spirits of God, the seven stars, has this to say: I know your conduct; I know the reputation you have of being alive, when in fact you are dead! Wake up, and strengthen what remains before it dies.

Sardis represents the deepest inner level of the Subconscious mind, the Mental Level. Here all imaged thoughts begin their journey toward physical manifestation. Each consciously created thought is recreated by the inner Subconscious mind. The developing process begins in the Mental Level of Consciousness and moves outward through the levels of the Subconscious mind, gaining substance, until what was imaged is reproduced in the physical life. Ignorance of this innate creative faculty in man leads him to believe that the physical comprises his entire existence — his life, when in Truth his existence comes from the Creator who gives life. Separation from the Creator is the first death of awareness. Until the consciousness is awakened to the Source, man perpetuates his entrapment in the physical which is known as *the second death.*

I find that the sum of your deeds is less than complete in the sight of my God. Call to mind how you accepted what you heard: keep to it, and repent. If you do not rouse yourselves I will come upon you like a thief, at a time you cannot know.

The purpose of the Subconscious mind or soul is to store the understandings of Creation. Activity in the mental level of consciousness is point of cause for what becomes manifested in our physical lives. From the mental level of consciousness, which understandings have been gained through physical lifetime experiences and what understandings have yet to be made a part of the soul can be perceived. The transformation of consciousness to

identify cause gives us the freedom to use reasoning to produce intuition, thus building permanent memory. Understandings which become a part of the soul's memory are integrated into the existence of man's consciousness. It is each individual's responsibility to expand awareness to include the direct grasp of Truth. When the awareness remains the same, unchanging, the Truth eludes us and another lifetime comes and goes.

I realize that you have in Sardis a few persons who have not soiled their garments; these shall walk with me in white because they are worthy. The victor shall go clothed in white, I will never erase his name from the book of the living, but will acknowledge him in the presence of my Father and his angels. Let him who has ears heed the Spirit's word to the churches!

Those who pursue awareness, whose ideal of life is constant opportunity for soul progression, refine their imaginative faculties. They understand the purpose for their existence is spiritual maturity. They know they are valuable as an offspring of the Creator. Each thought embodies these ideals and practices, and the nature of what the Bhagavad Gita calls the *Real Self* becomes known. Such a person communes with the Creator and his activities reflect a sacred service to God and all of mankind.

Verses seven through fourteen: To Philadelphia. To the presiding spirit of the church in Philadelphia, write this: The holy One, the true, who wields David's key, who opens and no one can close, who closes and no one can open, has this to say. I know your deeds; that is why I have left an open door before you which no one can close. I know that your strength is limited; yet you have held fast to my word and have not denied my name.

Philadelphia symbolizes the next inner level, the Causal Level of Consciousness. The Causal Level exists beyond the

Subconscious mind, in what we shall term the Superconscious mind. Here, an outpouring of life force energizes the inner levels of the Subconscious mind ultimately reaching the Conscious mind. By embracing the Universal Truth, *As Above, So Below,* the consciousness is expanded to understand the relationship of Self and others, reasoning and intuition, yesterday and tomorrow, light and darkness. What the Gita calls the pairs of opposites become part of the journey toward enlightenment.

I mean to make some of Satan's assembly, those self-styled Jews who are not really Jews but frauds, come and fall down at your feet; they will learn of my love for you in that way. Because you have kept my plea to stand fast, I will keep you safe in the time of trial which is coming on the whole world, to test all men on earth. I am coming soon. Hold fast to what you have lest someone rob you of your crown.

As awareness expands into this level of consciousness, the existence of Self beyond the physical is made known. The identity of who you are transcends the limits of the physical ego's motivations, entering the domain of motivation from the desire for enlightenment. Those who hold this singular vision use the Universal Law of Proper Perspective in each thought and action. What at one time was seen as an obstacle is transformed into a challenge; what were limitations become stepping stones on the journey toward the second coming of Christ.

I will make the victor a pillar in the temple of my God and he shall never leave it. I will inscribe on him the name of my God and the name of the city of my God, the new Jerusalem which he will send down from heaven, and my own name which is new. Let him who has ears heed the Spirit's word to the churches!

For those who remain steadfast in their journey, Spiritual

Man is a reality. Communion with the Creator becomes his greatest joy and consummate bliss fills his consciousness. He is truly in the world, but not of it. His identity is that of a Son of God, and his brilliance radiates in every thought and action.

Verses fourteen through twenty-two: To Laodicea. To the presiding spirit of the church in Laodicea, write this: The Amen, the faithful Witness and true, the Source of God's creation, has this to say.

Laodicea is the Christ Consciousness. The deepest level of mind, the Christ Consciousness or Buddha Consciousness or Cosmic Consciousness, is the part of Self closest to the Spiritual origin. When the awareness expands to include this level of consciousness the Source of creation is known and the aspirant stands in the presence of God. **This is the second coming of the Christ, the return with full awareness to our origin as a Thinker.**

I know your deeds; I know you are neither hot nor cold. How I wish you were one or the other - hot or cold! But because you are lukewarm, neither hot nor cold, I will spew you out of my mouth. You keep saying, 'I am so rich and secure that I want for nothing'. Little do you realize how wretched you are, how pitiable and poor, how blind and naked.

Awareness of Christ Consciousness transcends the pairs of opposites. The journey to full enlightenment requires that the aspirant be sentient of value and stability, perception and wisdom. An enthralling sense of humbleness fills the Self when this level of consciousness is experienced.

Take my advice. Buy from me gold refined by fire if you would be truly rich. Buy white garments in which to be clothed, if the shame of your nakedness is to be covered. Buy ointment to smear on your eyes, if you would see once more. Whoever is dear to me I reprove and chastise. Be earnest about it, therefore. Repent!

Through Self control and Self discipline, the *Real Self* is known. All energy is given freely and completely toward making the Self worthy of enlightenment, purifying wisdom and causing the perception to become whole. Living in accord with the Universal Laws reveals the purpose for our existence and the need for Spiritual discipline.

Here I stand, knocking at the door. If anyone hears me calling and opens the door, I will enter his house and have supper with him, and he with me. I will give the victor the right to sit with me on my throne, as I myself won the victory and took my seat beside my Father on his throne. Let him who has ears heed the Spirit's word to the churches!'

Reasoning Man's destiny for evolution is clear. The Superconscious mind holds the blueprint for each individual's evolution to become compatible to his Maker. This blueprint stimulates a constant inner urge toward enlightenment. As we discipline and still the outer consciousness, freeing our attention to be directed in the inner levels of consciousness, we gain the inner vision of this destiny. We become attentive to the true need of the Self by listening and responding to our inner urge. Through meditation and service, we can expect to *"Be still and know that I Am God."*

Chapter Four reveals the vision of Heavenly Worship and describes the preparation for the day of the Lord. Having knowledge of the inner levels of consciousness excites the desire for deeper states of Self awareness and opens the mind to the presence of divinity. The individual's readiness to receive this revelation depends upon his willingness toward Self control and Self discipline. By stilling the mind of activity, the ideal of wholeness and communion with the Creator is perceived. *The day of the Lord* is the Sabbath.

It is first referenced in the second chapter of the first book of the Bible, *God blessed the Sabbath day and made it holy, because on it he rested from all the work of creating that he had done.*

For the spiritual aspirant, the desire to be like the Spiritual Parent grows increasingly stronger with each meditation. Each moment devoted to communion with the Creator serves to prepare the consciousness for the spiritual work ahead. Through constant dedication, the ideal becomes clearer, the purpose more resolved, and the activity of creating reflects this illumined consciousness. Every thought and every action produces spiritual maturity and prepares the aspirant for the greater freedoms and responsibilities of becoming compatible to his Creator.

Reasoning is a sequence of events in thought producing experience which leads to understanding creation. It can be learned and taught. Intuition is also a sequence of events in thought characterized by drawing upon these permanent understandings. Intuition is the direct grasp of Truth demonstrated by one who has evolved to Spiritual Man. It can also be learned and taught. *The Book of Revelation* offers systematic instruction in the step-by-step transformation of Reasoning Man into Spiritual Man.

Chapter Four reveals the Spiritual ideal Man is to attain, therefore the purpose for his existence. The reasoner has prepared the Self by expanding his conscious awareness beyond only the physical existence. He has come to accept that he is a spiritual being entrusted with a physical lifetime which can, through Self transformation, lead to enlightenment and communion with his Maker. Knowing our spiritual ideal, we are now prepared for the next spiritual initiation which reveals the caliber of the aspirant who sincerely desires the second coming of the Christ, the Buddha, the Enlightened One.

Such a One realizes an inner urge for compatibility with the Creator in every part of His being. The singular purpose of

Enlightenment is shared by the I AM *(the One)* and the worth-filled individual *(the lamb)*, the authority of the Self is finally whole. Through virtue *(praise)*, esteem *(honor)*, awareness *(glory)*, and will power *(might)*, the alignment of the conscious identity or ego and the I AM Ego has been accomplished. This alignment will be respected by the inner workings of the Subconscious mind *(the four living creatures)* from this time forward. The Subconscious mind will reproduce what is necessary for the individual to achieve his earnest desire for Enlightenment, and will give all of its understandings toward that state of Being. Thus the seeker will know Self as made in the likeness and image of his Creator; the extent of his ability to create.

This initiation brings new awareness of the meaning and capacity for love. Because of this growth, the major aspects of the outer minds — the Conscious and Subconscious minds *(the elders)* — can now acknowledge the true meaning of love *(worship)* freed from attachment. The aspirant understands love from a point of cause and is no longer entrapped by its effects. Having understood experiences of conditional and unconditional love, he now knows love as a kelson of creation. As never before, he understands the reason for his Creator's creating; for he at last understands his own. Having arrived at this point of spiritual initiation, the individual is ready to expand his or her consciousness in the inner levels of mind revealed in Chapter Six.

Chapter Six

The First Six Seals. Then I watched while the Lamb broke open the first of the seven seals, and I heard one of the four living creatures cry out in a voice like thunder, "Come forward!"

The *I* in *Revelation* is the author, *John,* who symbolizes any individual who believes he is more than a physical being. He has faith in his destiny as an enlightened spiritual being; a Christ, a Buddha, a Zarathustra. In the Universal Language of Mind the *Lamb* represents the Conscious mind subject to the dictates of Universal Law. The *Lamb* is anyone who is moving away from compulsive thinking toward Self awareness, realizing thought as cause.

The *seven seals on the scroll* symbolize the keys that unlock permanent memory. What is stored in permanent memory are the understandings in each level of consciousness that are needed to be compatible to the Creator. The *opening of the first seal* addresses the understandings found in the physical level of consciousness. The *four living creatures* symbolize the inner workings of the Subconscious mind. These are the four qualities of the expression of energies: the *eagle* representing motion, the *lion* representing expansion, the *ox* representing contraction, and the *man* representing stability or inertia.

To my surprise I saw a white horse; its rider had a bow, and he was given a crown. He rode forth victorious to conquer yet again.

The *white horse* symbolizes the use of will power. Conscious will power, cultivated and developed, moves the individual (*the rider*) beyond compulsive thinking into Self awareness. Its *rider* had a bow indicates the Conscious mind has a desire or goal to be achieved. Each decision made in alignment with the spiritual ideal of becoming whole brings authority born from understanding to the individual and symbolized by the *crown*. *He rode forth victorious to conquer yet* again symbolizes the repeated process of rebirth or reincarnation. The inertia of rebirth, symbolized by the *living creature,* continues until karmic understandings are made a part of Self and the ideal is achieved.

When the Lamb broke open the second seal, I heard the second living creature cry out, 'Come forward!' Another horse came forth, a red one. Its rider was given the power to rob the earth of peace by allowing men to slaughter one another. For this he was given a huge sword.

The *second seal* symbolizes the understandings in the sixth level of consciousness, the emotional level. This level connects the inner Subconscious mind to the outer Conscious mind during incarnation. It enables the consciously imaged thoughts which have been reproduced through the subconscious levels to be manifested into the physical level. Therefore, the emotions act in the Subconscious mind and re-act in the Conscious mind. The *red horse* symbolizes the aspirant's will acting in the emotional level. Its *rider was given the power to rob the earth of peace* indicates the individual's ability to use or misuse emotion producing calmness or turmoil. The changes required for full mastery of the emotions will continue (*by allowing men to slaughter one another*) until all karmic obligations, symbolized by the huge sword, are fulfilled. This contraction of rebirth is symbolized by the *second living creature*.

When the Lamb broke open the third seal, I heard the third living creature cry out, "Come forward." This time I saw a black horse, the rider of which held a pair of scales in his hand. I heard what seemed to be a voice coming from in among the four living creatures. It said: "A day's pay for a ration of wheat and the same for three of barley! But spare the olive oil and the wine!"

The *third seal* symbolizes the understandings in the fifth level of consciousness, the lower spiritual level, which is the beginning of the physical. The *black horse* shows the receptive use of will, the individual's readiness to receive for intended action. The *rider holding a pair of scales in his hand* symbolizes the individual's understanding of the pairs of opposites. He understands the purpose of when to give and when to receive, when to act and when to expectantly wait. The *scales* also indicate an accounting of what has been completed and what has yet to be accomplished; what karma has been fulfilled and what obligations remain. This assessment is made at the end of each lifetime.

The *voice coming from in among the four living creatures* symbolizes consciousness expansion; the judgement of Self. This judgement is the assessment which includes *a day's pay for a ration of wheat* indicating the value of awareness gained during incarnation. *And the same for three of barley* shows the value of awareness is gained through what has been created with the knowledge gained. The *olive oil* and the *wine* symbolize the understandings gained through incarnation that have become a part of permanent memory and are thus spared. These understandings are now a part of the individual for all of eternity.

When the Lamb broke open the fourth seal, I heard the voice of the fourth living creature cry out, "Come forward!" Now I saw a pale horse. Its rider was named Death, and the nether world was in his train. They were given authority over one quarter of the earth, to kill with sword and famine and plague and the wild beasts of the earth.

The *fourth seal* symbolizes the understandings in the fourth level of consciousness, the higher spiritual level. The *pale horse* symbolizes the will in this level of consciousness which is the end of the mental consciousness. Its *rider was named Death* symbolizes the individual bound to the cycle of rebirth; his entrapment in the physical. Now the aspirant is aware that thought is cause and the physical is its manifest likeness symbolized by *the nether world was in his train.* The *four riders,* commonly called the four horsemen of the apocalypse, are *given authority over one quarter of the earth:*

the northern quarter, the western quarter, the southern quarter, and the eastern quarter, representing the four levels of the Subconscious mind. The will in these levels must be mastered to complete the cycle of rebirth *(kill with sword)*, to add knowledge of creation to Self *(famine)*, to become whole *(plague)*, and to become aware of Self as a Creator *(wild beasts of the earth)*.

When the Lamb broke open the fifth seal, I saw under the altar the spirits of those who had been martyred because of the witness they bore to the word of God. They cried out at the top of their voices; How long will it be, O Master, holy and true, before you judge our cause and avenge our blood among the inhabitants of the earth?

The *opening of the fifth seal* is realization of understandings held in the third level of consciousness, the mental level. This level is the innermost expression of energy in the Subconscious mind and is closest to the Superconscious mind which holds the blueprint for the individual's maturation as a Creator. In this level the attention *(altar)* is directed toward the completion of rebirth in the earthly plane. The individual's focus is nurturing and understanding his relationship with his Maker symbolized by those who had been martyred because of the witness they bore to the word of God. What is most important to the aspirant is the acceleration of spiritual evolution *(How long will it be, O Master, holy and true)*. The way to accomplish this is known — causing all aspects in the Conscious and Subconscious mind to work toward the ideal *(before you judge our cause and avenge our blood among the inhabitants of the earth.)*

Each of the martyrs was given a long white robe and they were told to be patient a little while longer until the quota was filled of their fellow servants and brothers to be slain, as they had been.

The *martyrs* symbolize the awareness of who I AM gained by sacrificing attachment for understanding that leads to enlightenment. Eventually all parts of Self *(their fellow servants and brothers to be slain)* will transcend the bounds of incarnation and enter into the awareness of omnipresence and eternal life.

When I saw the Lamb break open the sixth seal there was a violent earthquake; the sun turned black as a goat's hair tentcloth and the moon grew red as blood. The stars in the sky fell crashing to earth like figs shaken loose by a mighty wind. Then the sky disappeared as if it were a scroll being rolled up; every mountain and island was uprooted from its base.

The *sixth seal* symbolizes the understanding in one of the two levels of consciousness which comprise the Superconscious mind; the causal level of consciousness. The causal level provides the outpouring of spirit that energizes the outer parts of mind: the Subconscious mind and ultimately the Conscious mind. This outpouring produces changes in the substance of mind symbolized by a *violent earthquake*. The interactions of prana and akasha transform the outer, physical consciousness *(the stars in the sky fell crashing to earth)*. The awareness of the Superconscious mind *(the sun turned black as a goat's hair tentcloth)* and the Subconscious mind *(the moon grew red as blood)* are altered. Now the greater plan, housed in the Superconscious mind, is apparent indicated by the sky disappeared as if it were a scroll being rolled up. No longer do old limitations *(every mountain and island)* obscure the vision from the destiny as an offspring of the Creator. The individual has become aware of who he is and who he is to become as a spiritual being. He now understands what lies beyond the fulfillment of karmic obligations.

The kings of the earth, the nobles and those in command, the wealthy and powerful, the slave and the free — all hid themselves in caves and mountain crags. They cried out to the mountains and rocks,

"Fall on us! Hide us from the face of the One who sits on the throne and from the wrath of the Lamb! The great day of vengeance has come. Who can withstand it?"

This new awareness forever alters how the individual perceives himself and his world. He now knows the purpose for his existence. He realizes the need to fully control the senses *(kings of the earth)*, the intelligence *(nobles and those in command)*, the value and authority *(wealthy and powerful)*, the compulsiveness and creativity *(slave and free)* of Self. The *opening of the sixth seal* brings a new cooperation in fulfilling the spiritual ideal of Self that was previously unknown. All aspects of Self now yield to the greater purpose for existence that has been revealed *(hide us from the face of the One who sits on the throne and from the wrath of the Lamb)*. It is now time to return to the source with full awareness; a second coming of the Christ consciousness. This is the meaning of *the great day of vengeance.*

Chapter Six reveals the symbolic meaning of the first six seals, the understandings permanently stored in the six outer levels of the individuals consciousness. Awareness of these understandings precedes Enlightenment. This awareness of the inner parts of Self reveals the highest purpose for existence: a return to the Source, with full awareness, which is the second coming of the Christ or Buddha or Cosmic Consciousness.

Chapter Seven builds on this by revealing how the unity of Self is established toward a singular ideal and purpose. All parts of Self *(the 144,000)* are finally under the direction of the thinker, the Real Self, thus every part of Self responds to the vision of spiritual destiny now realized in the Conscious mind. All desire *(hunger and thirst)* is focused toward the ideal of becoming compatible to the Creator. All awareness *(the sun)* is aligned with the greater inner awareness of Christ consciousness. Now the individual *(the lamb)* is prepared to cause the forward motion which will complete the learning on the earthly plane, thus freeing the Self from the bonds of karmic indenture. As this occurs, the individual comes to know the nature and origin of life beyond the physical existence *(springs of life-giving water.)* The pleasure and pain of the physical learning, the pairs of opposites, are transcended and the essence of creation is perceived *(God will wipe every tear from their eyes.)*

Chapter Six of *Revelation* describes the opening of the *first six seals*. The *seven seals on the scroll* symbolize the keys that unlock permanent memory. The *Lamb* is any individual who realizes thought is cause and is moving toward Enlightenment and Illumination. It is not until Chapter Eight that the seventh and final seal is broken. The opening of *the seventh seal* is the realization of understandings held in the first level of consciousness, the Christ consciousness or Buddha consciousness or Cosmic consciousness. This is the innermost part of mind, the level of consciousness that is closest to the Source, the Creator. The *opening of this seal* is the second coming of the Christ. The *first coming* was the movement outward and away from the source which resulted in the creation of identity and all of mind. The *second coming* is the result of the Conscious mind's effort toward fulfilling the thinker's destiny of becoming compatible with his Maker. It is the returning with awareness to the Christ level of consciousness. The *silence in heaven for about half an hour* symbolizes the stilling of the whole mind which enables the aspirant to be One, to know God.

"Then, as I watched, the seven angels who minister in God's presence were given seven trumpets." Upon receiving this experience of being One, the aspirant now becomes aware of the means to create this wholeness at will. The *seven angels* who minister in God's presence symbolize the cause of creation — thought directed by God-intelligence. The *angels* are given *seven trumpets* which represent the means to transform the energy of

matter into thought. The aspirant will need this knowledge and ability to transcend the limits of physical matter and complete his earthly schooling. These *trumpets* are commonly referred to as the seven major chakras, seven energy transformers required for the continual functioning of man as a thinker.

Chapter Eight goes on to reveal the cause of creation as symbolized by the first four of seven *angels who minister in God's presence*. These angels each *blow a trumpet* which symbolizes what causes the transformation of thought into matter and matter into thought. There is a definite and intentional break between the first four angels and the remaining three that is revealed in Chapter Nine. This symbolizes the separateness of function between the physical Self and the spiritual Self, the four lower chakras and the three upper chakras. When the thinker has reached this point in awareness he is prepared to embrace thought as cause in every mental action, without hesitation or question. His consciousness is becoming identified with that of the Creator.

Chapter Nine

The Fifth Trumpet. Then the fifth angel blew his trumpet, and I saw a star fall from the sky to the earth. The star was given the key to the shaft of the abyss.

The *blowing of the trumpets* symbolizes the ability to transfer energy from thought to energy. The fifth trumpet is the opening of the Vissudha, the throat chakra. This *fifth angel* symbolizes the capacity to express Self through thought. By knowing the thoughts of Self awareness is born. By creating the thoughts Self awareness is matured. This is why *this star is given the key to the shaft of the abyss* symbolizing the will to mold the mind — to shape the Self.

He opened it and smoke poured out of the shaft like smoke from an enormous furnace. The sun and the air were darkened by the smoke from the shaft.

The initial attempts to set the direction of the mind *(opening the shaft)* leads to consciously misusing the will. Becoming caught up in physical pleasures and pains, people and possessions, leads to engrossment and the belief that the physical is all there is *(the sun and air were darkened...).*

Out of the smoke, onto the land, came locusts as powerful as scorpions in their sting. The locusts were commanded to do no harm to the grass in the land or to any plant or tree but only to those men who had not the seal of God on their foreheads.

When the will is employed the sense of the mind — the attention — is directed as symbolized by the smoke. The aspirant now embodies the Truth "You are where your attention is." The compulsive nature of instinct *(locusts)* has served man well throughout the first four stages of evolution thus no harm to the grass or to any plant or tree has been done. However in order for man to evolve from the fifth stage of Reasoning Man to the sixth stage of Intuitive Man, this instinct must be understood. The *seal of God on their foreheads* points to the pituitary gland, the master gland of the body, which is used by the mind of man for reasoning. Intuition is produced by the complete use of reasoning. This ability to rise above instinct is what separates man from all other animals and life forms. The ability is centered in man's conscious use of will.

The locusts were not allowed to kill them but only to torture them for five months; the pain they inflicted was like that of a scorpion's sting. During that time these men will seek death but will not find it; they will yearn to die but death will escape them.

As long as man remains compulsive in his thought and expression, he is subject to the dictates of animal instinct. Because man is capable of reasoning, instinct merely offers a stimulus for learning *(torture them for five months)*. When the stimulus is ignored there is pain because there is no change. Even when change *(death)* is desired it does not come until it is caused.

In appearance the locusts were like horses equipped for battle. On their heads they wore something like gold crowns; their faces were like men's faces but they had hair like women's hair. Their teeth were like the teeth of lions, their chests like iron breastplates. Their wings made a sound like the roar of many chariots and horses charging into battle. They had tails with stingers like scorpion's, in their tails was enough venom to harm men for five months.

Man's compulsiveness is a manifestation of will *(like horses)*. The value *(gold)* lies in the ability to use intelligence *(heads)* to direct the will, thus the power *(crown)* of decision and directing the mind. This fashions the expression *(faces)* of physical Self; the means of communicating who you are. When this is used well, all knowledge can be assimilated *(lion's teeth)* and made a permanent part *(breastplate)* of Self. Every challenge can and will be met until full awareness is attained symbolized by the *time period of five months.*

Acting as their king was the angel in charge of the abyss, whose name in Hebrew is Abaddon and in Greek Apollyon.

The righteous or correct use of the will can only be attained when the controlling thought *(angel)* is aligned with the Superconscious mind which is symbolized by Abaddon/Apollyon. Apollo was the Sun God representing the part of Self closest to the Creator which we identify as the Superconscious mind.

The Sixth Trumpet. The first woe is past, but beware! There are two more to come.

The *three woes* are the challenges that must be met and understood to become a Creator. The *first woe* symbolizes the righteous use of will and the freedom that brings; the end of entrapment in the cycle of rebirth. The *two woes* are revealed with the sixth and seventh trumpets.

Then the sixth angel blew his trumpet, and I heard a voice coming from between the horns of the altar of gold in God's presence. It said to the sixth angel, who was still holding his trumpet, Release the four angels who are tied up on the banks of the great river Euphrates.

The *sixth angel* is a thought arising from the Superconscious mind as symbolized by *the voice coming from...God's presence.* This is the desire to be like our Creator. The Euphrates is one of the four branches of the river which rises in Eden noted in *Genesis* Chapter 2. The *Euphrates* symbolizes the Kundalini, the creative power in man. The *four angels* are the governing thoughts of the four lower chakras discussed in the previous chapter of *Revelation.* Releasing these angels indicates the energy of the Heart, Solar Plexus, Adrenal/Spleen, and Root Chakras can now be dedicated to serving the destiny of the Self to become Enlightened. No longer are we bound to fulfillment of physical desires.

So the four angels were released; this was precisely the hour, the day, the month and the year for which they had been prepared, to kill a third of mankind. Their cavalry troops, whose count I heard, were two hundred million in number — a number I heard myself.

Enlightenment is the reason the lower chakras were created. Once man became entrapped in the physical there had to be a way to continue learning and achieve his destiny. The chakras enabled man to learn by manifesting his thoughts into physical reality where he can experience and gain understanding. The chakras return the energy used in manifestation back into the inner levels of mind, constantly replenishing the reservoirs for future creation and learning. The chakras are a means to *"see God face to face"* as Jacob did in the *Old Testament. Killing a third of mankind* symbolizes transforming the Conscious, physical mind through disciplining the will *(calvary troops)* to utilize the aggressive and receptive qualities with full understanding *(two million).*

Now in my vision, this is how I saw the horses and their riders. The breastplates they wore were fiery red, deep blue, and pale yellow. The horses' heads were like heads of lions, and out of their mouths came fire and sulphur and smoke. By these three plagues — the smoke and sulphur and fire which shot out of their mouths — a third of mankind was slain. The deadly power of the horses was not only in their mouths but in their tails, for their tails were like snakes with heads poised to strike.

The *sixth angel* is the opening of Ajna, the Brow Chakra. This is the inner urge toward insight. The Kundalini energy must be directed through insight, devoted to enlightenment. This is accomplished by the description of the horses and riders. When interpreted in the Universal Language of Mind, the way to gain insight is clear. The *riders* are the controlling thoughts of each chakra and the *horse* is the implementation of the thought through will. The *breastplates* are the understanding of body/emotion, spirit/spirituality, and mental/intelligence symbolized by the *three primary colors.* Intelligence *(heads)* and will *(horse)* spark the three ingredients of reasoning *(plagues):* imagination *(fire),* memory *(sulphur),* and attention *(smoke).* By employing reasoning, the Conscious mind changes; it matures *(one third mankind is slain). The deadly power* is wisdom *(like snakes).* Wisdom is gained when reasoning produces understandings that can then be shared in the life.

That part of mankind which escaped the plagues did not repent of the idols they had made. They did not give up the worship of demons, or of gods made from gold and silver, from bronze and stone and wood, which cannot see or hear or walk.

When reasoning is missing in the Conscious mind, stagnation occurs — the self remains unchanged. In such a state of mind we remain trapped by physical desires — erroneously believing a person, place, idea, possession, position, is more important than our relationship with our Creator. These physical objects are gods before our God — idols. *Worshipping demons* represents stubbornly holding onto old, egoic ways of thinking — refusing to change the identity.

Neither did they repent of their murders or their sorcery, their fornication or their thefts.

Therefore there is no change *(repent)* from the tendency to misuse God's laws; the Universal Laws of Creation. In *Exodus* in the *Old Testament,* many of those Laws are described in the ten commandments given to Moses: 1] Thou shalt not kill is the *murder* cited here, 2] *thou shalt have no other gods before me* is sorcery, 3] *thou shalt not commit adultery* is fornication, and 4] *thou shalt not steal* is the thefts.

In the language of mind these symbolize: 1] Constant awareness, everlasting life, realizing death is anything that keeps you from the presence of your Creator, for instance perpetuating your entrapment in the physical. 2] Honor your Spiritual heritage and strive toward maturity becoming like the Creator who brought you into existence. 3] Establish and live, in your Conscious and Subconscious minds, a commitment which leads toward enlightenment. Strive for complete understanding with every thought and deed. 4] Give and receive fully thus acknowledging the value and importance of service. These four are the changes yet to be made by one who desires complete Enlightenment.

In the tenth chapter of *Revelation,* the individual who is striving to evolve his consciousness to become Christ-like assumes the responsibility of who he is subconsciously and consciously, as a soul as well as a body. What has been made a part of Self throughout time and existence, the understandings gained and stored as permanent memory, comprise the aspirant's spiritual foundation of which he has become aware. Now the commitment must be made to use those understandings for the spiritual progression of Self and the betterment of humanity.

Once the commitment is made solely toward spiritual progression, the secrets of the Superconscious mind are revealed. Chapter Eleven describes these by relating the story, the history, of the Creator's gifts to mankind — existence and free will as symbolized by the *Two Witnesses.* Upon undertaking the celestial responsibility of one's spiritual evolution, all of mind is focused toward the fulfillment of destiny. This unlocks the transference of the highest energies available to man, symbolized by the Crown Chakra symbolized by the *seventh trumpet.* These energies reveal the Source of all Creation. Here you, as Jacob once did, *"meet God face to face"* and your life is spared. Self is now directed toward sacred service *(twenty-four elders)* because you know the history of the two witnesses and the secret of spiritual evolution.

This chapter is an assessment of the evolution of one's Spiritual being. It is an accounting of how the Self has progressed in maturing to become compatible with the Source of its existence; its Creator. The individual has always been empowered with the sense of his own existence and awareness of his right to choose because of this s/he must meet and conquer any limitation. The awareness that our spiritual evolution has been, is, and will always be in our own hands is awesome. To know that the attainment of peace and elimination of suffering is by our own choice is remarkable. It is this recognition who "I Am" that prepares the way for the transformation the ego must endure as revealed in Chapter Twelve. All of mind is now focused upon the ideal of Enlightenment — the fulfillment of spiritual destiny — as revealed in "The Woman and the Dragon."

Chapter Twelve

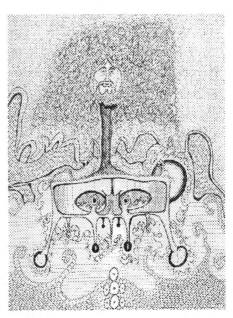

The Woman and the Dragon. A great sign appeared in the sky, a woman clothed with the sun, with the moon under her feet, and on her head a crown of twelve stars.

Because the full intention is now focused upon Self revelation the destiny becomes clearer. The seeker realizes his destiny *(great sign)* lies in the fulfillment of the seed idea of a fully matured Self; the Superconscious plan for Self *(appearing in the sky)* to become compatible to its maker. This destiny is awareness in the Conscious, waking mind *(woman)* of its origin in the Superconscious mind *(clothed with the sun)*. The Conscious mind exists only because there is a Superconscious mind. In other words, the Conscious mind would not exist were it not for the innermost Superconscious mind which is the divine spark from its Creator. When the Conscious mind is aware of its origin, it is also aware of the manifestations of consciousness which we have spoken of many times in our interpretations of *Revelation* as the levels of Subconscious mind and the physical. The Conscious mind symbolized by the *woman* represents the seeker who is aware of the subconscious *(moon)* spiritual foundation *(feet)* and who has gained control *(crown)* of creation in the physical *(twelve stars)*.

Because she was with child, she wailed aloud in pain as she labored to give birth.

As in *Genesis* when the Lord God told the woman she would bring forth children with pain, so the woman in *Revelation* labors to bear a child. In the Universal Language of Mind the *woman* symbolizes the Conscious, waking mind and her offspring are new ideas. Every idea conceived and imaged by the Conscious mind is a seed idea that is planted in the substance of the Subconscious mind. There the idea grows in and through subconsciousness until the seed is matured and ready for manifestation in your physical life. Here the Conscious mind is preparing to receive such an idea manifested from the inner levels of Self's consciousness.

Then another sign appeared in the sky: it was a huge dragon, flaming red, with seven heads and ten horns; on his heads were seven diadems.

To understand this new idea another part of the destiny *(great sign)* is revealed. This destiny is the role the ego *(huge dragon)*, or sense of identity, will play in the quest for Enlightenment. It is revealed the ego expresses through the e-motion *(flaming red)*, through all levels of consciousness *(the seven heads)*, and uses all forms of energy or chakras *(ten horns)*. Most revealing is the *crowns on the seven heads* indicating an understanding and control of identity in each level of consciousness. The aspirant now has some command of who he is beyond the present, beyond the physical identity, and this will cause a great transformation in how he sees himself.

His tail swept a third of the stars from the sky and hurled them down to the earth. Then the dragon stood before the woman about to give birth, ready to devour her child when it should be born. She gave birth to a son — a boy destined to shepherd all the nations with an iron rod. Her child was caught up to God and to his throne.

The duty of the ego is to motivate (*his tail swept...*), to stimulate the mind into action. This has been true since the moment of creation as Light, the point of origin of awareness. Outwardly, the ego's action is easily recognizable as tempting the Conscious mind to fulfill its duty; reasoning. This is demonstrated earlier in the Bible when the ego *(serpent)* stimulates the Conscious mind *(woman)* to remember (*Did God tell you not to eat of any of the fruit in the garden?"*) and to imagine (*"God knows well that when you eat of it your eyes will be opened and you will be as god"*). In *Revelation*, the individual's desire *"to be like"* — the expression of the ego — remains strong as Enlightenment draws closer thus the dragon stands ready to devour the woman's child. The new idea produced is aggressive or intent upon motion *(boy)* and specifically the motion is in alignment with the destiny of the Self *(caught up to God)*. This idea is the destiny of every individual: To aggressively direct all parts of Self *(nation)* to function in harmony with the laws of creation *(fron rod)*.

The woman herself fled into the desert, where a special place had been prepared for her by God, there she was taken care of for twelve hundred and sixty days.

Once this idea of governing the Self according to Universal

Law is produced in the Conscious mind, the consciousness is expanded *(woman fleeing to the desert)* to embrace all of creation *(place prepared by God).* It requires an understanding *(twelve)* of this expanded consciousness and an exercising of this consciousness through service *(sixty)* to others for it to become a permanent part of the awareness.

Then war broke out in heaven; Michael and his angels battled against the dragon. Although the dragon and his angels fought back, they were overpowered and lost their place in heaven.

When the new awareness is attained the Superconscious mind is experienced as never before. You are closer to God than ever before. Your ego is transformed as signified by the *conflict between Michael and his angels* (the true expression of Ego often referred to as I AM) and the *dragon* (the habitual expression of ego used to identify the self until this time). In Hindu teachings this war and the battle are described in many sacred passages as the pairs of opposites. Learning how to *"be in the world but not of it"* as Jesus taught is the essence of learning to bear the pairs of opposites with equanimity, acknowledging light and dark, pleasure and pain, hot and cold, without attachment to any of them. Such awareness brings understanding of the Law of Duality which is one part of Enlightenment.

The huge dragon, the ancient serpent known as the devil or Satan, the seducer of the whole world, was driven out; he was hurled down to earth and his minions with him.

In the Universal Language of Mind, this verse links the beginning of the Bible in *Genesis* to the end of the Bible in *Revelation.* The journey of one Self, one entity, one part of Creation, is described in great detail in the Bible beginning with *Genesis* which means "origin". Throughout the *Old Testament,* man's development from his creation as light through the evolution of Animal Man bodies — such as what is currently known as Neanderthal and Homo Sapiens — with the brain capacity for reasoning is revealed in symbolic language. The *New Testament* reveals how to live as a reasoning being to produce intuition and ultimately Enlightenment. This is told through the very early and very late years of the life of the Master Jesus who became known as the Christ. In this verse in *Revelation* we learn that the dragon of *Revelation* is the same as the ancient serpent who first appeared in the Garden of Eden in the book of *Genesis*. Both symbolize the urge for individual identity and independence characteristic of the ego. The word ego comes from the Latin meaning "I am." This urge toward self-expression has motivated all parts of Self *(the whole world)* throughout evolution for evolution. And this continues to be true as long as there is a need for the Conscious and Subconscious parts of mind *(the earth)*.

Then I heard a loud voice in heaven say: Now have salvation and power come, the reign of our God and the authority of his Anointed One. For the accuser of our brothers is cast out, who night and day accused them before our God. They defeated him by the blood of the Lamb and by the word of their testimony; love for life did not deter them from death. So rejoice, you heavens, and you that dwell therein! But woe to you, earth and sea, for the devil has come down upon you! His fury knows no limits, for he knows his time is short.

The individual never loses his ego. His ego dies many times in a figurative sense, changing with each stage of maturity like an adolescent who leaves childhood behind to embrace adulthood. However at this point the individual has achieved a major transformation in his understanding of his identity signified by the Anointed One. No longer is the aspirant dependent upon the ego for the motivation to reason and progress *(the accuser..)*. Rather now the seeker is desire motivated which means he reasons at will and is therefore in control of the rate of his evolution *(he knows his time is short).*

When the dragon saw that he had been cast down to the earth, he pursued the woman who had given birth to the boy. But the woman was given the wings of a gigantic eagle so that she could fly off to her place in the desert, where, far from the serpent she could be taken care of for a year and for two and a half years more.

Now the ego *(dragon)* will provide the momentum for the Conscious mind *(pursuing the woman)* who has given rise to the new idea *(the boy):* to aggressively direct all parts of Self to function in harmony with the laws of creation. The consciousness has been expanded to embrace all of creation so the Conscious mind now has a freedom of movement *(given wings).* This awareness of creation and your place in it is the quality that enables you to relinquish ego motivation and bring forth desire motivation that will lead to wisdom *(three and a half years).*

The serpent, however, spewed a torrent of water out of his mouth to search out the woman and sweep her away. The earth then came to the woman's rescue by opening its mouth and swallowing the flood which the dragon spewed out of his mouth. Enraged at her escape, the dragon went off to make war on the rest of her offspring, on those who keep God's commandments and give witness to Jesus. He took up his position by the shore of the sea.

The results of many ego-motivated, physical experiences *(torrent of water)* have been stored as part of the Subconscious mind substance or soul *(the earth opening up).* The ego has fulfilled its duty of ensuring soul progression until sufficient understanding brings about a Conscious mind that is willing to reason from desire rather than habit. From now forward, the Conscious mind — being desire motivated — will direct the ego. The ego will continue to provide motivation *(make war)* for the fulfillment of ideals *(her offspring)*. The identity of the Self at last transcends the physical-ness of men. It is now firmly seated in the spirit as an offspring of a Creator *(keep God's commandments)* who is to become a creator *(give witness to Jesus)*. From this time forward the sense of ego serves the whole Self *(taking his position)* and we are prepared — as is revealed in Chapter Thirteen — to use the Conscious mind in ways never before realized.

Chapter Thirteen

Verses one through ten: The First Beast. Then I saw a wild beast come out of the sea with ten horns and seven heads;
Here the imagery of *Revelation* truly comes alive. To transform the motivating power of the ego from physical satisfac-tion to spiritual fulfillment, we must understand how the ego manifests in our consciousness. The vivid descriptions in this chapter reveal the secrets of mind and consciousness, spirit and matter, evolution and creation. This beast comes out of the sea. As in a dream, this *beast* is an *animal* and in the Universal Language of Mind symbolizes a habit, a compulsion that is repeated with little or no thought. The origin of this habit is physical experience, symbolized by the *sea*. This *first beast* signifies the soul's attach-ment to the physical world. It is the habit of incarnation into matter. At last this compulsion is seen for what it is — a choice of the soul, a choice made on purpose and with purpose.

..on its horns were ten diadems and on its heads blasphemous names.
The *beast* is described as having *ten horns* which symbolize the ten energy transformers, or chakras, available to man each time

he incarns. Through repeated incarnation some control of energy and creation has been gained as symbolized by the *diadems on the horns*. The *beast has seven heads* signifying that the awareness of existence is in seven levels of consciousness at this point. The *blasphemous name* is identifying the Self with that which is temporal, that which is impermanent, that which is of the physical. As long as the physical ego is entrapped in what is transient the entire consciousness, including the soul and spirit, is engrossed. For the unaware, this identification happens every lifetime. From the time of incarnation, awareness and knowledge of the Real Self, the soul, fades until only things of the physical world are important. The habit of incarnation overshadows the soul and spirit thus the *blaspheming,* the denying of who you are, occurs again. And another lifetime comes and goes.

The beast I saw was like a leopard, but it had paws like a bear and the mouth of a lion. The dragon gave it his own power and throne, together with great authority. I noticed that one of the beast's heads seemed to have been mortally wounded, but this mortal wound was healed. In wonderment, the whole world followed after the beast.

The attachment to the physical world creates the soul who is entrapped in a physical animal-body.   In mobility *(leopard)*, purpose or instinct *(paws like a bear),* and expression *(mouth of lion),* the soul experiences the limitations inherent in the animal body. Man has a body that is similar to that of other animals.   The relationships within the animal kingdom, the animal bodies as they reveal progressive development, are the essence of scientific evolution. Too many theologians fight these scientific insights because they believe they contradict scriptural accounts of creation. Hopefully you will now see that science and religion are not at odds but are compatible means for understanding man's origin and destiny. This Truth is revealed as we interpret the meaning of the *two beasts* of

Revelation in the language of mind.

The consciousness of man uses the animal-body for a lifetime. Consciousness uses the body as a person uses a car, as a vehicle to transport the Self from one place to another. The outermost expression of consciousness, that which we refer to as the Conscious mind, forms the identity during a lifetime as symbolized by the *dragon giving its power and throne to the beast.* Each lifetime we begin anew, the conscious ego is built by our reaction to experience in the present time. As long as our awareness is determined by how our body reacts — does the experience bring pleasure? I want it again; does the experience bring pain? I want to avoid it — the soul, the ego of the Real Self, remains entrapped in the cycle of birth and rebirth. The outer, Conscious mind *(the head that was mortally wounded)* is compulsive, functioning from instinct only. No longer capable of learning through observation *(the whole world followed after the beast),* the mind must experience pleasure and pain in order to gain understanding *(mortal wound was healed).*

Men worshiped the dragon for giving his authority to the beast; they also worshipped the beast and said, Who can compare with the beast, or come forward to fight against it? The beast was given a mouth for uttering proud boasts and blasphemies, but the authority it received was to last only forty-two months.

As long as you believe *(men worship)* the physical is all there is, you are a slave to those limitations. Your ego *(dragon)* is defined by things of the physical: how you look, who you know, where you live, what you invest your time in. You fear death, for you do not know life. You give people, money, position the power to define who you are and to build or destroy your sense of Self worth. Whatever learning is gained by such a person transpires by hindsight, after the experience. This is a widely accepted concept today. "Life is for learning. Every experience brings a lesson. The important thing is to learn from everyone and everything." These are true, but they reflect the habitual thinking symbolized by *the first beast*. Something must happen physically, in your life, in order for you to react. You must experience something in order to learn anything. This thinking is compulsive and animalistic. Being ruled by consciously-formed habit keeps the soul entrapped.

It began to hurl blasphemies against God, reviling him and the members of his heavenly household as well. The beast was allowed to wage war against God's people and conquer them. It was likewise granted authority over every race and people, language and nation. The beast will be worshiped by all those inhabitants of earth who did not have their names written at the world's beginning in the book of the living, which belongs to the Lamb who was slain.

As long as you believe the physical is all there is, you deny your true origin as spirit *(blasphemies against God...)* and condemn your soul, for you bind it to what is not lasting. Many people believe there was a mistake made that condemned us all to the physical life we experience. For the Christian and Jew it is the "Fall of Man" and the concept of original sin, for the Hindu it is the bond of karma, for the Greek it was the opening of Pandora's jar. Yes, there was a point of origin for the soul's entrapment in the physical plane, but this entrapment is either perpetuated or resolved every moment. Since then each of us has continued to identify as a physical being thus *the beast has waged its war and had its authority,* time and time again. When we become aware of what is beyond the physical, we realize the relationship of soul and body, spirit and matter, permanent and transient.

While experiencing life we are not paying for something we did thousands of years ago, we are experiencing the effects of our own thought. Here, now. Today. Intention causes karma and understanding relieves it. Here, now. The understanding that we are souls temporarily experiencing through a physical body is the essence of the *book of the living.* Those spirits who have never become engrossed in the physical, souls who have never been entrapped, are those whose *names are in the book of the living.* These spirits learn through observing the physical world rather than being a participant in it. It is our immediate destiny as mankind to evolve beyond the need for physical learning and ascend once again to "the heights from which we have fallen."

Let him who has ears heed these words! If one is destined for captivity, into captivity he goes! If one is destined to be slain by the sword, by the sword he will be slain! Such is the faithful endurance that distinguishes God's holy people.

Destined for captivity is entrapment into the physical. *Destined to be slain by the sword* means to intentionally produce understandings. For those of us who experience incarnation, our destiny is to use the physical world as a schoolroom for learning the lessons brought to us by Universal Law and our individual karmic indentures. We will continue *(faithful endurance)* incarning to learn until all debts are paid and all understandings become a part of our soul's awareness *(distinguishes God's holy people).*

The Second Beast. Then I saw another wild beast come up out of the earth; it had two horns like a ram and it spoke like a dragon. It used the authority of the first beast to promote its interests by making the world and all its inhabitants worship the first beast, whose mortal wound had been healed.

The secret of how to accelerate soul progression is now revealed with the *second beast.* Unlike the first beast, this *beast comes up from the earth* signifying its origin as subconscious mind substance, the matter of the soul. The *first beast* is the compulsive ability to learn in the physical world. The *second beast* is the ability to cause that learning. This is achieved in three ways. 1] The development of the pituitary gland and pineal gland in the physical body of man *(the two horns)*. These glands enable the man's brain to function in ways that set him apart from all other animals. 2] The physical expression of the permanent understandings held within the soul *(spoke like a dragon)*. This enables man to call upon subconscious capabilities, displaying intuitive skill or the genius borne from understandings. 3] The full respect and utilization of the physical body and brain *(authority of the first beast)* for spiritual evolution *(to promote its interests)*.

It performed great prodigies; it could even make fire come down from heaven to earth as men looked on. Because of the prodigies it was allowed to perform by authority of the first beast, it led astray the earth's inhabitants, telling them to make an idol in honor of the beast that had been wounded by the sword and yet lived.

Here we learn what causes entrapment. The desire "to be like God" first stimulated in the woman in the Garden of Eden spoken of in *Genesis* or in the Greek myth of Pandora causes action which brings immediate expansion and overwhelming responsibility *(make fire come down from heaven to earth)*. The imagery of *fire coming down from heaven* conveys man's capability of manifesting his thoughts. When you think something and it happens, it is awesome, it is a wonder, it is often a miracle. To the uninitiated or unenlightened such an ability is a source of great speculation, and many times fear. We look for natural reasons to explain that which is super-natural, physical causes for the metaphysical. We make an *idol in honor of the beast.* In this way all aspects of self *(the earth's inhabitants)* are distracted from thought as cause *(led astray).* The best example of this in today's world is the common belief that the brain and the mind, or seat of consciousness, are one and the same therefore when the brain no longer exists nor does the individual.

The second wild beast was then permitted to give life to the beast's image, so that the image had the power of speech and of putting to death anyone who refused to worship it. It forced all men, small and great, rich and poor, slave and free, to accept a stamped image on their right hand or their forehead. Moreover, it did not allow a man to buy or sell anything unless he was first marked with the name of the beast or with the number that stood for its name.

The *second beast* is the ability to cause learning. Learning is initiated in the Conscious mind and is the product of reasoning which is the power of the Conscious mind. When you image a desire, your Subconscious mind seeks to recreate that image *(give life to the beast's image)* so the desire manifests in your life. Your Subconscious mind will bring to you the people, places, and things you need to fulfill that desire. It is the power of imagination in the Conscious mind which causes the creation of thought. The Conscious and Subconscious minds working together enable the expression of thought *(power of speech)* and the responsibility for what that thought causes *(putting to death anyone who refused to worship it)*.

In order for these two minds to work together, there must be a sufficient vehicle for the consciousness to use. The vehicle is the upright body of human man in combination with the juxtaposition ability of the fingers and thumb. This sets the body of man apart from all other animals. Look at the palm of your hand. You can hold a pencil. There's not another beast that can touch each of the fingers with the thumb, or form a fist, or grasp a tool. Even the primates use the first four fingers, they only use the thumb for suspending from a tree. The *mark of the beast* is the ability to make a fist or bring the fingers to the palm of the hand.

The *mark on the forehead* is the developed pituitary gland, the master gland of the body. Physically, this gland serves as the control center for the endocrine system. Mentally, it serves as the interpreter of the energies received through the five senses, what you see or hear or feel or taste or smell, and those coming from the inner levels of consciousness such as your nighttime dreams. The presence of this gland also sets man apart from all other animals because it enables him to rise above compulsion by using the power of reasoning.

All men, every human body, demonstrate both of these physical characteristics. The developed pituitary and the flexible, grasping hands give the soul inhabiting that body the ability to wield reasoning and the capability of using tools. These two physical abilities *(marked with the name of the beast)* are present only in the animal-man body and this body does identify its inhabitant as an advanced soul. These physical and mental abilities *(the number that stood for its name)* are necessary in order to give and receive *(buy or sell anything)* any thought and action. To create thought you must be able to reason, to rise above compulsion by adding imagination to memory. To respond to what you create with your thoughts you must be able to fashion and use the physical in ways far advanced from those of animals.

A certain wisdom is needed here; with a little ingenuity anyone can calculate the number of the beast, for it is a number that stands for a certain man. The man's number is six hundred sixty-six.

The *certain man* is not a singular person, nor is it male. The *certain man* is an evolved state of consciousness and also a time period. It is what students of metaphysics describe as Reasoning Man, *Genesis'* fifth day of creation, the current stage of evolution experienced by human beings. The number which represents this stage is *666*. Numerologically, the *six* symbolizes the universal truth "as above, so below", mind into matter, thought and manifestation. The number *six* represents the fulfillment of duty described so well in this chapter; the duty of the Conscious mind and the duty of the Subconscious mind one to the other in order to cause the learning and understanding that will bring about evolutionary soul growth. When the three sixes are added together they total 18 which digits to a nine, the number of completion. The *Real Self*, the soul and spirit that exist whether there is a physical body or not, meets his destiny through service to the highest Self until fulfillment is achieved.

Since the victory of Michael, the true Ego, in Chapter Thirteen of *Revelation* the seeker's consciousness has been firmly seated in the spirit, an offspring of a Creator who is to mature as a creator himself. This transformation is a change in how we identify Self. We no longer define our identity through experience in the physical world, rather we have come to know Self as a spiritual being, a child of the Creator whose duty is to mature in understanding and wisdom. The nature of that duty is revealed as the soul's assignment for learning and studying during a lifetime. The seeker is the closest he has ever been to realizing his dream of Enlightenment. What he receives from life no longer matters to him. His only concern is what he gives from his soul's understandings.

The *Lamb* that first appeared in Chapter Five reappears in Chapter 14. The *Lamb* symbolizes the Conscious, waking mind desiring guidance and instruction from the I AM, the offspring of the Creator. The *lamb* of *Revelation* is the culmination of the individual's preparedness for the expansion of consciousness that will bring awareness of the Christ consciousness. In Chapter Five we see the beginning of realization of the whole Self and the necessary commitment to transformation of Self's identity. The *lamb* appears here in Chapter Fourteen to emphasize the continued commitment to the growth of the whole Self. This is symbolized by *standing with the hundred and forty-four thousand who had his name and the name of his Father written on their foreheads on Mount Zion.* The challenges of evolutionary development, of maturing as an offspring of the Creator, have been met by the reasoner. They are no longer obstacles *(mountain),* for the aspects of Self *(the 144,000)* are now under the control of the individual seeking Enlightenment *(the lamb).*

Nearing the end of his journey on the wheel of birth and rebirth, the aspirant willingly meets the dictates of his duty, never failing to respond with the best he has to offer knowing that which he lacks will eventually be filled because of his giving. How his dharma unfolds is described in the *"last plagues"* in Chapter Fifteen. The aspirant willingly meets the dictates of his duty. He can release attachments to the material world because he is filling the soul with understandings. The transformations in every level of consciousness, symbolized in Chapter Fifteen as the *seven plagues*, transpire as a result of the need for the spirit to continue evolving. *God's wrath is brought to a climax* by these changes and the way the entrapped soul ascends becomes clear.

Chapter Sixteen

The Seven Bowls. I heard a mighty voice from the sanctuary say to the seven angels, Go and pour out upon the earth the seven bowls of God's wrath.

At last we have learned the lessons required in order for man to complete the cycle of birth and rebirth. Having gained understandings from experience in the material plane, the aspirant is free to return to evolution by learning through observation. These lessons are the *seven bowls of God's wrath*. Revealed through communication with the highest levels of consciousness *(angels)* known to man, the lessons unveil the plan for the end of reincarnation.

The first angel went out, and when he poured out his bowl on the earth, severe and festering boils broke out on the men who had accepted the mark of the beast or worshipped its image.

Message 1: Concerns responsibility for the Subconscious mind and the Conscious mind symbolized by *pouring out his bowl on the earth.* The misunderstandings that give rise to anger *(boils)* will be resolved by employing reasoning *(mark of the beast)* in physical experience *(worshipped its image).*

The second angel poured out his bowl on the sea. The sea turned to blood like that of a corpse, and every creature living in the sea died.

Message 2: Concerns the physical *(sea).* Truth will be revealed in the physical experiences *(sea turned to blood).* Universally, the Truth is the nature of the physical is change *(every creature living in the sea died).* To understand the nature of the Creator, we must transcend the physical. We must realize there is more to Self than the outer shell.

The third angel poured out his bowl on the rivers and springs. These also turned to blood. I heard the angel in charge of the waters cry out: "You are just, O holy One who is and who was, in passing this sentence! To those who shed the blood of saints and prophets you have given blood to drink, they deserve it." I heard the altar cry out:"Yes, Lord God Almighty, your judgments are true and just!"

Message 3: Concerns the energy flows that sustain life *(river and springs).* The Truth *(turned to blood)* is cosmic energy is the origin of what sustains life. Each individual is responsible for the energy received into the Self as life force *(the sentence of the holy One).* This cosmic energy connects Self with the rest of the universe *(shedding and drinking blood).* The Truth is thought is cause, this is the meaning of the *Lord's judgments being true and just.*

The fourth angel poured out his bowl on the sun. He was commissioned to burn men with fire. Those who were scorched by the intense heat blasphemed the name of God who had power to send these plagues, but they did not repent or give him due honor.

Message 4: Concerns the Superconscious mind *(sun)*. The plan for maturity of Self as a Creator is held in the Superconscious mind. Fulfillment of this plan requires an expansion of outer consciousness *(burn men with fire)*. Putting the quest for spiritual maturity first above all else produces the transformation in the identity that leads to the end of entrapment. Doing less — making the physical more important than the spiritual *(blaspheming)* and remaining compulsive, refusing to release and move forward *(repent and honor)* - retards evolution.

The fifth angel poured out his bowl on the throne of the beast. Its kingdom was plunged into darkness; men bit their tongues in pain and blasphemed the God of heaven because of their suffering and their boils. But they did not turn away from their wicked deeds.

Message 5: Concerns the power in the Conscious mind - reasoning. The *throne of the beast* is the power to learn. The *beast* is the soul's attachment to the physical world. It is the reasoning power which enables man to overcome the ignorance *(darkness)* of being separated from his Maker *(pain)* and blaming creation *(blaspheming)* instead of seeing the cause in Self. By mastering reasoning, man causes his own evolution into Spiritual, Intuitive Man.

The sixth angel poured out his bowl on the great river Euphrates. Its water was dried up to prepare the way for the kings of the East. I saw three unclean spirits like frogs come from the mouth of the dragon, from the mouth of the beast, and from the mouth of the false prophet. These spirits were devils who worked prodigies. They

*went out to assemble all the kings of the earth for battle on the great
day of God the Almighty.*

Message 6: Concerns the Kundalini, the creative energy
only available when man is entrapped in the physical *(Euphrates)*.
All desires have been fulfilled *(water dried up)* because we understand cause *(kings of the East)*. Any final physical habits concerning
the identity or who you are *(dragon)*, attachment or where you are
(beast), and physical thinking or where you are going *(false
prophets)* are admitted. They are recognized for what they are: the
product of engrossment in the senses *(kings of the earth)*. And with
awareness of the ideal of compatibility with the Creator, they are put
in perspective *(great day of God)*.

*(Be on guard, I come like a thief. Happy the man who stays wide
awake and fully clothed for fear of going naked and exposed for all
to see!) The devils then assembled the kings in a place called in
Hebrew 'Armageddon.'*

Constant awareness *(stays wide awake)* brings complete
understanding *(fully clothed)*, the omniscience of a Creator. The
physical *(Armageddon)* and its experiences can now be left behind
(assembling the kings).

*Finally, the seventh angel poured out his bowl on the empty air.
From the throne in the sanctuary came a loud voice which said, It
is finished! There followed lightning flashes and peals of thunder,
then a violent earthquake. Such was its violence that there has never
been one like it in all the time men have lived on the earth. The great
city was split into three parts, and the other Gentile cities also fell.
God remembered Babylon the great, giving her the cup filled with
the blazing wine of his wrath. Every island fled and mountains
disappeared. Giant hailstones like huge weights came crashing
down on mankind from the sky, and men blasphemed God for the*

plague of hailstones, because this plague was so severe.

Message 7: Concerns resurrection of the spirit this is why the final bowl is poured on the empty air. This is release from entrapment *(it is finished)*. The Enlightenment produced from countless lifetimes has finally come *(violence that there has never been one like it in all the time men have lived on the earth)*. Creation *(three parts)* now occurs in the Superconscious mind *(great city)*, no longer the Conscious mind *(Gentile cities fell)*. The physical *(Babylon the great)* has fulfilled its spiritual purpose *(cup of blazing wine of his wrath)*. Conscious *(island)* and subconscious *(mountains)* thoughts no longer exist. Self's awareness is now one within Superconscious mind. The Superconscious mind is the place for learning and the physical *(giant hailstones like huge weights came crashing down on mankind from the sky)* is once again a place to observe.

The Book of Revelation is a visionary account, told in universally symbolic language, of the final days of a soul's need for incarnation. The original plan for evolution was to learn through observation, not by engrossment in experience. The physical plane becomes the place of learning for those who have lost sight of this ideal. The entrapped soul must master himself through a series of incarnations, each presenting lessons to be understood. As he progresses, releasing attachments to the material world becomes easier because he is filling the soul with understandings.

This progression first occurs within the inner levels of consciousness, symbolized in Chapter Fifteen as the *seven plagues*. Transformations in the kind and quality of thought transpire as a result of the need for the spirit to continue evolving. At last we have learned the lessons required in order for man to complete the cycle of birth and rebirth. These lessons unveiling the plan for the end of reincarnation are *"the seven bowls of God's wrath"* described in

Chapter Sixteen. The aspirant who has come this far now functions from the superconscious part of Self. For him creation no longer occurs in the Conscious mind; the physical has fulfilled its spiritual purpose. Chapters Seventeen and Eighteen paint a clear picture of how this has come about.

The physical world symbolized in *Revelation* by *Babylon the Great* has dominated mankind's consciousness for a complete day of creation, one we term Reasoning Man. Reasoning Man is a time period, spanning tens of thousands of years and including the lands of Mu, Lemuria, Atlantis as well as our current world map. Reasoning Man is also a development in consciousness, the capacity for the discrimination of truth. In the current time we are witnessing the maturing of Reasoning Man, and the first inklings of humanity's next evolutionary impulse — Intuitive, Spiritual Man.

Babylon takes on whatever properties man endows her with - the power of life and death, happiness and sorrow, pleasure and pain. For thousands of years man has assigned physical causes for his experience thus missing the true meaning of life. This is why *Babylon* is described as a *harlot*, she fornicates irresponsibly, and so man has lifetime after lifetime used his Kundalini energy to fulfill one physical desire after another while his consciousness remains in darkness.

The unaware man is dominated by his sensory attachment to the finite world. His sense of "who am I?" constantly moves away from the soul and toward the physical personality and body. This identification with the material world slows his spiritual progress resulting in the creation of more lifetimes where he learns through direct physical experience.

The destiny of every man is to realize the purpose of physical existence. To answer the questions: Where did I come from? Why am I here? Where am I going? and Who am I? Eventually the answers come to each individual, at his or her own chosen rate of speed, at his own appointed time. We realize the material world exists for the increase of the soul and the maturing of the spirit.

Once on the wheel of rebirth, the soul repeatedly assumes an outer presentation that is both conscious and unconscious, realized and unaware. The capacity to learn comes as a result of the development of reasoning. The enrichment of the soul, the development of intuition, is the reward for repeated incarnation. Only then do we realize the truth of what we have gained reincarning; acquisition not of physical glory or wealth but of the wisdom that will aid us to become compatible to the Creator who brought us into existence.

Conscious and subconscious thoughts no longer exist. Self's awareness is now one within Superconscious mind. The Superconscious mind is once again the place for learning and the physical, a place to observe. The physical, *Babylon,* is viewed as it has never been seen before. It is amazing to realize the purpose for physical existence, to know that we are spirit first and last and only take on an outer physical shell as we put on a garment and cast it away when soiled or no longer fitting. This is *The Meaning of Beast and Harlot.* At last we are responding to the purpose for which we exist, and that changes our existence more than we expected.

The *end of the world*, the cessation of rebirth, comes when the individual has gained the wisdom to be a creator, he knows what it is to create with thought. The *Fall of Babylon* signifies the end of the need for physical incarnation to complete the ideal of becoming compatible with the One who brought us into being, our Creator.

Learning in the physical schoolroom has served its purpose and so is no longer needed by this aspirant. At this time you will no longer desire physical identity and what it affords. You will achieve what every Buddhist seeks - desirelessness. The Subconscious mind will be fulfilled. You will be free from the wheel of birth and rebirth, known to the Hindu. You, the Real Self, will no longer require incarnation for evolutionary growth. The Self has learned that freedom and responsibility are one, thus eternal life, the continuous awareness of existence has become part of the individual's awareness.

And we are completing what began in *Genesis:* the fulfillment of God's wrath on the man, woman, and serpent in *Genesis Chapter 3* and the initiation of awareness of the *tree of life*.

The spirit, the essence that is you, exists beyond the physical world.

Your essence is Light. It is as if you have been on a journey for a long, long time. A journey which brought to you opportunity for love, wisdom, truth, growth, most of all fulfillment. Your journey to become like your Creator has led you to a place, a place described well in the final chapters of *Revelation*.

By the time a soul reaches the stage of progression described in *Revelation* 20, the outer desires have left and only the inner desire remains. By aligning the Self with Universal Law the truth has become known. As it was in the beginning and throughout Light's evolution until the entrapment of Animal Man, now, once again, the spirit is centered in the Superconscious existence, learning through observation of the physical rather than direct experience. The conscious awareness and the Superconscious mind become one in identity and action. The creative urge is focused solely on understanding the singular identity of Self, the I AM. All creative movement is devoted to becoming like our Creator.

In *Revelation* is the great answer to the oracle of all times. Why would such enlightened beings – particularly Jesus, Gandhi, and others who were martyred – return to the earth if they did not have to? A possible answer is here in the final teaching. Once ascended awareness overtakes the Self, each individual has the opportunity to return back into the physical to pass on what is learned. It would seem that this was the motivating force and great passion of every great Master of consciousness, to teach, to aid others.

In the final chapters of *Revelation* we receive a glimpse of how this metaphysically beneficent consciousness can exist in the world human man has created.

Chapter Twenty

Verses one through ten: **Thousand Year Reign.** *Then I saw an angel come down from heaven, holding the key to the abyss and a huge chain in his hand.*

How the spirit can manifest itself in the physical world without becoming entrapped in it once again. This guidance is revealed in the form of an *angel from heaven.* The Superconscious part of mind has always had dominion *(chain)* of the outer worlds *(the abyss).* From the Superconscious mind sprung the levels of consciousness in Subconscious and Conscious minds. The *key to the abyss* is the way your thoughts work, the way energy expresses itself in outer creation. *The chain* is how you use the thoughts you create.

Now that the final attachment to the physical world has been understood, a new identity *(dragon, serpent, devil)* can be born. This *angel* reflects the new way of thinking we are assuming now that we are no longer subject to natural laws that bind the soul to the body.

He seized the dragon, the ancient serpent, who is the devil or Satan, and chained him up for a thousand years. The angel hurled him into the abyss, which he closed and sealed over him. He did this so that the dragon might not lead the nations astray until the thousand years are over. After this, the dragon is to be released for a short time.

We can now understand the development of identity throughout the previous stage of our evolutionary development, the creation of reasoning. We realize the urge, the motivation, has been consistent throughout time. Whether it be experiences with the serpent in the Garden of Eden or Jesus's adversary Satan or the dragon in *Revelation* 12, each is the reflection of the desire to be like the Creator. Now we can more clearly see how the identity, the ego, has matured through the stages of man. We have moved from infancy into adolescence into adulthood into wisdom *(chained him up for a thousand years).*

The urge to mature, to be like, has existed in the outer mind, constantly influencing the Conscious and Subconscious minds *(...into the abyss, which he closed and sealed over him)* toward growth and understanding through the infancy and adolescence of reasoning. Lifetime after lifetime. Every thought deals with developing the identity of the mind toward becoming a whole, functioning Self. An Enlightened One.

When adulthood is reached, the ego matures as symbolized by the *dragon. Seizing the dragon* is taking control of the ego at this stage of its development. Now the conscious ego and the superconscious ego have only one goal. This one goal is to be a part of the identity, the I Am. Making this new identity part of the awareness results in the releasing of the Conscious **and** the Subconscious mind. The identity of the whole Self *(the dragon is released for a short time)* is finally developed.

Then I saw some thrones. Those who were sitting on them were empowered to pass judgment. I also saw the spirits of those who had been beheaded for their witness to Jesus and the word of God, those who had never worshiped the beast or its image nor accepted its mark on their foreheads or their hands. They came to life again and reigned with Christ for a thousand years. The others who were dead did not come to life till the thousand years were over. This is the first resurrection;

The resurrection addresses the revisiting of the Christ consciousness. When we "resurrect" we revive the practice, use and memory of.

The movement of spirit outward from the I AM into mind is the first experience of this Cosmic Consciousness, Buddha Consciousness. The more engrossed we became in physical matter *(others who were dead),* the more we lost sight of this expanded consciousness.

The return to this awareness at once signifies and requires the maturing of the Self *(thrones, those sitting on them.)* It also enables us to realize the parts of self that exist beyond entrapment, all of Self beyond the outer realm. Now the superconscious worlds are open to us *(came to life again)* and we are Cosmic Conscious *(reigned with Christ...)* again.

..happy and holy are they who were in the first resurrection! The second death will have no claim on them; they shall serve God and Christ as priests, and shall reign with him for a thousand years.

These are the Christs and Buddhas and atmans. The Enlightened who walk among us in wisdom for the purpose of serving all of humanity through their teachings.

When the thousand years are over, Satan will be released from his prison. He will go out to seduce the nations in all four corners of the earth, and muster for war the troops of Gog and Magog, numerous as the sands of the sea. They invaded the whole country and surrounded the beloved city where God's people were encamped; but fire came down from heaven and devoured them. The devil who had led them astray was hurled into the pool of burning sulphur, where the beast and the false prophet had also been thrown. There they will be tortured day and night, forever and ever.

When the identity is unified in Christ Consciousness, the outer ego and the I Am ego are one, a new motivation *(Satan)* affects all parts of mind *(seduce the nations in all four corners of the earth)*. Our understanding of the reason for creation *(troops of Gog and Magog)* is forever expanded *(fire came down from heaven and devoured them.... pool of burning sulphur)*. We will never be the same again. We are born anew.

Verses 11-15: **The Last Judgement.** *Next I saw a large white throne and the One who sat on it. The earth and the sky fled from his presence until they could no longer be seen. I saw the dead, the great and the lowly, standing before the throne. Lastly, among the scrolls, the book of the living was opened.*

The new identity enables the aspirant to know the true Ego, the *One seated on the throne* spoken of since the first chapter of the *Revelation*. This essence of Self, the One, is omniscient, knowing where the spirit has been, where the spirit is, and where the spirit is to go. Only the present matters *(earth and the sky fled from his presence)* . This is the accounting, the day of judgement.

What has come before is now seen, the entrapment *(the dead)*. the experiences in the pairs of opposites *(the great and the lowly)* are realized for their value. In all the memories in the akasha *(lastly, among the scrolls)* only those which produced understanding for the whole self, the permanent memories *(the book of the living)* have been called upon to forge the new identity.

The dead were judged according to their conduct as recorded on the scrolls. The sea gave up its dead; then death and the nether world gave up their dead. Each person was judged according to his conduct.

The intentions *(conduct)* can now become part of the identity. What has been built through the physical experiences *(sea)* and through the subconscious *(netherworld)* experiences are now freed to become a permanent part of the identity.

Then death and the nether world were hurled into the pool of fire, which is the second death; anyone whose name was not found inscribed in the book of the living was hurled into this pool of fire.

When the new identity is assumed, our sense of Self is the Christ Consciousness of the One. The Conscious and the Subconscious mind *(second death)* and the learning through separation they embody are no longer needed. We are now connected to all.

Chapter Twenty-One

VI: NEW CREATION

Verses 1-8: New Heavens and New Earth. Then I saw new heavens and a new earth. The former heavens and the former earth had passed away, and the sea was no longer.

How we relate to Self will be transformed. As foreshadowed in Chapter 19, we are never the same again. Where we have become accustomed to existing, in the vehicle of the mind, will change. It is like the change that happens seemingly overnight when a child comes to you, you are transformed, you are never the same again. Or when you shed the mortal body at the end of a life, accepting a new body in a new life. The old body, the old life, the old you, is no more. It has passed away and a new you begins fresh.

When this time comes the Superconscious mind (*former heavens*), the Subconscious mind (*earth*) and the Conscious mind (*sea*) will no longer exist **as we knew them** throughout the period of building reasoning, the experiences of entrapment. A trans-

formed, a *new heavens and earth,* consciousness will be made known.

I also saw a new Jerusalem, the holy city coming down out of heaven from God, beautiful as a bride prepared to meet her husband. I heard a loud voice from the throne cry out: This is God's dwelling among men. He shall dwell with them and they shall be his people and he shall be their God who is always with them. He shall wipe every tear from their eyes, and there shall be no more death or mourning, crying out or pain, for the former world has passed away.

The new consciousness is described. It is a complete expression of Self from the I Am (*holy city*) existing in the physical (*new Jerusalem*). A single awareness so often spoken of in the gospels. Receptive and committed (*bride prepared...*).

The I Am (*voice from the throne*) expresses the first inklings of connectedness realizing the union of all (*dwell...always with them*) that has resulted from the experiences gained during the development of Reasoning Man *(death...former world).*

The One who sat on the throne said to me, See I make all things new! Then he said, "Write these matters down for the words are trustworthy and true!"

The One signifies the I Am. At one time the whole mind was without experience. The journey, the evolution of I Am is described in the whole text of the <u>Bible</u>.

How we were brought into being is described in the first chapter of *Genesis.* The formation of mind as a vehicle for I Am to gain experience in order to mature and become compatible to its Creator is in chapters 2 and 3. Later dividing the mind was symbolized by the description of *the flood, Noah* and his three sons, by *Abraham* and the description of his heirs including *Isaac* and *Jacob.* In the Universal Language of Mind, these passages tell us how the mind was separated into divisions.

The four gospels, four different accounts of the birth of Jesus of Nazareth and the last three years of his adult life, reveal the maturing wisdom of Reasoning Man that brings into being a new stage of growth we term Spiritual Man. Jesus teaches us how to live as Reasoning Man.

Now, in *Revelation,* we have put it all back together so that the mind works as a whole once again. It isn't so much that the Conscious mind and Subconscious mind will be released and no longer exist. What will occur is they will no longer be recognized as divisions of the mind, rather they will be a part of the whole *(One who sat on the throne and said to me, "See, I make all things new!)*

This change is in alignment with the Universal Laws of creation *(trustworthy and true)* that now is made a part of the whole self *(write down...).* To make this come about in your life, to make all things new, you've got to identify with the whole because before that time we are certainly identifying with the separate parts.

He went on to say: These words are already fulfilled! I am the Alpha and the Omega, the Beginning and the End. To anyone who thirsts I will give to drink without cost from the spring of life-giving water.

In the second chapter of *Genesis "a stream was welling up out of the earth and was watering all the surface of the ground."* This is the *spring of life-giving water*, the connection to the source which nourishes and energizes. Now we can access the endless supply of cosmic energy directly, we no longer need to consume lower root races, animals or plants or even air, to exist. When there is union *(I am...)* we can live directly from cosmic energy.

He who wins the victory shall inherit these gifts; I will be his God and he shall be my son.

This is the promise of our future. Once we have completed our understanding of reasoning *(victory)* and brought forward its off-spring intuition we will know ourselves as Creators *(I will be his God...).*

As for the cowards and traitors to the faith, the depraved and murderers, the fornicators and sorcerers, the idol-worshippers and deceivers of every sort — their lot is the fiery pool of burning sulphur, the second death.

Only we can prolong our separation, our entrapment symbolized by the *second death*. Through failing to believe *(coward)* or act upon our beliefs *(traitors)*, through intentionally doing wrong *(depraved, murderers)*, through craving sense gratification *(fornicators)* and ego glorification *(sorcerers)*, we have prolonged our separation *(deceivers)* from the Creator *(idol-worshippers. .).* As long as those identifications into the separate parts remain, there is still some attachment to the physical and our destiny will be delayed.

*Verses nine through twenty-seven: **The New Jerusalem.** "One of the seven angels who held the seven bowls filled with the seven last plagues came and said to me, 'Come, I will show you the woman who is the bride of the Lamb.' He carried me away in spirit to the top of a very high mountain and showed me the holy city Jerusalem coming down out of heaven from God. It gleamed with the splendor of God. The city had the radiance of a precious jewel that sparkled like a diamond. Its wall, massive and high, had twelve gates at which twelve angels were stationed. Twelve names were written on the gates, the names of the twelve tribes of Israel."*

The revelations concerning the resurrection of the spirit *(seven angels)* are a part of the new identity. This is the coming together of the receptive *(bride)* and aggressive *(he)* aspects that unite to create. When we come to this point in our evolution we will understand creation as a Creator *(splendor of God).*

There are no longer divisions in the mind, only communion symbolized by the *holy city.* The Self will now be described as one city, with particular attributes that in the language of mind reveal the consciousness we can look forward to living.

The repetition of *"12"* indicates this mind has mastery of creation.

Twelve gates are the points of giving and receiving in the new mind; the *angels*, the twelve intelligences guiding movement.

The completion of what has long been desired is reflected in the *names written on the gates.* The twelve tribes of Israel first appear in *Genesis* and *Exodus.* By noting the way each expresses himself and where each was stationed in the columns of the exodus from Egypt, you can identify what each of these governing aspects are. All serve the Mastery of the whole Self *(Israel)* which is revealed in the last book of the <u>Bible</u>.

In *Revelation* we find the fulfillment of the destiny of the tribes.

There were three gates facing east, three north, three south, and three west.

This indicates mastery in creation in all elements.

The wall of the city had twelve courses of stones as its foundation, on which were written the names of the twelve apostles of the Lamb.

This mind's mastery has been built upon the utilization of the imagination and will.

The one who spoke to me held a rod of gold for measuring the city, its gates, and its wall. The city is perfectly square, its length and its width being the same. He measured the city with the rod and found it twelve thousand furlongs in length, in width, and in height.

Twelve thousand reveals the **power** of creation this mind now possesses. This mind values Universal Law *(rod of Gold)* existing in harmony with it.

Its wall measured a hundred and forty-four cubits in height by the unit of measurement the angle used.

The building of the will is complete symbolized by the *144* that reduces to nine, the number of completion. This mind understands the place will holds in mastering creation. *One hundred and forty-four* is twelve times twelve.

"The wall was constructed of jasper; the city was of pure gold, crystal-clear.

Jasper is a quartz stone known for its healing properties. The use of this stone to describe the substance of the city's wall reflects how the will has been used to create the wholeness now experienced. This has given the new mind clarity in its worth and value.

*The foundation of the city wall was ornate with precious stones of
every sort: the first course of stones was jasper, the second sapphire,
the third chalcedony, the fourth emerald, the fifth sardonyx, the sixth
carnelian, the seventh chrysolite, the eighth beryl, the ninth topaz,
the tenth chrysoprase, the eleventh hyacinth and the twelfth amethyst.
The twelve gates were twelve pearls, each made of a single pearl;
and the streets of the city were of pure gold, transparent as glass.*

The developed spiritual will is described by *precious stones*, by what
the will power has built. Again there are twelve, symbolizing the
mastery of the will to create. They also reflect the full color
spectrum, even beyond what the physical eye registers, produced as
the will is employed for awareness.

The gates being *made of pearls* signify they were constructed
from physical experiences. This is how a pearl is made. A pearl is
made of a grain of sand that aggravates an oyster, so it begins to build
something around it to relieve the aggravation. This is the way *the
gates* into the Superconscious mind were made, by overcoming
obstacles in the physical.

The *streets being paved with pure gold* tells you that eventually
everything you have experienced will be worth it. All of the activity
that you took, all that you are taking now, and all that you are going
to take in the future will be valuable.

*I saw no temple in the city. The Lord, God the Almighty, is its temple
— he and the Lamb.*

Throughout the <u>Bible</u> the *temple* has symbolized spiritual consciousness. When you reach Spiritual Man, the Christ or Cosmic or
Buddha consciousness will be yours.

*The city had no need for sun or moon, for the glory of God gave it
light, and its lamp was the Lamb.*

The time of the old divisions of mind, once needed for spiritual progression, is passed. The new mind knows creation is awareness and its impetus is receptivity.

The nations shall walk by its light; to it the kings of the earth shall bring their treasures.

The impetus is no longer derived from receptivity in the physical, as experienced by the five senses throughout Reasoning Man. What has been learned of creation through the senses is a part of the new mind. Awareness guides the urge to create.

During the day its gates shall never be shut, and there shall be no night.

Awareness is constant. Timeless.

The treasures and wealth of the nations shall be brought there, but nothing profane shall enter it, nor anyone who is a liar or has done a detestable act. Only those shall enter whose names are inscribed in the book of the living kept by the Lamb.

Every wisdom, all that is worthy, is known to the new mind. Being connected with all, all illusions drop away. Leaving the identity that is ready to understand eternity and creation.

We reach the final chapter of the *Revelation* of John. A meditative dream of what is to come. A fulfilled destiny of what has come before. A prophecy of what must now occur for mankind to spiritually progress.

These latter chapters of Revelation give us a hope-filled glimpse of what is to come. Evolution is a series of developing identities, changing egos. Whether thought of in one lifetime as a person moves from childhood to adulthood to old age, or seen in a more magnified sense of the soul taking on incarnation again and again, the spirit is enriched through experiences that mature.

Revelation tells of one maturing. The growth spurred through wise reasoning. This brings the direct grasp of truth known as intuition. As the intuitive sense is developed, it becomes a skill to master just as reasoning was previously. This process changes our ideas of who we are and where we came from, ultimately producing a transformation in how we know Self.

When the new identity is assumed, our sense of Self will be the Christ Consciousness of the One. Our awareness will be constant, the will fully realized, and alignment with Law secure. The description in the Universal Language of Mind of this new consciousness begins in Chapter 21 and concludes in the first few verses of Chapter 22. The Mastery of consciousness is described in vivid imagery of a new Heaven and a new Earth. All the work we have invested in opening our minds, cultivating wisdom, and harmonizing with Universal law will be rewarded by a total transformation of our consciousness. Destinies are fulfilled that were initiated in *Genesis*. The old divisions of mind fall away, replaced by a new mind that is whole, connected, and spiritually realized.

The description of this new mind, the mind of Spiritual Man continues.

Chapter Twenty-Two

Verses one through five: The angel then showed me the river of life-giving water, clear as crystal, which issued from the throne of God and of the Lamb and flowed down the middle of the streets. On either side of the river grew the trees of life which produce fruit twelve times a year, once each month; their leaves serve as medicine for the nations.

What began as a *spring of life-giving water* in *Genesis* has evolved. It is now the *river of life-giving water* flowing in the streets of the new Heaven and new Earth. This symbolizes a transformation in our connection to the energy Source. Our union enables us to exist as cosmic energy throughout eternity *(trees of life,)* empowering us to continuing gaining mastery as creators *(12 times year.)*

Nothing deserving a curse shall be found there.

The old dictates of responsibility for thought in action, so characteristic of our present stage of evolution, are passed. Karmic law ceases to apply to the one who has achieved this level of spiritual awareness.

The throne of God and of the Lamb shall be there, and his servants shall serve him faithfully. They shall see him face to face and bear his name on their foreheads.

This describes the time when we realize we are achieving compatibility with our Creator as symbolized by the *throne of God* and the *Lamb* existing together. As Spiritual Man we will function in harmony with the Universal Laws *(servants)*. We will realize our compatibility with God, as a child who grows into an adult begins to recognize his own maturity with his physical parents. We will know ourselves as matured offspring of our Maker, the Source of our Spirit.

The night shall be no more. They will need no light from lamps or the sun, for the Lord God shall give them light, and they shall reign forever.

The consciousness is One, the awareness fully realized as I Am. Future experience is guided by the urge for compatibility, for bringing into being universes of our own.

Verses six through twenty-one: The angel said to me: These words

are trustworthy and true; the Lord, the God of prophetic spirits, has
sent his angel to show his servants what must happen very soon.

These final images of the Epilogue bring us back to the present time, the present state of awareness, which is John's, the receiver of this dream. These are the final thoughts to the one who believes Spiritual Man is a reality. For such a believer, knowing is close at hand.

These are spiritual thoughts coming from Superconscious mind. Reminding us that all is evolving according to Universal Law. The identity of Self is moving toward its destiny of becoming compatible to its Maker.

Remember, I am coming soon! Happy the man who heeds the
prophetic message of this book!

This is the ideal to hold in mind, to strive for, to serve.

It is I, John, who heard and saw these things, and when I heard and
saw them I fell down to worship at the feet of the angel who showed
them to me. But he said to me: No, get up! I am merely a fellow
servant with you and your brothers the prophets and those who heed
the message of this book. Worship God alone!

Believing is born from experience. We believe we will grow as tall as our mother or father. We believe we will pass a test or land a job. We believe we will be healthy all the days of our lives. To make these beliefs reality, to move them from thoughts to experience, we must learn to create like our Maker. We must *worship God.*

Then someone said to me: "Do not seal up the prophetic words of
this book, for the appointed time is near! Let the wicked continue
in their wicked ways, the depraved in their depravity! The virtuous
must live on in their virtue and the holy ones in their holiness!"

Admit and accept where you are in your evolution. Know that

Spiritual Man is at hand. Humanity is on the threshold of spiritual progression. Some will progress faster than others, all will progress. Know where you are, both productive and destructive. Through admittance you will know where you have come from and through acceptance you will be able to see where you are to go.

"Remember, I am coming soon! I bring with me the reward that will be given to each man as his conduct deserves."

We are evolving into connectedness *(I am coming soon)*. This cycle, this stage of evolution called reasoning, is almost complete and each Subconscious mind will receive its just rewards.

"I am the Alpha and the Omega, the First and the Last, the Beginning and the End!"

The symbol for infinity is the number 8 on its side. This shows perpetual motion. The figure has its beginning and its ending. So it is with Spirit. *I am the first and the last.* Wherever you are on any place of infinity, it is the end of the past and the beginning of the future. The beginning is whole and complete but without experience, the journey leads back to the same place, now whole and complete with experience.

Happy are they who wash their robes so as to have free access to the tree of life and enter the city through its gates!

Peace of mind exists for one who expresses infinity for it brings eternal *(tree of life)* consciousness. When you exist in the eternal now, the past and present and future become one in your consciousness. You are becoming whole, aligning your outer consciousness with Superconsciousness *(enter city through its gates)*.

Outside are the dogs and sorcerers, the fornicators and murderers, the idol-worshippers and all who love falsehood.

Truth has become the sole passion of the seeker, the believer, the knower, the One who is to come. Any limitations previously acceptable are separated, left behind, starved. They cease to exist from lack of attention. The need for habitual activities that mind goes through in order to learn how to be a mental creator *(dogs, sorcerers)* is passing. The old identity that created for no purpose, for ill purposes, or selfish purposes *(fornicators, murderers, idol-worshippers)* is passed. With Truth as a compass these old ways of learning become passe.

It is I, Jesus, who have sent my angel to give you this testimony about the churches, I am the Root and Offspring of David, the Morning Star shining bright.

The root and offspring of David is reasoning. Our identity is no longer as Animal Man but as Reasoning Man. *Jesus* reflects mastery of reasoning and the birth of Spiritual Man. When we reach this stage of growth we realize intuition is the product, the offspring, of reasoning. This changes our identity. Our awareness as the most beautiful angel of heaven, Lucifer, *the morning star*, comes back to us in its purity and glory.

The Spirit and the Bride say, Come! Let him who hears answer, Come. Let him who is thirsty come forward; let all who desire it accept the gift of life-giving water.

The invitation to evolve is ever present. Any who desires spiritual progression and who acts upon that desire will have whatever energy is needed to fulfill that desire.

I myself give witness to all who hear the prophetic words of this book.

By acting upon belief, we bring experience to ourselves. Thought is cause. Ideas precede manifestation. Believing and

Knowing predicts and fulfills the future.

If anyone adds to these words, God will visit him with all the plagues described herein! If anyone takes from the words of this book, God will take away his share in the tree of life and the holy city described here!"

Each of us must experience *(adds...)* fruition by bringing our thoughts into reality *(God visit him)*. This has been so since the time of our choosing the physical world as our schoolroom, the wheel of rebirth *(plagues)*. Refusing to experience, denying the power of your thoughts and responsibility as a creator for them, only delays your evolution *(God will take...)*. Such ignorance delays awareness of what is beyond the physical world, your own superconsciousness.

As one of my teachers was fond of saying, "Use it or lose it!"

The One who gives this testimony says, "Yes, I am coming soon!" Amen! Come, Lord Jesus! The grace of the Lord Jesus be with you all. Amen!

So be it. We are preparing for a transformation in consciousness that will transcend the sorrow of separation, uniting the whole Self. We will evolve, freeing us to live the next *day of creation,* the sixth day, for the making of the Spiritual Man *(grace of the Lord Jesus)*.

May we wisely follow the teachings and examples of Jesus and all great Masters of consciousness who have come before us.•

These interpretations of the *Book of Revelation* are reprinted from *Thresholds Quarterly,* the journal for School of Metaphysics Associate members, with permission from the Board of Governors of the School of Metaphysics.

Interpreting Holy Scriptures in Dream Symbols

"A thought is produced in the conscious mind of the individual. Words are chosen and formulated in such a way as to describe the mental image. The mental image, the thought, that has been described in the conscious mind of the person with words is next expressed as verbal sounds through the mouth of the thinker. These verbal sounds then travel as vibration through the air as sound waves. These air or sound waves may be received in the ear of the listener, the receiving individual, striking the ear drum and causing a like vibration in the inner ear where it is then transformed into electrochemical units of coded energy that report to the brain. The electro-chemical units of coded energy are "decoded" by the pituitary gland in the brain which then draws stored images of memory together in order to formulate a workable image similar to the image originally verbalized.

The degree of accuracy with which the recreated mental image or thought is formulated in the receiver's (listener's) conscious mind and brain is the degree to which effective communication transpires. At times the receiver's mental image may closely resemble the speaker's mental image. In other situations the two images may be worlds apart. The latter leads to confusion, reaction, frustration and, in general, inefficiency.

The language of the subconscious mind, which dreams and scriptures of Holy books such as the <u>Bible</u> use for communication, is also initiated with a mental image. However, in the process of dream communication the mental image is relayed from subconscious mind directly to the conscious mind via the pituitary gland in the brain. The pituitary gland is the part of the brain that has as its function to interpret energies. It is the interpreter of energies. The pituitary, having received the mental image from the subconscious mind, then draws out of the brain a collection of stored mental images called memory of past events. This memory, these mental images stored in the brain, are then chosen, collected, orchestrated in such a fashion as to form a collective, moving image or message of the communication which the inner or subconscious mind is attempting to convey to the conscious waking mind.

Since mind to mind communication, such as one's subconscious mind to one's conscious mind, does not require the inefficient vehicle of words, the message is given in symbolic or picture image form and is received in like or similar manner. Therefore, it is of utmost importance that each individual, each person, come to understand this Universal Language of Mind which is the language of mental images, pictures or symbols.

The Bible, and in fact any truly Holy book or scripture, can be and is to be accurately interpreted in the universal, symbolic, language of mind for its deepest spiritual and evolutionary significance. This is the language of picture-images. This book uses exactly that interpretation in the language of mind. It recognizes the universal symbols and connects them to form a mental image of creation and evolution to our ultimate quest --- Enlightenment."

–from **The Universal Language of Mind: Book of Matthew Interpreted**

About the Authors

Barbara Condron interpreted the *Book of Revelation* throughout the last decade of the 20th century. Her efforts appeared in *Thresholds Quarterly*, the journal for School of Metaphysics Associates (SOMA) worldwide. This is the only compilation of that work. Whether teaching, lecturing, or writing about the development of man's potential as a creator (her painting *Creation* appears on the back cover of this book), she has stimulated thousands to open their minds and hearts to greater Self awareness. As the granddaughter of a faith-healing evangelist, working with *Revelation* was particularly fulfilling as both a prophecy and a destiny for her. Today, Dr. Barbara makes a home with her husband Daniel and their son Hezekiah on the campus of the College of Metaphysics, an ever-growing community of people dedicated to living Spiritual Renaissance.

Daniel R. Condron wrote this interpretation of *The Song of Solomon* in 1981. Since that time he has gone on to write many books including **The Universal Language of Mind: The Book of Matthew Interpreted.** Dr. Daniel has devoted the past thirty years of his life to Self awareness and to understanding the Universal Language of Mind. Serving as a teacher of mind and spirit, he has shared his knowledge and research with thousands through formal study, seminars and conferences, and all forms of media. His major address on *Permanent Healing - Breakthrough to Awareness* was enthusiastically received at the 1993 Parliament of the World's Religions in Chicago and his influence continues to reach around the globe as a conductor of intuitive reports including the Intuitive Health Analyses, offered through the institute. Dr. Condron serves as Chancellor of the College of Metaphysics where he teaches every day.

Gayle B. Matthes wrote **Discovering the Kingdom of Heaven** in 1981 and dedicated her work to her newly born nephew. This remarkable volume reflects more than Dr. Matthes' experience and understanding of the life of Jesus, it remains a statement of one individual's journey from belief into knowing. Her subsequent book about the ego, **From a Caterpillar to a Butterfly**, is available only on audio tape. Dr. Matthes earned all degrees from the School of Metaphysics and served for a number of years, including a four-year-term as board president, through the organization before leaving in 1989.

Jerry L. Rothermel penned these earliest interpretations of the *Book of Genesis* in 1973. They are a testament to the first recorded efforts to understand the Bible in light of the dream language. His interpretations of the first eighteen chapters of Genesis appeared, one per issue, in the initial years of *Thresholds Magazine*. Dr. Rothermel was one of the founding members of the School of Metaphysics serving as its first president in the latter 1970's and traveling extensively helping to open branch schools. In the 1980's he settled in Missouri, teaching the first students at the College of Metaphysics until the end of his life in 1990.

About our Artists

Born in Wheatridge, Colorado, in 1979, John Crainshaw is our youngest artist. His painting (on the front cover) of the resurrecting Christ was inspired "by my love of the **Bible** and a desire for humanity to be enlightened."

In 1989, Dianne G. Brady heard that Dr. Jerry Rothermel planned to write a book about the Biblical *Revelation*. Dr. Rothermel died before doing so, but Dianne's striking rendition of Chapter 12, The Woman and the Dragon graces our cover in a way truly reflective of the nature of dreams.

Born in Czechoslovakia, Sharka Glet graduated from the Art Institute in Prague before emigrating to the United States in the late 1960's. Currently she teaches art at a Chicago college and plans to develop the Metaphysical Arts training at the College of Metaphysics in Missouri in the next few years.

A metaphysician, artist, and self-described recovering Englishman, Ben Wheatley lives in Kansas City with his wife Dory and daughter Iris. "My inspiration was found in meditation and in the esoteric art of ancient China and Egypt; however none of those sources accounts for the unplanned appearance of the dollar bill in two of the drawings" for the *Song of Solomon*.

Born in 1976 in Tulsa, Oklahoma, Adam Campbell is currently expanding his already considerable artistic talent through applied studies at the College of Metaphysics. "I chose to depict *Genesis* using a mandala because a circle is whole, as is God's plan of creation."

Greg Brown was born in Manhattan, Kansas, and has been drawing since the age of five. For *Revelation* he "focussed on capturing the essence of the free flow still motion" characteristic of the narrative.

Charles C. Nealon hails from New York State and now lives in Kansas City with wife Angela and son Jordin. His *Revelation* illustration reflects an "urge deep within me to express self through artwork and other forms of illustration."

Additional titles available from SOM Publishing include:

Spiritual Renaissance
Elevating Your Consciousness for the Common Good
Dr. Barbara Condron ISGN: 0994386-22-9 $15.00

Superconscious Meditation
Kundalini & the Understanding of the Whole Mind
Dr. Daniel R. Condron ISBN 0944386-21-0 $13.00

First Opinion
Wholistic Health Care in the 21st Century
Dr. Barbara Condron ISBN 0944386-18-0 $15.00

The Dreamer's Dictionary
Dr. Barbara Condron ISBN 0944386-16-4 $15.00

The Work of the Soul
Past Life Recall & Enlightenment
Dr. Barbara Condron, ed. ISBN 0944386-17-2 $13.00

Uncommon Knowledge
Past Life & Health Readings
Dr. Barbara Condron, ed. ISBN 0944386-19-9 $13.00

The Universal Language of Mind
Book of Matthew Interpreted
Dr. Daniel R. Condron   ISBN 0944386-15-6 $13.00

Permanent Healing
Dr. Daniel R. Condron   ISBN 0944386-12-1 $13.00

Dreams of the Soul
Yogi Sutras of Patanjali
Dr. Daniel R. Condron   ISBN 0944386-11-3 $9.95

Kundalini Rising
Mastering Your Creative Energies
Dr. Barbara Condron   ISBN 0944386-13-X $13.00

To order write:

> School of Metaphysics World Headquarters
> HCR 1, Box 15
> Windyville, Missouri 65783 U.S.A.

Enclose a check or money order payable in U.S. funds to SOM with any order. Please include $4.00 for postage and handling of books, $8 for international orders.

Visit us on the Internet at *http://www.som.org*
e-mail: som@som.org
for more on dreams... http://www.dreamschool.org

About the School of Metaphysics

We invite you to become a special part of our efforts to aid in enhancing and quickening the process of spiritual growth and mental evolution of the people of the world. The School of Metaphysics, a not-for-profit educational and service organization, has been in existence for more than two decades. During that time, we have taught tens of thousands directly through our course of study in applied metaphysics. We have elevated the awareness of millions through the many services we offer. If you would like to pursue the study of mind and the transformation of Self to a higher level of being and consciousness, you are invited to write to us at the School of Metaphysics National Headquarters in Windyville, Missouri 65783.

The heart of the School of Metaphysics is a four-tiered program of study. Lessons introduce you to the Universal Laws and Truths which guide spiritual and physical evolution. Consciousness is explored and developed through mental and spiritual disciplines which enhance your physical life and enrich your soul progression. We teach concentration, visualization (focused imagery), meditation, and control of life force and creative energies. As a student, you will develop an understanding of the purpose of life and your purpose for this lifetime.

Experts in the Universal Language of Mind, we teach how to remember and understand the inner communication received through dreams. We are the sponsors of the National Dream Hotline®, an annual educational service offered the last weekend in April. Study centers are located throughout the Midwestern United States. If there is not a center near you, you can receive the first series of lessons through correspondence with a teacher at our headquarters.

For those desiring spiritual renewal, weekends at our Moon Valley Ranch offer calmness and clarity. Each Spiritual Renaissance Weekend's mentor gives thematic instruction and guidance which enriches the Spirit and changes lives. One weekend may center on transcendent meditation, another on creative genius, another on wholistic health or understanding your dreams. Please feel free to contact us about upcoming sessions.

The Universal Hour of Peace was initiated by the School of Metaphysics at noon Universal Time (GMT) on October 24, 1995 in conjunction with the 50th anniversary of the United Nations. We believe that peace on earth is an idea whose time has come. To realize this dream, we invite you to join with others throughout the world by dedicating your thoughts and actions to peace for one hour beginning at noon [UT] on the first of January each year. Living peaceably begins by thinking peacefully. We invite SOMA® members to convene Circles of Love in their cities during this hour. Please contact us about how you can participate.

There is the opportunity to aid in the growth and fulfillment of our work. Donations supporting the expansion of the School of Metaphysics' efforts are a valuable way for you to aid humanity. As a not-for-profit publishing house, SOM Publishing is dedicated to the continuing publication of research findings that promote peace, understanding and good will for all of Mankind. It is dependent upon the kindness and generosity of sponsors to do so. Authors donate their work and receive no royalties. We have many excellent manuscripts awaiting a benefactor.

One hundred percent of the donations made to the School of Metaphysics are used to expand our services. Donations are being received for Project Octagon, the first educational building on the College of Metaphysics campus. The land for the proposed campus is located in the beautiful Ozark Mountains of Missouri. This proposed multipurpose structure will include an auditorium, classrooms, library and study areas, a cafeteria, and potential living quarters for up to 100 people. We expect to finance this structure through corporate grants and personal endowments. Donations to the School of Metaphysics are tax-exempt under 501 (c) (3) of the Internal Revenue Code. We appreciate any contribution you are free to make. With the help of people like you, our dream of a place where anyone desiring Self awareness can receive wholistic education will become a reality.

We send you our Circle of Love.